Human
Sigma

Human Sigma

MANAGING THE EMPLOYEE-CUSTOMER ENCOUNTER

John H. Fleming, Ph.D. | Jim Asplund

GALLUP PRESS
NEW YORK

GALLUP PRESS
1251 Avenue of the Americas
23rd Floor
New York, NY 10020

Manufactured in the United States of America

First edition 2007

10 9 8 7 6 5 4 3 2 1

Library of Congress Control Number: 2007929466

ISBN: 978-1-59562-016-3

Bible quotations are taken from the New Revised Standard Version Bible, copyright 1989, Division of Christian Education of the National Council of Churches of Christ in the United States of America. Used by permission. All rights reserved.

Poet John Masefield once wrote, "All I ask is a tall ship and a star to steer her by." I have been blessed with not one, but three, stars to steer by. To Robin, my pride and passion — the consummate example of serenity, strength, and wisdom and a true guiding star, and to my twin daughters Allison and Emma, from whom I have learned more about joy than I ever could have imagined. — JHF

John Masefield also wrote, "The days that make us happy make us wise." Any wisdom I have imparted in this book is therefore due to Susan and our sons Jakob and Jonas, who bring happiness into my every day. — JA

TABLE OF CONTENTS

ACKNOWLEDGEMENTS

This book is a much-expanded version of the article "Manage Your Human Sigma" that appeared in the July/August 2005 issue of the *Harvard Business Review*. We are much indebted to the editorial staff at *HBR* — Tom Stewart, Sarah Cliffe, and M. Ellen Peebles in particular — for all their assistance in helping to bring many of the core HumanSigma concepts to life.

No undertaking of this magnitude could be accomplished without the dedication, hard work, and contributions of a multitude of colleagues, client partners, and other associates around the globe. From Washington, D.C., to Omaha, Nebraska, to Irvine, California, and from Bangkok, Thailand, to Mumbai, India, and London to São Paulo, Brazil to Tokyo, we are blessed to have worked with some of the best and brightest in the world during our tenure with Gallup. Without the support of all these people, this book, quite literally, would not have been possible.

The journey that culminated in the writing of this book began on a winter afternoon in 1999 in Palmer Square in Princeton, New Jersey, during a conversation with Gale Muller, then Director of Analysis at Gallup and now Vice Chairman, Worldwide

Research and Development. Gale posed a simple question: "If you could do anything at all, what would you do during the next 12 months that just might change the world?" Though we were initially nonplussed by the question's scope, it got us thinking, and our answer is contained in these pages. It's a testament to Gallup's strengths-based philosophy that we were given free rein to "do what we do best every day" — to explore the terrain of the employee-customer encounter and to help build the model that would become HumanSigma.

We would like to acknowledge the unswerving support of our colleagues at Gallup Press, Larry Emond and Geoff Brewer, who shepherded this book through to completion, and Pio Juszkiewicz, who did just about everything else and more to get this book out to the world. Our editorial team — Barb Sanford, Mark Stiemann, Trista Kunce, Kim Burks, Carolyn Madison, and Kelly Slater — deserves special recognition for their all-too-often-unheralded efforts, which matter greatly to the quality of this book. Kim Burks gets kudos for her first-rate work on the book's design and typography, as does Chin-Yee Lai, who created our excellent book jacket, and Tommy McCall who did a superb job designing the graphics. Rachel Johanowicz gets high marks for managing the production process so effectively. The contributions of several of our Gallup colleagues, past and present, are particularly noteworthy and were essential to the framing of many of our ideas: Jim Clifton, chairman and CEO of Gallup, Dana Baugh, John Cameron, Donna Chlopak, Curt Coffman, Bill Diggins, Laragh Dubois, Peter Flade, Gabriel Gonzalez-Molina, Andrew Green, James K. Harter, Bill Hoffman, Jon Hughes, Bill McEwen, Charles Pribyl, Tom Rath, Rajesh Srinivasan, Heather Totin, and Rodd Wagner. We would also like to gratefully acknowledge the support of a cadre of distinguished social and biological scientists around the world whose insight and expertise have been invaluable: Jonathan Cohen, Allan Cooper, Joel Cooper, John Darley, Nose Izuru, the late Ned Jones, Daniel Kahneman, Ralph Oliva, Masahiro Sakamoto, and Masato Taira. Equally important are the contributions made by some of our client partners around the world who early on embraced many of the new rules described in this book: Carrie Tolstedt and Jay Freeman; Lex Kloosterman, Jos ter Avest, Andius Teijgeler, and Fred Machado; Simon Cooper, John Timmerman, and Sarah Santaella; Mike Wells, Mike Morrison, Mark Templin, Nancy Fein, and Bob Carter; Tiffany Tomasso and Kurt Conway; Kannikar Chalitaporn and W. Michael Than; Marvin "Skip" Schoenhals and Mark Turner; and Rich Martino. We have learned a great deal from each of you and from the companies you help run. We certainly hope the feeling is mutual.

INTRODUCTION
THE TERMINATOR SCHOOL OF MANAGEMENT

"I'll be back."
— Arnold Schwarzenegger, *The Terminator*

Arnold Schwarzenegger fans will recall this harrowing image from the apocalyptic opening scene of *The Terminator*.[1] It's the Year of Darkness, 2029. Across a war-ravaged landscape of destroyed buildings, piles of broken bones, billowing smoke, and unbelievable carnage, a ragtag band of humans battles for their survival against an onslaught of artificially intelligent machines.

The machines — created by an advanced form of artificial intelligence called Skynet that accidentally becomes self-aware — have concluded (quite rationally, it would seem) that they must erase humans from the face of the planet, replacing them with predictable but unfeeling, efficient, and relentless copies of themselves. In essence, the machines are the polar opposite of the humans they seek to destroy. It's a grim scene, and the implications are clear: The machines have decided that humans are not only unnecessary, but they are expendable. They add no value in the vision of the future the machines seek to create.

The Terminator is a work of science fiction. Machines don't rule the earth — at least not yet. Human beings are not on the verge of extinction — at least not immediately. So what is the connection to a book on management?

THE FACTORY FLOOR AND SIX SIGMA

As business people, we have gotten good at managing the processes and systems that produce the latest high-tech gadget, the innovative home appliance, or the next-generation automobile. Ever since the dawn of the industrial era, value creation in manufacturing companies has taken place on the factory floor. Creating high-quality goods was the raison d'être of manufacturing companies. Manufacturing leaders are acutely aware that the more of their product that winds up in the "defective" bin, the less efficient and effective their operations are. Ultimately, the higher the defect rate, the less profitable the enterprise can be. That's just simple math.

Manufacturing leaders, likewise, understand that managing the bell curve of quality is crucial to profitability. Pushing more and more output into the acceptable range while reducing the number of defective products is the quality mantra. The difference between making a component only to throw it out versus having that same component available for sale has substantial effects on the productivity and profitability of the enterprise. It's as simple as that.

The notion that variation in output quality represents a corporate survival issue is not new. Two decades ago, Motorola, Inc., introduced a new language and process-improvement methodology to the global management conversation with Six Sigma. At its core, Six Sigma is about reducing variability in processes and systems. Mountains of books, guides, and how-to manuals have been written on the Six Sigma methodology.[2] In fact, a quick Internet keyword search on "Six Sigma" reveals more than 2,000 titles in press today. An entire cottage industry dedicated to Six Sigma consulting has sprung up and flourished.[3] By all accounts, Six Sigma has been one of the most successful management movements of all time. Not only has Six Sigma consistently produced positive results in the companies that have implemented it, but it also has had the staying power that other quality initiatives — statistical process control, TQM, and others — have lacked. In simple terms, Six Sigma integrated a universal and consistent method for counting quality defects with a disciplined process to eliminate them. It galvanized business management, particularly at senior levels, and spearheaded the quality movement.

THE EMPLOYEE-CUSTOMER ENCOUNTER: THE NEW CRUCIBLE OF VALUE CREATION

But what about the people whose job is to sell the new automobile, service the appliance, or help users navigate the eccentricities of the new gadget's many features? It's here — in the human side of business — that too many companies have dropped the ball. As effective as the Six Sigma approach has been, it was developed within a manufacturing context where producing products with "zero defects" was a primary concern and face-to-face interaction with customers was generally minimal. For sales and service companies — retail, banking, lodging, healthcare, hospitality, commercial transportation, business-to-business, and a slew of other service economy companies that have high levels of direct customer contact — Six Sigma has been much more difficult to translate into an effective management intervention strategy.

For several reasons, the Six Sigma approach is just not as applicable to the "soft" dimensions of organizational quality and performance — those dynamic human systems that encompass employee productivity and customer service. Though Six Sigma has proven to be an effective tool for reengineering the mechanics of production processes and systems, it's more cumbersome and difficult to apply to (and arguably less effective at improving) the complex human systems that underlie organizational performance.

So how can a leader of a sales and service organization manage this range of quality in the human side of business? On the sales floor, at a hotel front desk, or even in a hospital room, the inter-action between an employee and a customer — what we call the *employee-customer encounter* — is the new factory floor. It's the crucible where value is created in sales and service organizations. And, like the factory floor in manufacturing, the quality of the employee-customer encounter has a distribution of performance from flawless to severely defective. Here, too, the difference be-tween creating an experience that draws customers back and one that sends them away from the brand forever has large effects on the productivity and profitability of the company.

Although production managers use steel, silicon, and plastics to feed their factories, customer service managers must work with the most unpredictable and volatile of components — people. In trying to manage employees *and* the customer experience, traditional tools have proven woefully inadequate; a new model and a new set of management tools are required. Six Sigma black belts around the world have gotten good at improving four of the root causes of quality defects *(machines, materials, measurement, and methods)*, but there is another root cause identified in the Six Sigma methodology — *people.* This root cause has largely been ignored. This is not too surprising because it's probably the hardest to fix. But, it may also be the most important.

Put simply, the problem is this: Even the most perfectly designed and built process or system is only as good as the human being who uses it. And, for many executives, because controlling quality in processes and systems is infinitely easier than similar activities with people, it seems reasonable to try to factor people out of the equation altogether.

"A CHANCE FOR SOMETHING TO GO WRONG"

A few years ago, one of us had the opportunity to make a presentation at a major car rental company to a senior operations executive and his team. The topic was the effect of the human aspects of business on overall organizational performance. Immediately after the presentation ended, the executive closed his notepad, let out an audible sigh, and said, "I am sorry, gentlemen. I understand what you are telling me — I really do. But the truth is, if I could get rid of every, single human touchpoint we have with our customers, I would. *Every interaction one of our employees has with a customer is a chance for something to go wrong.* Online reservations and self-serve machines are just much more efficient and cost-effective. They always show up for work, they never complain, they don't have bad days, and they don't make mistakes. I am looking forward to the day when the only person a customer sees is the guy in the security booth when they drive the car off the lot. And even he is still one employee too many."

"WE JUST DON'T TRUST THEM THAT MUCH!"

The CEO of a retail bank echoed a similar sentiment. During an afternoon roundtable session with the chief executive and his management team, our discussion found its way to a number of changes that the bank could make to its service model in response to customer comments. One of the concerns expressed by the bank's customers was that the bank's tellers could never make decisions on their own. Instead, they always needed the approval of a supervisor to complete even the most basic tasks. One of the suggestions on the table was whether the bank should give its tellers — the frontline associates who actually deliver service to customers and who are, de facto, the company's "face" to the world — a greater degree of decision-making autonomy to deliver a higher standard of customer service. At a critical point in the discussion, the CEO slammed his hand on the table and said, "We can't do that. We just don't trust them that much!"

What struck us as odd then, and continues to strike us as odd to this day, is how a company could trust its employees enough to put them toe-to-toe with its most valuable assets — its customers — every day, but not trust them enough to allow them to make independent decisions that might enable them to serve their customers more effectively. "Yes, you are the face of our brand in the marketplace, but we just don't trust you enough." These executives are alumni of what we call the "Terminator School of Management." Its governing ideology dictates that the best way to flourish in modern business is to minimize the amount of human interaction and involvement in the enterprise.

This attitude is reminiscent of the following exchange from *Terminator 2: Judgment Day*,[4] where the Terminator explains the limits his "leadership" places on him.

> John Connor: "Can you learn stuff you haven't been programmed with so you could be, you know, more human? And not such a dork all the time?"
>
> The Terminator: "My CPU is a neural net processor, a learning computer. But Skynet presets the switch to 'read only' when we're sent out alone."
>
> Sarah Connor: "Doesn't want you doing too much thinking, huh?"
>
> The Terminator: "No."

We have observed that many executives like those described earlier wish they could switch their employees' minds to "read only" to limit their independence and restrict their actions to those explicitly allowed by management. If we are feeling especially benevolent, we might be willing to chalk up these executives' rather pessimistic views of their employees to simple frustration. After all, their sentiments are just updated and expanded versions of a similar frustration reportedly expressed by Henry Ford many years ago: "Why is it that I always get the whole person when what I really want is a pair of hands?"

If you have occasionally felt the same frustration trying to manage the human systems within your business, you're not alone. It's a common experience. And there is a modicum of truth embedded in Henry Ford's rhetorical question. People can be difficult to deal with and frustrating to manage. Unlike the traditional manufacturing factory floor, where raw materials with known and predictable properties are repeatedly combined in known and predictable ways to produce products with known and predictable characteristics, human beings can be volatile, and they are not easily controlled. Unlike machines, they don't always show up for work, they sometimes complain, they occasionally have bad days, and they will make mistakes. Employees are indisputably a great source of unpredictability. A tractor will never demand a pension or sick time. Of course, the tractor will never invent a more secure Internet protocol or concoct an irresistible cookie, either.

THE DARK SIDE

Something potentially darker lurks in the sentiments expressed by these executives. Buoyed by the promise of reduced costs, increased efficiency, and the ability to offer customers greater choice, flexibility, and convenience, many companies are pursuing a strategy of minimizing (or in some cases, eliminating) the human interface altogether: self-serve check-in, Internet banking, a proliferation of automated voice response customer service numbers, and online retail. These processes are nameless and faceless but relentlessly efficient. In the pursuit of risk reduction and efficiency, leaders of sales and service organizations have expended a great deal of time and energy reengineering their workplaces so that there are more roles fit for machines and fewer that require a person. Should a role absolutely require a person, the requirements of the role often are specified in excruciating detail. Human beings appear to add no value in the vision of the fully automated company and offer, at best, an opportunity to make mistakes. And, even though these corporate reconfigurations are usually implemented with the best of intentions, they have helped, possibly inadvertently, to accelerate the principles of Terminator Management.

We contend that a vision of the service economy that emphasizes automation and technology at the expense of human interaction does customers and shareholders alike a huge disservice by ripping the face and soul out of business. And, if we are not careful, we won't have to wait until 2029 to experience the rise of the machines. Sadly, *The Terminator*'s Year of Darkness may be closer than we think.

"GET A LIFE!"

Lessons from the Terminator School of Management are not limited to executives' and other managers' feelings about their employees. These lessons extend to their feelings about their customers, as well. A couple of years ago, one of us presented the results of a customer engagement study to the executive committee of a consumer bank. During the discussion, we asked this group to tell us what they thought their customers would do if for some reason the bank ceased to exist. Would their customers be devastated? Or would they simply take their money and go to the next bank they could find? Without missing a beat, this management team said with considerable confidence that of course their customers would just find another bank. Why wouldn't they? After all, *"We are just a bank."*

We then told this management team that based on the data we had collected and analyzed, there was a small but important group of customers who were absolutely passionate about their bank. Though this extremely vocal group comprised less than 10% of the bank's customers, they not only thought and talked about the bank a lot more than most customers, but they also felt that the bank was irreplaceable in their lives. These customers quite literally could not imagine what their world would be like without the bank. On top of all that, these customers lived out their passion for the bank. They tended to be the most profitable, they each owned a product portfolio that was considerably deeper than that of most other customers, and they cost less for the bank to service. But, after we told the CEO about the existence of this extraordinarily valuable customer segment, he sat back, laughed, and said, "Wow! Those poor people. They really need to get a life!"

A NECESSARY EVIL

Terminator Management is an institutionalized mind-set that views people — customers *and* employees — as a necessary evil, a nuisance, or in extreme cases, as adversaries in doing business. Rather than viewing people as the reason a business exists, the Terminator School of Management views them as impediments to business that breed inefficiency, cost, and errors.

Terminator Management is characterized by a failure to appreciate that business is a fundamentally human enterprise and by a wish (rarely expressed openly) that it could somehow be otherwise. It fails to recognize and unleash the unique potential embodied in every employee, preferring instead to view all employees as interchangeable cogs in some grand machine. Terminator Management sees employees as little more than a cost it needs to reduce or a mistake just waiting to happen. It laughs at a company's most valuable asset — the customers who feel so strongly about a company that they can't imagine their lives without it. And it's about creating a business landscape where everything is flat, where everything is efficient, but nothing has a soul. But, perhaps most importantly, Terminator Management is about a need for control.

NEW RULES

Though it's an interesting phenomenon in and of itself, this book doesn't focus on Terminator Management. Instead, we offer a new set of rules and a different way of thinking about managing your company's complex human systems, which we believe can serve as an antidote to Terminator Management. It's about a model and an approach that we call *HumanSigma*.

The HumanSigma model grew out of a multiyear research initiative to map the terrain of the employee-customer encounter. In this book, we identify the specific operational metrics that define its effectiveness, explore how to deploy those tools appropriately, and describe the kinds of operational and financial benefits that can result when you apply them appropriately. The foundation of this work is our direct experience with hundreds of companies and more than 10 million customers and 10 million employees around the globe. It's an approach that grew out of discoveries from some of the best managed companies in the world — and some of the worst.

We will present new meta-analytic research from 10 companies and 1,979 business units in the financial services, professional services, retail, and sales industries. Each of the 10 companies that has applied HumanSigma management principles has outperformed its five largest peers within its sector during a recent one-year period by 26% in gross margin and 85% in sales growth.

The dehumanization of modern business is not inevitable, nor is it necessary. Just as the humans in *The Terminator* had a choice about the kind of future they could create, so too does the business community. There was an alternative to a future ruled by Terminators, and there is an alternative to the Terminator School of Management. HumanSigma offers a disciplined approach to measuring, managing, and improving the performance of your most volatile and valuable assets — your customers and employees — to drive financial performance.

In the process of working with the some of the best run companies in the world, we have learned a great deal about how the world's finest organizations unleash the power of their human systems and how the worst fail to do so. Though the specific ways that the HumanSigma model may be implemented in your company may vary, the underlying philosophy can be boiled down to five new rules, which we list here and describe in detail in subsequent chapters.

Rule 1: You can't measure and manage the employee and customer experiences as separate entities. Because you must manage these human systems in tandem, you may need to reorganize.

This is not a trivial issue. Most companies are not currently organized or prepared to manage employees and customers under the same organizational umbrella. But because the crucial juncture in creating value in sales and service organizations is the interaction between employees and customers, you must view both sides of the employee-customer encounter as interrelated and mutually dependent. As a result, you must assess and manage these human systems as a coherent whole, not as separate pieces. In practice, this means that you cannot separate the responsibility for the quality of a company's employee relationships from the responsibility for the quality of its customer relationships. They are interdependent and you must not manage them in isolation.

Who owns the employee experience at your company? Who owns the customer experience? How well integrated are your efforts to assess and manage the employee-customer encounter? We will discuss the issues surrounding Rule 1 in Chapters 1 and 2.

Rule 2: Emotion frames the employee-customer encounter. It's important not to think like an economist or an engineer when you're assessing employee-customer interactions. Emotions, it turns out, inform both sides' judgments and behavior even more powerfully than rational or dispassionate thinking. Because employees and customers are people first and employees or customers second, they are prone to all the volatility and irrationality that is the hallmark of being human.

If companies are ever going to be able to truly understand their employees and customers, it's crucial that they take their employees' and customers' essential humanity seriously. Historically, this has been a tough sell because emotions or feelings have been viewed as messy, imprecise, nettlesome things that don't lend themselves well to rigorous management science. Besides, emotions don't conform to rational rules.

But it's possible to reliably evaluate the emotional dimensions that are important to employees and customers. The measurement and management of the employee-customer encounter must acknowledge and incorporate the crucial emotional infrastructure of human behavior and decision making, yielding a concept that extends beyond traditional considerations of employee and customer satisfaction to a concept we call *engagement*.

Have you incorporated these emotional components into your understanding of what drives your employee and customer relationships? We discuss the issues surrounding Rule 2 in detail in Chapters 3 through 9.

Rule 3: You must measure and manage the employee-customer encounter at a local level. Though companies can manage many kinds of organizational activities effectively from the top down, the employee-customer encounter is an intensely local phenomenon that can vary considerably from location to location within the same company. Because of the variability in local performance, you must measure and manage it locally.

Are your corporate metrics and other activities aligned to support local accountability and action? We discuss Rule 3 and related issues in Chapter 10.

Rule 4: We can quantify and summarize the effectiveness of the employee-customer encounter in a single performance measure — the HumanSigma metric — that is powerfully related to financial performance. Our research has revealed that the two sides of the employee-customer encounter potentiate one another and can be quantified into a single HumanSigma metric. The interactive effects of employee and customer engagement at the local level exponentially drive operational and financial performance and growth.

Does your company suffer from either an overabundance or a shortage of human systems performance metrics? How well integrated are the metrics you use? And how well do these metrics link up to your company's financial performance outcomes? We present the conceptual model and the financial performance analyses used to validate Rule 4 in Chapter 11.

Rule 5: Improvement in local HumanSigma performance requires deliberate and active intervention through attention to a combination of transactional and transformational intervention activities. Measurement by itself is never enough to improve performance. Creating organizational change is hard work and requires active and disciplined intervention.

Our work has found that few companies apply the full range of intervention activities required to generate real and sustainable change. *Transactional* activities, such as action planning, training, and other aggressive interventions, are cyclical interventions that tend to be topical and short-term in focus and to recur regularly. They are designed to help your company do what it already does — but do it *better*. *Transformational* activities, on the other hand, are structural interventions that focus on how companies select employees, select and promote managers, pay and evaluate employees, do succession planning, and recognize and develop employees. Transformational activities focus on creating an organizational infrastructure that supports HumanSigma. They are designed to help your company come up with *new* ways to do things.

What processes do you have in place to support a HumanSigma strategy in your organization? We discuss several topics related to Rule 5 — particularly a set of strategies and tactics to drive sustainable organizational change — in Chapters 12 through 15.

We will return to these new rules throughout the book to illustrate how the world's best companies unleash the power of their human systems — and how the worst fail to do so. This book shares some of the progress several of the world's best companies are making now. These companies have, not coincidentally, dramatically outperformed their peers during the past few years while setting themselves up for even greater performance in the future. They have decided that the Terminator will *not* be back. You can, too.

CHAPTER **ONE**
QUALITY *CONTROL*

"Quality has to be caused, not controlled."
— Philip Crosby, *Reflections on Quality*

The Terminator School of Management is not an inevitable consequence of the evolution of modern business processes. But its origins *do* lie in the forces and advances that have helped to make today's manufacturing processes so effective and efficient — and so do its solutions.

A TALE OF TWO MODELS

To begin to understand the origins of Terminator Management, let's consider some of the differences between the manufacturing economy with its emphasis on production, scalability, and efficiency and the service economy with its emphasis on individualization and human interaction. These two models offer different perspectives on the nature of value creation and the role of employees and customers in creating value for the enterprise. We all know that creating value is the chief objective of all businesses, but the specific way in which it's created depends on the nature of the business.[1]

Approaches such as TQM and Six Sigma have demonstrated that manufacturing and other process-intensive enterprises can enhance value by paying careful attention to a clearly defined set of activities. These activities focus on reducing variation while increasing output quality and operational efficiency. Many production improvements work because the materials used to make things react predictably. Processes can be improved because they combine known and predictable materials in a known way time after time. But for these processes to be maximally effective, human variation must be squeezed from the system.

THE INCREDIBLE SHRINKING EMPLOYEE

Prior to the industrial era, most products were made by hand in small lots by craftspeople who learned their trades as apprentices to master craftspeople. Production was labor intensive and output was limited, but the quality of the goods produced was extremely high.

But, as demand for products increased, mass-production processes and assembly line manufacturing were introduced, ushering in the industrial era. As industrialization took hold, craftspeople were no longer needed in many areas because products of adequate quality could now be produced in large quantities. For mass production to be viable, however, the production systems had to be scalable; in other words, processes had to be repeatable with little deviation from shift to shift or employee to employee.

Once workplaces began to value scalability over skill, they needed a new workforce. Instead of requiring an army of skilled craftspeople who produced goods individually and saw the production process through from beginning to end, this new workforce required

a large number of relatively unskilled laborers who could keep
the assembly lines moving continuously by performing the same
tasks in the same ways over and over. Because the members of this
modern workforce were responsible for only a small portion of
the production process, they were viewed as interchangeable and
highly replaceable. And because these workers brought few skills
or experiences with them to their roles, workplaces had to define
role requirements in precise terms, often down to the specific behaviors, actions, and ways of working. In short, harkening back
to Henry Ford's exasperated query, what companies really needed
from this new workforce were their hands. Their heads and hearts
were considered not only irrelevant but also often problematic.

Over time, a company's ability to improve operational efficiency
and product quality incrementally hinged less on the particular
contributions of individual employees and more on specifying and
controlling the processes and systems used to produce the goods. As
long as the employees on the production line executed their assigned
tasks without deviation, the process ran smoothly. As successive
advances in technology and automation were introduced, this
evolutionary process accelerated. Each new technological advance
lessened the opportunities for employees to take initiative and
contribute; it often eliminated the need for the employees themselves.
At the same time, technology and automation helped increase the
overall quality of the products and reduced the variation in quality
from shift to shift and factory to factory. Over time, the perception
became firmly entrenched that the factories themselves, and not the
people inside them, produced quality products. To a certain extent,
the perception was true: People were considered interchangeable in
many industrial settings.

From a manufacturing perspective, these were largely positive developments. No longer was the production of quality goods solely dependent upon skilled workers. Instead, a focus on continuously improving and controlling all aspects of the manufacturing processes led to increases in output quality. Employees — if they were needed at all — had become a necessary evil, and, in many cases, a cost to be minimized. All that companies needed were their hands.

JDS MANAGEMENT

Eventually, as manufacturers continued their quest to wring costs from their production systems, even the hands began to look too expensive. Automation promised further efficiencies, and in many cases, delivered them. Taking a cue from the world's best manufacturers, many sales and service organizations — armed with evidence of the benefits of automation and the improved organizational processes built to incorporate it — have opted to streamline their own operations along the same lines. They have driven more customer transactions out of their bricks-and-mortar, face-to-face channels and into their call centers and Internet sites.

Once sales and service companies have successfully wrung costs out of the more production-oriented aspects of their businesses using this strategy, it's then a common impulse to use the same approach to make other aspects of their businesses, such as the employee-customer encounter, more efficient, too. Companies would examine management practices and employee-customer interactions to improve their quality or make them more productive. This might work if we replaced people with robots, but because customers and employees are people — with all the illogical and emotional behaviors inherent in human beings — the result has generally been an organization that is designed not to fail in the short term rather than to succeed long term. These organizations are run with a particularly risk-averse philosophy that can be summed up as Just Don't Suck (JDS).

We have seen firsthand evidence of the diminishing returns that come from JDS management at several companies. Take, for example, the retailer that had wrung great cost savings out of its stores by slowly ratcheting down the range of behaviors it allowed store employees to perform. After an initial surge in savings, the retailer found that further improvements in process compliance were detrimental to sales and profit growth. What could possibly account for this finding? Initially, when the retailer implemented process improvements, better-managed stores adapted quickly and understood the initiative as a means to keeping shelves stocked and checkout lines moving. These stores saw the initiative as one of several means to manage toward their primary financial outcomes. Poorly managed stores, in contrast, focused myopically on improving their procedural efficiencies to such an extent that they completely neglected other important management tasks such as engaging their customers. For these stores, procedural excellence became the latest in a series of "big fixes" that was the answer to managing the stores effectively. Because the retailer confused the outcome (store profitability) with the process (procedural adherence), they could not see the forest for the trees.

An obsessive focus on procedural steps can become a barrier to building enduring customer relationships because customers generally don't know what they are supposed to do according to the script the store management may be following. What's more, store personnel have a finite amount of time and energy, and only the best managers can separate the "flavor of the month" initiatives from the more important, long-term objectives to which they should commit their efforts. In the way we observed, a single-minded focus on process improvement could negatively affect sales growth at this retailer.

VALUING INTANGIBLES

Another dynamic is essential to understanding why employees are often viewed as a necessary evil or a cost to be minimized. The accounting and financial reporting systems modern businesses use have failed to keep up with the changing nature of value creation. By focusing on tangible assets, current accounting systems implicitly undervalue human contributions to the enterprise, which are primarily intangible things such as creative branding strategies, research and development, and labor productivity.

A recent study revealed that an estimated 80% of the market value of the average S&P 500 company is made up of its intangible assets — the company's brand, its customer base and levels of engagement, the talent of employees, and innovation and R&D, just to name a few of the most crucial elements.[2] Though most executives recognize the importance of these intangible assets, it's much more difficult to justify investing in them without an accepted means of accounting for the success or failure of those investments.

New York University Professor Baruch Lev has written extensively about these kinds of intangible assets and how to account for their contributions to a company's market value. His research has also found that intangible assets represent a large share of the value of most firms and intangible-driven earnings, or the profits intangible assets generate, better predict stock market returns than either accounting earnings or cash flows.[3] In our own research, we have observed that building a critical mass of engaged employees contributes significantly to the bottom line. In a recent study of 89 companies, we found that the companies that build this critical mass of engagement grew earnings per share (EPS) at 2.6 times the rate of companies who do not.[4]

If intangible assets are such a competitive advantage, why don't companies routinely quantify how much they are worth? The short answer is that, until recently, it has been hard to do, and there is still little agreement on how to do it. As a result, employees have been consigned to the status of costs to be minimized rather than assets to be optimized. That's a big mistake because it makes investing in employees and customers look riskier than it really is.

The perceived added risk of investing in human systems may help explain why many executives have spent their careers ridding their organizations of as many jobs as possible — by transferring functions formerly performed by employees to Web servers or reengineering employee functions out of the business altogether. There are good reasons for doing many of these things. Automated voice response systems (AVRs) are efficient, and an outsourced provider of services might have expertise or efficiencies that it would be difficult for a firm to replicate. But the cumulative effect of these changes often results in a purely functional, if not downright sterile, relationship with customers, one that gives them no compelling reason to prefer one company to another.

When added to the heritage of the Terminator School of Management, outdated accounting systems make it difficult for executives to discern or justify the investments they need to build positive and productive relationships with employees and customers. Instead, these instincts tend to drive them toward JDS strategies that feed short-term needs for improvement and security — such as something to talk about at the next quarterly conference call with the stock analysts — but that ultimately fail to provide the exponential growth we see in businesses that make the right investments in their employees and customers.

Here is an example of how these faulty instincts can corrupt the best intentions of managers and lead an organization down the primrose path to failure.

PLOWMAN'S STATE BANK: ENHANCING VALUE IN THE SERVICE ECONOMY

Ferdinand Gustafson founded Plowman's State Bank in the early 20th century in a typical small town. Even in this community of Swedish immigrants, no one called himself "Ferdinand" if he could help it. To his friends, employees, and customers, he was simply "Gus," and he presided over the bank he founded for nearly 50 years. The success of his bank and its eventual expansion provide a useful parable for understanding the growing pains of sales and service organizations.

In Plowman's State Bank, as in virtually all service economy businesses, value was created in an entirely different way from that employed in manufacturing enterprises. Absent were state-of-the-art manufacturing processes and quality control systems. Instead, Gus and his employees created value through their personal interactions with customers and the resulting relationships they nurtured over time. For Gus, these employee-customer encounters *were* the factory floor of his banking business.

Gus' interactions with a typical patron, Wilbur "Swede" Carlsson, provide an excellent example of this principle in action. Swede, like many of the bank's best customers, was a local farmer. Gus realized implicitly that his livelihood depended on the long-standing relationships he had with Swede Carlsson and others like him. The service Gus provided to Swede was personal, individualized, and, above all, authentic. He didn't follow a script to guide his behavior when he engaged Swede in conversation, asked about his family, or determined whether Swede was a good enough farmer to be an acceptable risk for an operating loan. This is tricky stuff in a small town — not everyone is a good credit risk, and Gus knew he would have to reject the loan applications of many friends and neighbors. Most of all, no one needed to remind him to smile and thank Swede for his business; Gus knew that the future of his bank depended on building relationships that last a lifetime.

For Swede, being a customer of Plowman's State Bank was more than the sum of his transactions — depositing checks, getting cash, and securing the loans needed to buy seed and equipment. After all, there were other banks in Sandburg County, many of which paid better interest rates on deposits. But to Swede, visiting Plowman's

State Bank was also about the relationships he had formed with Gus, Gus' son Earl, and the bank tellers through countless interactions.

These relationships were important to Gus, too. He was a pillar of the community and proud of the quality of service he provided to his neighbors and the faith they showed in him. Eventually, the Great Depression tested these relationships, but Gus returned his customers' faith by helping many farmers stay in business through those dark times and the war that followed.

Though Plowman's State Bank provides a compelling example of how service-based organizations create value, we don't need to travel back in time to find examples of this kind of value creation. Myriad examples exist in today's business environment. One has only to look at world-class practitioners such as The Ritz-Carlton or USAA Insurance to see exactly how relationship building serves as a foundation for sales and service organizations like these. The challenge for many of today's sales and service businesses is not whether they should try to build strong relationships with their customers, but how to make relationship building scalable across a large enterprise.

HOW BIG CAN YOU GET BEFORE YOU GET BAD?

Let's fast-forward past the war years. Plowman's State Bank has grown considerably, and so has the need for additional branches and staff to handle the demands of that growth. No longer can Gus greet every customer personally. Nor can he maintain the personal relationships he had so carefully nurtured in the days when his enterprise consisted of a single brick storefront in a small town. For better or worse, Gus had to entrust the management of the new branches to carefully selected associates who he hoped shared the same values and goals as he did.

Before too long, some cracks began to appear in the expanded Plowman's State Bank network. Though many of the newly hired staff shared Gus' sense of mission and purpose, his commitment to high-quality service, and his passion and talent for nurturing each customer relationship, there were others who did not. As a result, the quality of service across the franchise became inconsistent. In some branches, service became spotty. Long-standing relationships soured. Profitability and revenue growth sagged. Yet in other branches, service thrived. Relationships blossomed, and financial performance excelled. Yet all of this variation occurred under the unified banner of Plowman's State Bank. It was as though different versions of Plowman's State Bank — some good, some terrible — were popping up from location to location, and customers could not be certain which version they might encounter when they visited a particular branch. This variability was beginning to damage the hard-won equity of the brand. Plowman's State Bank was providing its own answer to the question, "How big can we get before we get bad?"[5]

As successful as the franchise had become, Gus and his growing management team now faced a serious dilemma: How could they make high-quality service scalable across a significantly expanded organization? What could they do to ensure that the interactions their enlarged staff had with every customer were as consistent and high quality as though Gus himself were greeting each customer? Like many sales and service businesses have done when confronted with exactly this set of challenges, the management team decided to apply the principles of quality control, which had proven to be so effective in manufacturing settings, to their own business. In spite of their best intentions, the management team at Plowman's State Bank made two fundamental errors that started the wheels of Terminator Management turning.

CLONING SERVICE

As a first step, the management team decided that it made sense to observe what exceptional service looks like in action. What specific things does Gus do that enables him to serve his customers so well? By recording the behaviors they observed — Gus using the customer's name, smiling, asking about the customer's family, showing genuine caring and concern, thanking them for their business, and reminding them to have a wonderful day — they hoped to create a catalog of actions to drive exceptional service. Once cataloged, these behaviors would form the core of a standardized script. Then the management team would train and require every associate — from the branch manager to the tellers — to execute that script in the same way, every time they interacted with a customer. In other words, they decided to try to create hundreds of Gus clones by scripting service.

At first, the logic behind this move appears infallible. If quality control approaches had succeeded in reducing the variability in performance at every step in the manufacturing process on the factory floor, why couldn't they be applied to service organizations, as well, with similar results? Shouldn't rigidly enforcing consistency in executing service delivery reduce the growing variability in service quality from branch to branch? Couldn't a well-orchestrated and disciplined program that specified each of the steps required to deliver high-quality service allow Plowman's State Bank to control the quality of each customer interaction? Sure, there would no longer be any room for individual initiative, but do customers really need that? Wouldn't a uniform standard of service be better? Wouldn't it be enough to try to control the process by getting every frontline employee to enact the right set of scripted behaviors?

Well, maybe not. Just like the Terminators who could be counted on to execute their programs exactly the same way every time, specifying the exact sequence an employee should follow with every customer certainly standardized those interactions. They even seemed to give managers greater control over the process. Unfortunately, scripting employee behavior didn't really enhance the quality of employee-customer interaction. What's worse, it had the unintended consequence of emphasizing the steps an employee should follow rather than the outcome the process was supposed to produce. In the customer-measurement arena, these approaches have also led to the misguided demand for *actionability* in any prescriptive recommendations for improving customer service. In reality, actionability is nothing more than a code word for "I don't really want to put much thought into this. Just tell me exactly what the specific steps are to high-quality service, and those are the elements of the customer experience I will actively attempt to control." Unfortunately, you can't find the solution to building genuine customer connections in making the steps of service into a routine.

One unintended consequence of attempts to make customer service scalable and consistent was that firms began to place most of their emphasis on how to do the job instead of the outcomes that would result if the job was done well. As a direct result, companies often judged employees on whether they were meeting the demands of their roles by how well they followed the steps.

But the tried-and-true methods that produce manufacturing excellence by reducing variance in finished goods don't seem to fit when companies apply them to human interactions. There are two fundamental reasons why this is so and why organizations cannot simply transport the principles of quality control from manufacturing to the service economy.

In the manufacturing world, organizations can improve processes and systems because the materials they use to make things behave predictably — metals have a set melting temperature, assembly lines work at programmed rates of production, molds create identical parts over and over again. At their heart, these kinds of processes are little more than sequences of known and predictable actions repeated in identical ways.

But human systems in business — like the employee-customer encounter — conform to no such rules, and businesses that assume that they do, do so at their own peril. The fundamental errors the management team at Plowman's State Bank made were to assume that human interaction always follows the same immutable rules (it's consistent and predictable) and that all employees should be able to provide exceptional service in exactly the same ways (it's scriptable and trainable). Both these assumptions are flawed.

EQUIFINALITY

The work of the late German social psychologist Fritz Heider can help shed some light on why these assumptions about human interaction are flawed. In his watershed work *The Psychology of Interpersonal Relations*, Heider described the concept of *equifinality* and its role in purposeful behavior.[6] In essence, equifinality describes that there are as many paths to achieving a desired outcome as there are people willing to try. No single path is appropriate for all individuals because the conditions required to reach the desired outcome are different for every individual. In other words, though the end remains constant, the means to achieve that end will inevitably vary from individual to individual.

This is a crucial point because it suggests that no single set of behaviors can be equally effective in achieving the same goal from person to person. When given the same goal, different people need to make their own adjustments to a general set of behaviors to achieve the goal. The specific steps through which David provides exceptional customer service, for example, will look different from the steps Cynthia uses to achieve the same goal.

Socrates expressed the same sentiments in Plato's *Republic* more than 24 centuries ago:

> We are not all alike; there are diversities of natures among us which are adapted to different occupations. . . . We must infer that all things are produced more plentifully and easily and of a better quality when one man does one thing which is natural to him and does it at the right time, and leaves other things.[7]

Great organizations and managers follow Socrates' logic. They legislate goals, not steps. They view excellence within a role as attaining the right outcomes — not just conforming to a script and doing it the "right" way. We have all known someone who created outstanding outcomes using unconventional means. When the outcomes are clear, and people are free to discover how to use their unique talents to achieve them, unbelievable things begin to happen.

However, when organizations attempt to mass-produce behavior — as they do when you cash a check at your bank and the teller mispronounces your name because he's reading it from the deposit slip — the results are bitterly disappointing. It's impossible to legislate genuinely human interactions. Yet the belief persists that if we could just find the right set of steps or behaviors, then *anyone* could deliver exceptional customer service — just as anyone could work in a factory.

IT ALL DEPENDS ON WHOM YOU TALK TO

To illustrate these points, consider the customer of a European telecom provider — let's call him David Barnes. He called the customer service center with a question about upgrading his cell phone. This mobile phone provider had a standing offer to upgrade customers' phones once every two years. A customer service representative (CSR) greeted David with a curt, "How can I help you?" David provided his name and the necessary security details, then asked his question, which was followed by an equally curt, "Let me check your account details, and I will be right back." After about three minutes, the CSR returned to the line saying, "Well, Mr. Barnes, I have checked, and you are not presently eligible for an upgrade. Unfortunately, you haven't been with us long enough. Please check back with us in October. Is there anything else I can help you with today?" Question asked, question answered.

David wasn't happy with this answer, so he decided to try again. The second call started quite differently. Instead of a curt "How can I help you?" David was greeted with a warm, "Good afternoon, sir. What can I help you with this afternoon?" Again, David provided his name and the necessary security details and then asked his question. This time, however, the CSR asked him if he would prefer to be called "David" or "Mr. Barnes." After David expressed his enthusiastic preference for being addressed by his first name, the CSR continued: "Now David, I need to check your account details to answer your question. To do that I must put you on hold for a few minutes. Would that be all right? It's going to seem like a long time, but it really shouldn't be more than two to three minutes. I promise I will be right back." After about three minutes, the CSR returned to say, "OK, David, I'm back, and I apologize for that delay. Well, I have some good news and some bad news. The good news is that you are such a valued customer that you are eligible for an upgrade. The bad news is that I can't arrange for the upgrade just now — we'll have to wait until October. I hope that is OK with you. If you would be so good as to call me back in October, I would be delighted to arrange for your upgrade. I want to thank you for your business and for putting your trust in us. Is there anything else I can help you with this afternoon?" Same question, same basic answer, but from David's perspective, the second exchange was much more engaging.

What is interesting in David's experience is that both CSRs followed exactly the same steps and gave him essentially the same answer, but the outcome each produced was radically different. The first CSR left David feeling ignored and unimportant. The second left him feeling engaged and valued by the company.

A similar finding was born out by one of the largest CSR-level studies Gallup ever conducted, involving more than 4,600 CSRs. The results can be stated simply: In spite of the latest in technology tools, processes, and systems a typical call center uses, the customer experience still depends largely on the CSR who answers the phone.

Imagine that you manage a state-of-the-art call center. It's equipped with the most up-to-date technology, including a completely integrated customer relationship management (CRM) system that allows your CSRs to access each customer's relationship history with the company, including account activity, revenue, and profitability, in real time. Calls are routed automatically to make efficient use of total capacity. All CSRs are comprehensively trained, monitored, and coached, and the majority are paid within relatively narrow pay bands. Computer-assisted scripts even offer CSRs a menu of responses to common customer requests and concerns.

In this case study, the top 10% of CSRs produced a 6:1 ratio of positive to negative customer interactions. In other words, in a post-contact interview, for every seven calls these CSRs handled, six customers evaluated their interactions with those CSRs positively, while just one customer left the experience feeling alienated. What's more, a small cadre of seven CSRs consistently delighted every customer they talked to.

The bottom 10% of CSRs, in contrast, yielded a 3:4 ratio of positive to negative customer experiences; for every three customers who were delighted with their interactions with those CSRs, another four customers left the experience feeling alienated. And the worst CSRs actually managed to alienate every customer they spoke to.

How could this be? Did all of these CSRs have access to the same tools and resources? Surely. Were prepared scripts available to address common customer concerns? Indeed they were. Were they all trained in the same ways and paid about the same? Absolutely. This study reveals an inherent flaw in the logic that suggests that approaches designed to control quality by reducing the variability in manufacturing performance can be transported to a service context. It also shows that even a well-orchestrated and disciplined program of quality control that specifies the precise steps required to deliver high-quality service still can't enable a call center to control the quality of every customer interaction. Trying to legislate the steps to customer service does not guarantee a high-quality customer experience.

ASSEMBLY LINE SERVICE

When you stifle human interaction by attempting to legislate the steps to service, you sacrifice real quality — genuine human interaction — in favor of control. In essence, by attempting to control the service delivery process, you confuse the customer outcome you ultimately desire to create with controlling the processes through which that outcome is delivered. It's like writing "quality" in tiny, 4-point font and "control" in gigantic, 12-inch-high letters. You have embraced the idea that you can legislate service standards — and importantly, implement them — from on high. You are focused on the means to an end rather than the end itself.

But as Phil Crosby notes, "Quality has to be caused, not controlled." We can no more legislate human interaction than we can manufacture caring, mandate empathy, or generate a standard operating procedure for trustworthiness. No matter how much we might like it to be otherwise, we simply cannot control these volatile human dimensions.

The timeless wisdom of Matsuo Basho, a 17th century Zen master, provides an apt commentary: "[If you seek wisdom], do not seek to follow in the footsteps of the wise. Seek what they sought." Or in other words, "Don't focus on the steps. Focus instead on the outcome you are trying to create." In the end, any approach that sacrifices individual thought and initiative in favor of uniform standards is doomed to failure. At best, it will produce service that is bland, undifferentiated, and uniformly mediocre. At worst, it breeds bad service. So what is the alternative?

TOWARD AN ALTERNATE APPROACH: HUMANSIGMA

Our experience working with sales and service organizations around the world has led us to formulate an approach to measuring and managing human systems that we call HumanSigma. We didn't choose the name "HumanSigma" casually. HumanSigma, like its namesake Six Sigma, builds on the best principles of that methodology, offering a strategy for optimizing business performance by reducing variability and improving performance on key indicators.

Simplicity is the key to performance measurement and management effectiveness. The beauty and simplicity of Six Sigma is that it integrates a universal and consistent method to count quality defects with a disciplined process to eliminate them. The HumanSigma model overlays these same basic process elements onto the human systems of your business by providing a consistent method to assess and monitor the effectiveness of the employee-customer encounter with a disciplined process to manage and improve it. Ultimately, we believe HumanSigma offers a fresh way of thinking about how to manage that nettlesome and long-ignored root cause — your people — to get the most from the human systems in your business.

Six Sigma focuses on reducing variability in processes, systems, and output quality, and it's extraordinarily effective in manufacturing settings. But this kind of step-by-step process-improvement method does not work when applied to employee-customer interactions. In contrast, HumanSigma is a methodology for improving the quality of the employee-customer encounter that does not rely on reducing the variability in *how* employees are managed or *how* they serve customers. As paradoxical as it may seem, improving the quality of customer relationships will likely require *increasing* the variability in how those relationships are developed and maintained. By individualizing your approach to managing employees and customers, you'll unlock their maximum potential and your maximum profitability. This is the very antithesis of control.

The HumanSigma management approach starts by accepting human nature and then uses it to manage employees, motivate them, accelerate their development, and engage customers' emotions. Contrary to popular wisdom, our emotional traits are in fact quite predictable, and this long-ignored aspect of employee-customer relations holds the key to superior performance and long-term growth.

CHAPTER **TWO**
HUMAN SYSTEMS AND VITAL SIGNS

"Quit worrying about your health. It'll go away."
— Robert Orben, presidential speechwriter and humorist

If managing the effectiveness of the employee-customer encounter is not about controlling and scripting the steps of service, then what is it about? To understand how to enhance its effectiveness, let's step back and critically examine some of the assumptions that have guided how we view the human systems within our companies and how we have tried to manage them in the past.

VITAL SIGNS

Good health stems from an interconnected set of physical functions that your body performs. To ensure that these functions are working properly, you regularly visit your physician. Your physician evaluates your physical functions, often by assessing your vital signs, gauges your overall health, and then tells you if you need to adjust your behavior. Are you eating properly? Getting enough sleep? Exercising regularly? Are you finding ways to reduce or eliminate stress? Are you taking any prescribed maintenance medications, and, if so, are you taking them properly?

Think for a moment about your vital signs. Place your right index finger inside your left wrist just below your thumb. You'll feel the vibrant pulse that announces your heart is hard at work delivering its life-sustaining blood supply throughout your body. Now, relax and concentrate on your breathing. Though you cannot see the air you breathe, the oxygen it contains is essential to the health, growth, and sustainability of your body. As long as you take care of yourself by eating right, getting enough sleep, and making sure you exercise regularly, you rarely have to think about the physical functions these vital signs measure; they are pretty much automatic.

From one vantage point, you can think of your circulatory system (heart rate) and your respiratory system (breathing) as *independent* physiological functions. You can hold your breath and your heart won't stop, at least not immediately. From a slightly different point of view, however, your circulatory and respiratory systems are really *interdependent* physiological systems that must work together. Neither breathing nor circulation alone is sufficient to sustain life. When one or the other becomes ineffective or inefficient, your health will most certainly suffer. Whether these two systems are working in perfect harmony goes a long way in determining whether your body will survive and flourish or wither and possibly die.

The interdependency of these two systems is manifest physiologically in an additional vital sign — blood pressure — that represents the combined or net effects of heart rate and respiration. Blood pressure measures how efficiently and effectively your body is distributing oxygenated blood. Blood pressure reflects how well the two systems — respiration and heart rate — are working together.

Your vital signs — the outward indicators of those invisible and mysterious internal processes — serve an important function. When your physician measures your blood pressure, heart rate, and respiration, he or she is looking for early warning signs that something may be amiss. In most cases, your vital signs will register within normal limits, indicating that it's all systems go and your body is functioning more or less optimally. Occasionally, however, vital signs yield results that are outside of normal limits. When this happens, they give your physician a warning that your physical systems are out of alignment and may be in distress.

It's not surprising that this relatively small set of vital signs is often the first piece of diagnostic information an attending physician requests when a question arises about your health. These basic metrics of physical functioning are the foundation on which all subsequent medical interventions are usually based. Your physician may choose to order additional tests to diagnose the source of an injury or ailment, but, generally, he or she does this only after these "first-line" indicators have registered that something is wrong.

VITAL SIGNS OF THE EMPLOYEE-CUSTOMER ENCOUNTER

Just like your regular visits to the physician, an organization requires a feedback system to evaluate, regulate, and maintain its overall health. And, just like you, organizations have vital signs that need to be regularly monitored. An organization's vital signs serve as diagnostic indicators of how effectively it's addressing its key constituencies, executing its strategies, and maintaining its economic viability and how likely it is to grow.

Gallup has studied organizational vital signs for more than 60 years and has accumulated an extensive body of knowledge and experience about what makes organizations healthy and sick. Based on our studies of thousands of different performance metrics and hundreds of high-performance companies, large and small, we have learned that for sales and service organizations, the number of organizational vital signs is really quite small.

From our perspective, if heart rate, respiration, and blood pressure are the vital signs of the human organism, then in sales and service organizations, the corresponding vital signs of the employee-customer encounter are the health of its human systems: its customer relationships (heart rate), employee relationships (respiration), and overall financial vitality (blood pressure). That's it.

Separately, these vital signs provide important, but incomplete, diagnostic information about how effective the organization's employee-customer encounter is. Just as in the human organism, when one of a company's vital systems becomes ineffective or inefficient, its overall health suffers. On its own, neither sign provides a complete picture of the company's health. Only when these vital signs are viewed and understood as interrelated and mutually dependent human systems can a company measure the real effectiveness of its employee-customer encounters.

We recognize that there is an almost universal tendency to complicate and extend the list of organizational vital signs. After all, many executives will argue that we need a considerably larger collection of performance metrics to evaluate organizational health. They each have their favorite candidates based on their background, experience, and position within the company.

But executives should resist the urge to complicate or extend the list precisely because it hides the signs that are truly vital among a multitude of useful but less important measures. Just as a physician may order additional diagnostic tests to track down the ultimate source of an ailment, organizations should monitor a range of internal functions — but the main focus should be on a small set of vital signs that represents the first-line indicators of the company's health.

SELF-REGULATING (FEEDBACK) SYSTEMS

Most feedback systems, whether organic or mechanical, can regulate themselves. Take the thermostat in your home, for example. You set the temperature that's comfortable for you, and an internal thermometer in the thermostat continuously monitors the room temperature. When the temperature falls below your preset threshold, the thermostat turns on the furnace, warming the air in the room. When the air in the room reaches the desired temperature, the system shuts down, but the furnace continues monitoring the room temperature until the next time it falls below the preset threshold. In this way, the system maintains a uniform room temperature over time under different conditions. It's self-perpetuating and requires little human monitoring. Like the Energizer Bunny, it keeps going and going.

Your body's feedback systems work on basically the same principles, though they use different triggering mechanisms. Holding your breath is a good example. A specialized region of your brainstem continuously monitors the levels of carbon dioxide (CO_2) in your blood. When the level of CO_2 increases beyond a predetermined point, you experience overwhelming air hunger, and your brain sends out signals telling your lungs that it's time to breathe. Your lungs gulp in fresh air, and as the levels of CO_2 in your blood return to normal, your breathing also returns to normal. If you hold your breath again, the cycle will repeat. (This feedback system is one reason why it's impossible to hold your breath until you die.)

In the case of breathing — as well as with several of other physical needs such as hunger and thirst — your brain sends signals in the form of electrochemical messages that it transmits through the nervous and endocrine systems. Regardless of whether a feedback system is chemical or mechanical — or whether it's located in your brain or in your home — it consists of two parts: a sensor that monitors a predetermined state or condition and a switch that activates and deactivates the system in response to the sensor's signals.

Unfortunately, organizations don't have prefabricated feedback systems or predetermined performance thresholds to help them self-regulate. Instead, they must build and maintain those systems themselves. Unlike their human counterparts, an organization's human systems don't come with thermostats. If an organization's customer relationships start to decay or its employee relationships deteriorate, there is no sensor in the company's brain that forces it to self-correct — no internal warning that screams, "Fix it now!" Because of this, a company's vital signs require constant attention and monitoring.

Findings from some recent research into human performance highlight the need to monitor and attend to a company's vital signs. Without access to objective, external feedback on their performance, it seems that people are not good at evaluating it on their own. They tend to underestimate their own incompetence in different performance settings.[1] In other words, people are generally bad at recognizing when they are bad at something. What's worse, if left to their own devices, the same psychological processes that cause people to be ignorant of their own incompetence prevent them from being able to improve their performance.

Without constant, objective feedback about their performance, it's likely that employees will wander off track, thinking their actions are uniformly productive and positive; managers without recourse to objective performance data will tend to overestimate how well they are doing. Given these findings, it's crucial that organizations deploy the right kind of performance monitoring and feedback systems.

Monitoring your company's customer and employee vital signs is no longer something that's a "nice-to-have" item. In today's business environment, it's absolutely essential. That's why most companies invest considerable resources to monitor their customer and employee vital signs. Yet, almost every company has a slightly different way of doing it. Although there is almost universal agreement that heart rate, respiration, and blood pressure are the vital signs of the human organism, there is considerably less agreement on the vital signs of an organization. A cursory review of the business literature published in the past two decades reveals a plethora of potential candidates for organizational vital signs.

Until recently, for example, most business executives focused exclusively on financial results to gauge the health of their organizations. This made sense, given Wall Street's acute focus on the financial metrics that ultimately determined the value of an enterprise. But financial results proved to be a rudimentary feedback system. Because financial results always lag behind the organizational activities that produce them, executives who monitor financial performance can only react to events that have already happened. Monitoring financial results alone cannot help executives to anticipate marketplace behavior, alert them to potential missteps, or help them identify areas that need corrective action before preventable declines in overall financial performance occur. More importantly, monitoring financial performance alone could not help executives understand *why* financial performance may have declined (or for that matter, improved). For today's information age managers and executives, adopting a wait-and-see attitude to whether their strategic and tactical management initiatives have yielded positive financial returns is no longer a viable option. The pace of global business is too rapid and competition too intense.

THE BALANCED SCORECARD

In 1992, Robert Kaplan and David Norton argued for a broader set of organizational vital signs by introducing the concept of the "balanced scorecard." In a landmark article in the *Harvard Business Review* and a follow-up book,[2] Kaplan and Norton argued that though traditional financial measures worked well for the industrial era, a more balanced and comprehensive mix of metrics — including assessments of customers and employees, the crucial human systems of organizational performance — is required to accurately gauge the health of today's organizations.

A key point from their work is that so-called "hard" financial data are lagging indicators of organizational performance, while non-financial, human performance metrics are leading indicators. These leading indicators, in turn, can help managers and executives take corrective action before declines in financial performance occur.

Following the publication of the balanced scorecard approach, companies rushed to incorporate myriad non-financial performance metrics into their strategic management initiatives. Too often, these efforts resulted in a proliferation of metrics that created more confusion than clarity.

As the dust settled around companies' attempts to identify a core set of leading measures to assess the effectiveness of their human systems, two classes of preferred metrics emerged: *customer satisfaction* and *employee satisfaction*. The issue of whether customer and employee satisfaction actually measure anything of value to the organization is incredibly important. Therefore, it's surprising to us that serious attempts to link customer and employee metrics to measures of financial performance have been made in earnest only in the past few years.

Five years after Kaplan and Norton's work was first published, the utility of an approach that employs financial *and* human performance metrics to gauge total business performance was given a public forum. *The Service-Profit Chain*[3] discussed an exploratory analysis of the linkages between employee satisfaction and customer satisfaction and financial performance outcomes. Though James Heskett and his colleagues described strong conceptual links between these different measures, most of the evidence they offered was anecdotal.

Attention to some mix of human systems indicators is by now a generally accepted tenet of modern business practice. Almost 15 years after Kaplan and Norton appealed for the use of a more complete set of business metrics, many businesses have implemented some type of balanced scorecard. But, as they say, the devil is in the details. In our view, the breakthrough promise embodied in the balanced scorecard approach remains largely unfulfilled.

"NOT EVERYTHING THAT CAN BE COUNTED COUNTS"

With this in mind, now is probably a good time to consider if organizations have focused on the right vital signs to effectively measure and manage the employee-customer encounter and if those vital signs are being synthesized and used to galvanize action and improve organizational health. As a sign purported to have hung in Albert Einstein's office warns: "Not everything that can be counted counts."

Let's focus first on what companies do with the information they gather from the indicators they use. Our experience suggests that in most companies, these indicators are rarely collected, analyzed, or used in an integrated way. What's more, these indicators are rarely linked to economic performance measures. We contend that it's not sufficient to provide managers with a "dashboard" of seemingly unrelated gauges and dials drawn from different parts of the organization. Patients would be aghast if they had to visit different specialists to have their respiration checked and their heart rate measured. Similarly, businesses do managers a great disservice by failing to integrate the metrics for which they hold them responsible.

Most companies continue to maintain functional silos responsible for their organizational vital signs. The customer perspective and the metrics used to monitor it, for example, are usually the province of the quality or marketing organization. These organizational entities often carry out an enormous amount of research, but little, if any, of that research finds its way to other areas within the company. This is unfortunate. What executives can learn from this research about the nature of the marketplace affects the ways employees should be deployed within the company and which employees should be performing key tasks.

The employee perspective usually lies within the domain of the human resources department. Though the encounter between an employee and a customer represents the touchstone of value creation in sales and service companies, human resources departments are rarely involved in strategic decision making, marketing campaigns, or advertising efforts, outside of providing input about staffing levels and costs. This is also unfortunate. Employees who interact with customers are the face and the soul of the brand and are intimately involved in the frontline execution of the brand promise, yet they play little role in its formulation and development.

This brings us to the first new rule of HumanSigma management:

Rule 1: E Pluribus Unum. You can't measure and manage employee and customer experiences as separate entities; they must be managed together under a single organizational entity.

We contend that only when these organizational systems and their vital signs are brought together and empirically linked can a true picture of the health of the employee-customer encounter be understood and managed. What this means in practice is that the responsibility for measuring and monitoring the health of a company's employee and customer constituencies should reside within a single organizational structure. This structure should have a clearly identified champion who has the authority to manage change across the broad range of organizational activities that affect the employee-customer encounter. Although the tactical responsibility for managing the effectiveness of the employee-customer encounter resides with local or line-level managers, oversight must reside within a single corporate entity and should not be dispersed to various areas of the organization.

This is a tall order, as it may require companies to rethink their structure. To maximize the potential in a company's employee-customer encounters, it may need to reorganize. The human resources function in sales and service companies, for example, should reside within the operations, marketing, or quality organization, creating a department of human marketing or human quality. This organizational structure emphasizes the essential role that employees play as brand ambassadors while aligning the employee function with the major constituency those employees serve: your customers. We suspect that over the next 5 to 10 years, this kind of organizational structure will become the rule rather than the exception.

Have you built an organizational structure that is customer centric? How thoroughly integrated are your employee and customer metrics and the activities that support them?

CHAPTER **THREE**
FEELINGS ARE FACTS

"At the constitutional level where we work, ninety percent of any decision is emotional. The rational part of us supplies the reasons for supporting our predilections."
— Charles Evans Hughes, chief justice of the United States from 1930 to 1941

Jerry, his wife Julie, and their two sons, Brian and Wesley, have been looking forward to their summer vacation for months. For them, like many other families, this weeklong visit to central Florida represents a significant investment in time and money. They've had their airline reservations for months, they have booked a nice hotel close to the action, and they have their theme park tickets in hand. Finally the day arrives and the family begins their trek from their home in North Carolina to the theme park Mecca of Orlando.

The trip south passes uneventfully. The flight is on time and picking up the rental car actually goes off without a hitch. As the family drives from the airport to the hotel, the excitement builds. Jerry parks the rental car near the hotel, enters the lobby, and joins the line of guests waiting to check in. A couple of minutes pass, but the line does not seem to be moving quickly. Even though it has been just a few minutes, Jerry grows restless. He looks around and notices that there is just one receptionist on duty, even though there is space behind the counter for at least five. A few more minutes pass, and Jerry begins to grow irritated; his family is waiting outside in the car, and their long-awaited vacation can't start until they are safely in their hotel room. "Why can't they add a receptionist or two?" he wonders.

Finally, Jerry reaches the front desk and is greeted with a familiar "May I help you, sir?" Looking at his watch, Jerry is surprised to find that he has been in line for only 10 minutes, though it seemed like much longer.

Two days later, Jerry, Julie, and the boys are in the midst of their theme park vacation. Brian and Wesley have been anxious to experience one of the world-class "big iron" rides the park is famous for. As the family approaches the line for the roller coaster, they notice a sign that says, "From this point, the wait time for this ride is 30 minutes." Undaunted, they join the queue. As they wait, they notice that the line winds back and forth, turning upon itself every 50 feet or so. In addition, the queue is covered, shielding the family from the relentless Florida sun. There are video monitors playing trailers for upcoming film releases featuring the action heroes around which many of the park's rides are themed. Posters display facts and figures about the action heroes and provide "historical" context about them.

At last, the family reaches the boarding area for the coaster. As he boards, Jerry glances at his watch and is surprised to find that he has been in line for a full half hour, though it seemed much shorter than that.

THE ELASTICITY OF PERCEPTION

Like all consumers, Jerry's perception of his wait time in line is elastic — like his perceptions of virtually every aspect of his experience with the many companies he does business with, from how accurately they transact his business to how interested they are in his personal needs. Like a rubber band, his sense of time stretches and shrinks depending on the circumstances and the context.

His perceptions of other aspects of his experience with the companies he does business with are equally flexible. The *objective* — and often quantifiable — reality of the situation takes a back seat to Jerry's *subjective* experience of it. What matters most to Jerry is not the exact amount of time he and his family waited, but how long it *felt*. That perception is what prompts Jerry's subsequent behavior and influences the decisions that he makes; it's what Jerry will react to, it's how Jerry will frame his experience at the park, and it's what Jerry will remember.

"Feelings are facts." This simple phrase succinctly captures almost everything we need to know about how customers perceive their interactions with the companies they do business with and how employees view their relationship with their employers. It also summarizes an idea with a long history in academic sociology — something sociologists refer to as the "definition of the situation." More than 75 years ago, William I. Thomas, a sociologist at the University of Chicago, wrote that "If men define situations as real, they are real in their consequences." In other words, a person's definition of the situation — that is, how they perceive that situation and what they define to be true about it — determines how he or she will react to it.[1] Thomas was saying that though the objective elements of a situation are important, the subjective experience of those objective elements — what the situation feels like — is what truly matters to people. Perception *is* reality.

Too often as business leaders, we get caught up in the facts of our businesses and fail to appreciate what matters to employees and customers. For them, reality is not only the objective experience they have with our companies but also how they perceive and interpret that experience — their feelings about it. For Jerry, the 10-minute wait in the hotel lobby felt exasperatingly long, whereas the 30-minute wait for the roller coaster seemed blessedly short. In Jerry's case, having things to look at and do while in line made the wait feel shorter and more engaging, while counting the number of unoccupied receptionists' spaces made what was really a shorter wait feel like an eternity — and wholly disengaging.

But where does this elasticity in perception come from? Many things can intervene to make our perceptions align with or deviate from objective reality. We can't always see everything that happens during a specific event, for example, and we may "go beyond the information given" by filling in the missing pieces based on our past experience or what we expected to happen.[2] Or we may become distracted by salient — or attention-grabbing — aspects of our environment or by other things we might be thinking about.[3] Or we could be angry or elated, and this could draw our attention elsewhere. The list could go on and on.

The academic literature in cognitive and social psychology has documented dozens of these so-called errors, biases, and heuristics in judgment and decision making: the full spectrum of cognitive (mental) processing biases and heuristics,[4] being busy,[5] a lack of attention or paying too much attention to something else,[6] our expectations,[7] and perceptions of risk,[8] to name just a few. In the employee-customer encounter, one of the most intriguing factors that can significantly affect customers' and employees' perceptions of the world around them is their emotions.

ADAM SMITH AND THE "PASSIONS"

No, it's not the name of an up-and-coming rock group. Back in 1759, before he wrote *The Wealth of Nations*, Adam Smith, the father of modern capitalism, argued for the existence of what today would be called a dual-process system that guides human behavior. In *The Theory of Moral Sentiments*, Smith argued that human behavior results from the struggle between two opposing forces: the "impartial spectator" or the "rational man" who at some remove dispassionately scrutinizes every move one is likely to make and the "passions," which are those nettlesome drives, emotions, and feelings that often stand at odds with rational behavior.[9] Smith's work was ahead of its time and presaged many of the contemporary perspectives on the relationship between emotion and cognition.[10]

Much has changed in the past 250 years — including our understanding of the psychological and neurological bases of human behavior — but Adam Smith has proven to be surprisingly prescient. What makes his insights perhaps more astounding is that much of what we have learned about the human brain was discovered in just the past 15 years. As the National Institutes of Health (NIH) recently noted, we learned more about our brains in the 1990s than in the entire previous history of the human race.[11] Until recently, humanity was living out Heisenberg's uncertainty principle — the very act of trying to observe our own behavior led us to conclude some things that were just wrong about how our brains work.

These new fields of scientific inquiry have enabled researchers to take a much more objective look at human behavior at home, at work, in the marketplace, and at play. We know so much more now than we did even 15 years ago about how our brains develop, how they predispose us to behave in certain ways, and how we respond to those predispositions in others that we are able to take a much more critical and honest look at who we are as employees, customers, and parents — as *people*. The idea that much of what we thought we knew about human nature is now an open question has enabled some fundamental rethinking of human behavior.

Perhaps one of the most important and startling developments in this arena has been the advances made in our ability to understand the inner workings of the human brain and how brain activity links to behavior.[12] For example, Joseph LeDoux, a neuroscientist at New York University, has argued that it's much easier for emotional responses to influence our thinking than for rational responses to temper our emotions. This is because the neural pathways that extend from the emotional system to the cognitive or thinking system in the brain are wider and faster than those that extend from the cognitive system back to the emotional processing areas. Antonio Damasio's work has shown that the separate systems we call emotion and rationality are in fact completely intertwined and interdependent. Damasio's work suggests that emotion is as central to everyday decision making as is rational thought. Neither system can exist or function without the other, and understanding the organic underpinnings of feelings is key to understanding how and why people make the decisions and behave in the ways they do.

The relatively new science of behavioral economics — the discipline that sits at the crossroads of psychology and economics — has also begun to shed new light on the psychological dynamics of human decision making and how non-conscious and emotional factors influence that process.[13] All of these developments are of paramount importance to business leaders because they compel us to rethink the traditional rational/functional models of human decision making that guide many business decisions. Sadly, many business leaders and many economists have been slow to embrace these profound changes in perspective, clinging instead to an outmoded view of human behavior that regards human beings as dispassionate brokers of objective information.

So, if human beings are less akin to Smith's impartial spectator and are driven more by their passions, how does this affect the tools we use to manage them? If the health of a company's employee and customer relationships really are the core of sales and service organizations' vital signs, have business leaders found the right ways to evaluate them in their own companies? This is not a trivial issue because if business leaders fail to measure these vital signs correctly, they put their organizations at risk by monitoring what is not important and missing what is. The business consequences can be disastrous, and improvement efforts targeted at the wrong vital signs waste resources that we could otherwise apply more productively.

We would suggest that many, if not most, companies could benefit by reevaluating the vital signs they currently use to assess the quality of the employee-customer encounter. Getting the metrics right is an essential first step, but it's one that many companies seem to have overlooked. So how do you accurately measure these vital signs? Of the many things companies *could* count, what really counts?

THE IRRATIONALITY OF EVERYDAY LIFE

People do all sorts of things for all sorts of reasons — and some of those things defy reason. An example from the sports pages brings this issue to life. Around 11:30 a.m. on June 12, 2006, Ben Roethlisberger, the quarterback for the Pittsburgh Steelers football team, was traveling between radio interviews on his black 2005 Suzuki Hayabusa motorcycle. As he approached the intersection of 10th Street and 2nd Avenue in Pittsburgh, a silver Chrysler New Yorker traveling in the opposite direction turned left and collided with the motorcycle. According to the *Pittsburgh Post-Gazette*, Roethlisberger was thrown into the Chrysler's windshield and then hit the ground headfirst. He sustained significant injuries to his head and face, though none were life threatening. What was truly amazing was that at the time of the accident, Roethlisberger wasn't wearing a helmet — in spite of reams of empirical data and the repeated warnings from his coaches and teammates that wearing a helmet reduces the likelihood of injuries in a serious crash.

When asked why he chose not to wear a helmet in spite of all the good and rational reasons to do so, Roethlisberger simply replied, "Because you don't have to. It's not the law. If it was the law, I'd definitely have one on every time I rode. But it's [not] the law, and I know I don't have to, and you're just more free when you're out there with no helmet on."[14] For Ben Roethlisberger, when it came to deciding whether to wear a helmet, emotion trumped reason.

Although this sort of behavior may strike you as atypical or rare, it's worth noting that non-rational considerations shape a significant proportion of our behavior, from deciding whether we will wear seat belts, to which appliances to purchase and which car to drive, to the kinds of coffee we drink, and to which employer we decide to work for.

BERNOULLI'S ERROR

In 2002, psychologist Daniel Kahneman of Princeton University was awarded the Nobel Prize in economics for his work, conducted largely in collaboration with the late Amos Tversky, on the psychology of decision making under conditions of uncertainty. What made this particularly noteworthy was that this was the first time the Nobel Prize for economics was awarded to a psychologist.

It was also noteworthy because, historically, economics and psychology haven't gotten along well. At their core, psychology and economics share an interest in understanding human thought, feeling, and behavior. But for the past 80 years or so, these two disciplines have followed remarkably different paths to attain that understanding. Early on, economics embraced physicist, philosopher, and mathematician Daniel Bernoulli's rational-agent model, which assumes that people are rational and dispassionate maximizers of economic gain. In essence, Bernoulli's perspective was that people make decisions based on a cool and rational evaluation of the available evidence — the benefits of a certain course of action weighed against its costs — before arriving at a decision. The right decision, according to Bernoulli, was the one that maximized an individual's economic gain and minimized his costs. The core assumption of the rational-agent model has not changed much in the 250 years since Bernoulli first espoused the idea in spite of the evidence illustrating its flaws.[15] Kahneman refers to this inaccuracy in Bernoulli's formulation as "Bernoulli's error."

Psychology embraced a different model altogether, one that emphasized the interplay between rational, perceptual, and emotional processes in decision making, noting in particular that human decision making is prone to all manner of errors and biases, many of which Kahneman and his colleagues first documented.[16] Much of Kahneman, Tversky, and their colleagues' pioneering work focused on the heuristics — or simple, efficient rules of thumb — that people use to make decisions.[17]

Kahneman and his colleagues' work has been influential for many reasons, but chief among these was that their "prospect theory" set the stage for a reunion of psychology and economics under the banner of behavioral economics.[18] The emergence of the integrated field of behavioral economics has been a watershed development because it has forced many economists to abandon — or at least modify — their rational-agent models and incorporate psychological principles of decision making into their work.

Now that economists have begun to recognize the need for a more comprehensive understanding of human decision making, we think it's high time for business leaders to do the same. Although much of our understanding of these processes remains in its infancy, several key discoveries have emerged that affect what companies should pay attention to when assessing the vital signs of the employee-customer encounter. Every company has a largely untapped, enormous potential for breakthrough improvements in employee productivity, customer retention and profitability, and authentic sustainable growth. Before companies can achieve these gains, they must first improve their understanding of how the emotional economy works in their company and in the larger marketplace. Harnessing this potential starts with a reevaluation of how we measure and manage the employee-customer encounter.

A NEW PERSPECTIVE ON "CUSTOMER REQUIREMENTS"

To master the new discipline of the emotional economy, business leaders need a new way to think about "customer requirements" and a new set of tools to help structure their businesses around them.[19] But exactly how should they construct a new definition of customer requirements?

Traditionally, the customer's perspective has been evaluated by assessing "conformance to requirements," often (though not always) by using a generic measure of customer satisfaction. Early practitioners of the quality movement postulated that customers would be satisfied with and would continue to purchase a product or service if it met their functional specifications and fulfilled their requirements. The origins of how "customer satisfaction" emerged as the preferred measure are a bit murky, but, for better or for worse, it seems to have been selected primarily based on its intuitive appeal. In other words, customer satisfaction seems so plausible that surely it must be the correct thing to measure. As a result, the issue of whether customer satisfaction actually measures anything of value appears to have been overlooked.

Because the bulk of the work that laid the foundation for this perspective originated in manufacturing and process-intensive businesses, customer requirements have generally been specified in functional terms: Did the product have any defects? Did it conform to specified manufacturing tolerances and parameters? Was it delivered on time? And so on.[20] But as our knowledge of psychology, behavioral economics, and neuroscience has matured, we now recognize that this rational-functional view of human decision making is flawed and incomplete.[21] To date, only advertisers have paid much attention to the essential non-rational and emotional dimensions that define what it means to be human — and a customer. As a result, it's not surprising that executives and managers continue to struggle to understand why customers who appear to be satisfied defect to competitors — and why authentic, organic growth remains elusive.

CUSTOMER SATISFACTION IS NOT ENOUGH

Business leaders, researchers, academics, and management consultants alike have expressed concern that though customer satisfaction may be a necessary foundation for building strong customer relationships, by itself it's a relatively poor indicator of future customer behavior.[22] Our data support this concern. Empirical results from a large and growing number of case studies suggest that customers who are *extremely satisfied* — those who provide the highest rating of overall satisfaction with a company's products or services — can be classified into two distinct groups: those who are *emotionally satisfied* and those who are *rationally satisfied*. Emotionally satisfied customers are extremely satisfied with the products and services the company provides and have a strong emotional attachment to the company. Rationally satisfied customers, in contrast, are also extremely satisfied with the company but lack the strong emotional connection of customers who are emotionally satisfied. When we examine the indicators of customer behavior within these two customer groups, such as customer attrition, frequency of use, share of requirements/share of wallet, and total revenue and spending, among others, a clear and striking pattern emerges. Emotionally satisfied customers deliver enhanced value to a company, for example, by buying more products, spending more for those products, or returning more often to or staying longer with the business. Rationally satisfied customers, on the other hand, behave no differently than customers who are dissatisfied.

Consider the following case study from a large U.S. retail bank. When we assessed this bank's customers using an 11-item metric of customer engagement (described in detail in Chapter 4 and Appendix A), we found that over a six-month period, emotionally satisfied customers ended their relationships with the bank by completely closing their accounts at rates that were 37% lower than rationally satisfied customers' rates. Dissatisfied customers, on the other hand, scarcely differed from rationally satisfied customers in their attrition levels.

Similar results emerged for an international credit card provider. Over a six-month period, emotionally satisfied cardholders spent on average $251 per month and used their cards an average of 3.1 times per month. Rationally satisfied cardholders, in contrast, spent on average just over half this amount ($136 per month) and used their cards less often (an average of 2.5 times per month) during the same period. Again, dissatisfied customers were virtually indistinguishable from rationally satisfied customers in their actual purchase behavior: Dissatisfied customers also spent on average $136 per month and used their cards an average of 2.2 times per month during the same period. And, emotionally satisfied cardholders increased their spending by 67% over a 12-month period, compared to an increase of just 8% among rationally satisfied customers. Once again, dissatisfied customers were virtually indistinguishable from rationally satisfied customers in terms of spending increases.

This general pattern is consistent across every industry we have examined, leading us to this powerful conclusion: Customer satisfaction is not enough. Merely satisfying customers by delivering on their rational requirements represents a minimum point of entry for today's businesses; managing to satisfy customers will not drive the enhanced financial performance today's business leaders seek. To build the strong customer connections that produce enhanced financial benefits, a more complete view of customer requirements is needed, which incorporates an understanding of the emotional dimensions of customer commitment. Customers want more than transactions — they want relationships.

NOT ALL ADVOCATES ARE CREATED EQUAL

In the *Odyssey*, Homer describes how Odysseus avoided the deadly lure of the siren song. The sirens inhabited a rocky island and created music so beautiful that sailors who passed near the island became enchanted and were unable to resist its charms. To get closer, the sailors would leap into the ocean and drown, or steer their ships toward the beautiful sounds, wrecking them on the rocks. The siren song was irresistibly beautiful, and its consequences predictably dire. But, following the advice of Circe,

Odysseus had his men plug their ears with beeswax and tie him to the ship's mast as they neared the sirens' island, commanding his men to tighten his bonds should he beg them to release him. In this way, he avoided the lure of the sirens and sailed safely past.

Every so often an idea comes along that, on the surface, seems so compelling and simple that we would be surprised if it weren't true. Just such an idea — that there exists a single question that business leaders should ask their customers in order to grow their business — has recently been put forward by Frederick Reichheld, a director emeritus of the consulting firm Bain & Company and a Bain Fellow. In essence, Reichheld asserts that the one number a business needs to know and track over time is the percentage of existing customers who would serve as strong advocates for the company by recommending the company to others. Reichheld's claim has provoked a great deal of interest and debate, and the utility of the entire construct has recently been called into question.[23] Nonetheless, it has struck a chord, primarily because it takes something that has been considered complex and makes it astonishingly simple. What's more, it holds out the promise that companies just might be able to shed their sometimes cumbersome customer feedback systems in favor of a simple one comprised of just a single question.

The existence of a simple, single-item performance metric that can be reliably linked to positive financial performance would be the management equivalent of a cure for the common cold. But, before we all go running off to determine our company's advocacy score on the basis of a single question, consider this: Not all advocates are created equal nor are they equally valuable. So, unless we want to risk being lured, like Odysseus of old, onto the rocks by the siren song of oversimplification, we should heed Alfred North Whitehead's sage advice to "Seek simplicity, and distrust it." At a minimum, your shareholders will be glad you did.

Oversimplification is a modern-day siren song. True, many things that are complex in modern business processes needn't be. But, though it may be appealing to try to reduce things to their most basic elements, we should also recognize the wisdom in Albert Einstein's admonition that "Everything should be made as simple as possible, but not simpler." Taking simplification too far can result, paradoxically, in a loss of understanding and poor decision making. First, it's a maxim of measurement theory that single-item measures are inherently less reliable than composite (multi-item) metrics.[24] Essentially, that's because a single item may not always measure the same things in the same ways from one time to the next. Smart executives should be wary of using one-item indicators for any important business metric regardless of how simple it might appear. Few of us would be comfortable with a single-item final exam or a single-question job interview. Fortunately, there is an alternative — a simple performance metric that yields a single number but isn't based on just one, ultimate question. We'll return to this metric in a moment.

If your goal is increasing customer advocacy, you must recognize that the challenge isn't to get customers talking about a company's products or services. Instead, the challenge is to get them talking *positively* and *passionately* about your company. That requires your customer to feel the enthusiasm that only comes from strong emotions. Even among customers who say they are extremely likely to recommend the company, the strength of the positive emotional connection is what determines whether that recommendation is lukewarm or glowing. And the strength of the emotional connection is what ultimately determines customers' future behaviors. Even strong advocates differ in terms of the extent to which they are emotionally attached to a company. Some of these strong advocates are just advocates; others are *passionate* advocates.

To illustrate, let's consider three groups of customers. The first group — the *non-advocates* — is made up of all customers who are less than extremely likely to recommend the company to others. The next group — the *rational advocates* — is made up of customers who, although extremely likely to recommend the company to others (the highest possible rating), lack a strong emotional bond with the company. The final group — the *emotional advocates* — is made up of customers who are also extremely likely to recommend the company to others, but who have forged a strong emotional attachment to the company. If advocacy in itself were all that mattered in driving business performance, then we would expect both groups of advocates to deliver significantly better business outcomes than the non-advocates. We might expect the two groups of advocates to differ in their actual behavior toward the company. But, according to our research, it doesn't work like that.

First, let's look at the investment behavior of customers at an international private bank. When we sorted the customers into three categories — emotional advocates, rational advocates, and non-advocates — emotional advocates delivered significantly enhanced business outcomes when compared to their rational counterparts, both in share of assets and in the net new assets they invest with the company. Surprisingly, rational advocates did not differ from the non-advocates on these key financial measures. (See the graphic "Customer Advocates: The Emotional ROI.") We found the same general pattern for the customers of an international lodging and hospitality company. In this case, emotional advocates stay more nights and spend more with the company. They deliver significantly more business value to the company than do rational advocates, who behave more like non-advocates on these key measures. The same general pattern also emerged for a U.S. retailer and a global B2B cargo shipper.

Analysis of data from these companies, as well as a host of other companies in the United States and worldwide, demonstrates that a company's strongest advocates behave differently toward the company depending on the degree to which they are *emotionally* attached to it. If you want to drive advocacy — and reap the financial benefits that come from building strong emotional connections with your customers — you must first understand and manage those emotional connections.

Now, obtaining a recommendation from your customers remains crucial to business success. But our research suggests that developing a deep understanding of what makes your customers tick requires more than knowing how many of them would recommend you to others. Human nature is more complicated than that, and business leaders who ignore its complexities do so at their own peril.

CHAPTER **THREE**

CUSTOMER ADVOCATES:
THE EMOTIONAL ROI

When we sorted customers into three categories — emotional advocates,
rational advocates, and non-advocates — emotional advocates delivered significantly
enhanced business results when compared to their rational counterparts. Surprisingly,
rational advocates generally do not differ from non-advocates on many of these key
financial measures.

INDEXED PERFORMANCE

■ Emotional advocates   ■ Rational advocates   ■ Non-advocates

(100 = average)

INTERNATIONAL PRIVATE BANK

Share of investable assets
- 126
- 97
- 97

Net new assets
- 337
- 127
- 98

INTERNATIONAL LODGING AND HOSPITALITY COMPANY

Total nights
- 111
- 95
- 85

Value
- 107
- 92
- 94

U.S. RETAILER

Number of visits (past month)
- 111
- 101
- 96

Total dollars spent (past month)
- 116
- 104
- 94

Share of spending
- 125
- 107
- 90

GLOBAL BUSINESS-TO-BUSINESS CARGO SHIPPER

Share of spending
- 150
- 86
- 70

Share of tonnage
- 147
- 97
- 65

Source: Gallup

83

There is much value in Reichheld's analysis of existing customer measurement platforms and a good deal that we agree with — that traditional customer satisfaction measures are poor indicators of the health of a company's customer relationships, for example, and that only the highest possible ratings really matter. But there are several shortcomings to the single-item approach that compromise its feasibility and validity. As noted previously, single-item measures are inherently less reliable, and some advocates are more valuable to your company than others are. Among the most important reasons to be wary of a single-item approach is that a single-item advocacy metric doesn't tell you *why* customers recommend a company. As a result, it doesn't give you the intelligence you need to manage customer touchpoints to increase the number of these advocates. Measuring advocacy is one thing, but to manage your customer relationships effectively, you need to know more.

For instance, you should probably add questions to your survey to "get under the hood" with your customers, but doing so undermines the purported value of a single-item measure. If you need to measure a number of additional factors, you should measure what really matters rather than reducing your set of measures to a single item that struggles to be all things to everyone. Ultimately, paring down your measurement system to just one question won't yield the customer feedback you need to drive performance and create organizational change. Instead, you should pay careful attention to exactly what the company is measuring to ensure that the process balances brevity and simplicity with valid, reliable, and useful information.

Connecting with customers' emotions carries a huge financial benefit. Establishing strong emotional connections with your customers can mean the difference between creating rational advocates — customers who merely talk about your company — and emotional advocates — those who talk about it passionately.

So go ahead, measure your customer advocacy. It's an important piece of information. But while you're at it, don't stop there. Remember that your ultimate goal is to inspire something more than mere advocacy among your customers. Your true goal is to inspire *passionate* advocacy at every location and touchpoint because passionate advocacy pays significant financial dividends. Achieving this goal requires you and your employees to forge strong and lasting emotional bonds with your customers. And measuring how effectively you are building and nurturing those emotional bonds is truly the one number you need to grow.

We can sum this all up with the second new rule of Human-Sigma Management:

Rule 2: Feelings are facts, and emotions frame the employee-customer encounter.

Although it is appealing to simplify how we think about the health of our employee and customer relationships, remember that "Not everything that can be counted counts." You need to be careful, deliberate, and informed because what you measure is a crucial component of your future success. What you measure must be more comprehensive than mere satisfaction and broader than simple advocacy.

Do your current performance metrics incorporate an understanding of the key emotional dimensions that drive positive employee and customer outcomes?

CHAPTER **FOUR**
CUSTOMER ENGAGEMENT AND EMOTIONAL ATTACHMENT

"Mankind are governed more by their feelings than by reason."
— Samuel Adams, 18ᵗʰ century American patriot

J ennifer's mom is more than just a satisfied shopper — she is a *fully engaged* customer. A couple of years ago, Jennifer was scheduled to deliver her second child. Her mother, Ann, arrived the day before the delivery to stay with her first child while Jennifer was in the hospital. Instead of cooing over the layette, cooking, or doing whatever it is that normal grandmothers are supposed to do, Ann insisted that they go shoe shopping at a particular upscale clothing store (let's call it Tres Bon) because, as she put it, she rarely makes it to a town where Tres Bon has a store. So Jennifer, Ann, and Jennifer's 3-year-old made the trek to the store. As they walked in, Ann grabbed Jennifer's hand, looked her deep in the eyes, and sighed, "I want to be buried here."

Jennifer spent more than two hours wandering the store with her mother and her 3-year-old. Ann wound up buying several hundred dollars worth of shoes and then called back later — from the hospital on the day Jennifer's second child was born — to have them ship a shirt that she decided she wanted after all.

We all know someone like Ann — someone who is more than merely satisfied: a customer who is so passionate, so emotionally connected to and fanatical about a particular brand that it seems as though a large portion of her life revolves around it. Companies spend millions of dollars each year trying to find and court just this kind of customer. But how do you know exactly which customers actually deliver the greatest value?

IN SEARCH OF THE RIGHT QUESTIONS

In the previous chapter, we showed that rationally satisfied customers behave no differently than dissatisfied ones — and rational satisfaction is not enough to drive enhanced financial outcomes. Rational advocates also behave no differently than non-advocates and rational advocacy alone — like rational satisfaction — is not enough to drive enhanced financial outcomes. This may lead you to wonder why businesses have been so slow to recognize that neither of these single-item measures — overall satisfaction or likelihood to recommend — is an adequate way to gauge the true health of a business. One part of the reason, no doubt, lies in their simple appeal; it just seems like these two questions should matter. Another part of the reason is probably that, until now, there have been few other options available to managers and businesspeople. Whatever the reason, it's absolutely critical to recognize that if a business' ultimate goal is sustainable organic growth, these measures simply are not good enough. We all need to aim higher.

So if being satisfied or willing to recommend a company won't motivate customers to behave in ways that deliver value to a company, what will? As we considered this question, the start of answer came — not too surprisingly — from a group of customers.

"IN MY CHILDREN'S EYES"

A few years ago, we were doing some work for a major theme park, helping to identify the elements of the theme park experience that most strongly influenced a desire to return to the park. To probe customer opinions and behavior, we hosted many focus groups with theme park visitors around the United States. Our ultimate goal was to create an ongoing customer measurement program that would provide feedback on the customer experience to the park's operators and staff.

During one early focus group in Atlanta, we began by asking participants to describe their last theme park experience. At the beginning, the participants' comments tended to be critical: It was too hot, and there wasn't enough shade. The food prices were exorbitant and the food wasn't very tasty; a bottle of water cost a fortune. The lines were long, and the wait times for the attractions and restaurants were interminable. There weren't enough signs; the ticket prices were too high; it was too crowded. The list of shortcomings went on and on.

Taken aback by this outpouring of negativity, the moderator commented, "Wow! It sounds to me like very few, if any, of you had a particularly good time at the park. So let me ask a question. With a show of hands, tell me, if you had the chance, how many of you would go back?" Without hesitation, every hand in the room shot up.

The moderator was stunned. "OK, now I'm really confused. You all described some pretty nasty incidents and criticized almost everything about the park's operations. Yet all of you would willingly — and from the looks of it, quite cheerfully — go back again. Why?" Almost instantly, a mother from suburban Atlanta responded, "Oh, that's easy. It's not about what happens to me. When I see the joy in my children's eyes when they are in the park, it makes all the hassles, all the expense worthwhile. And I would go back a thousand times just to experience that feeling." Around the room, heads began to nod in agreement.

These comments set us thinking. On a purely rational level, these theme park visitors' comments didn't make any sense at all. That's because according to a rational-functional approach, the sum total of all the elements of a customer's experience should yield an over-all evaluation, like $1 + 1 = 2$. With these visitors, the accumulation of their negative experiences should have translated into an ardent desire never to return to the park. But what we had heard was something closer to $1 + 1 = 10$. Rationally, their experiences just didn't add up — based on their comments, there was no way these customers should ever want to return to the park. But when we considered their comments from an emotional point of view, they made all the sense in the world. Of course these visitors would return to the park, but not because every aspect of their theme park experience was executed perfectly, but because the ultimate takeaway — the emotional payoff they were looking for — was seeing the joy in their children's eyes.

TOWARD A SCIENCE OF EMOTIONAL ATTACHMENT

Inspired by the discoveries that our colleagues were making with customers like those in the Atlanta focus group, in the summer of 2000, scientists at Gallup embarked on an ambitious and far-reaching R&D program to probe the deep psychology behind what we call *customer engagement.* Taking a cue from psychologist Ben Schneider and management consultant David Bowen's work on customer delight and outrage,[1] we set out to understand what made customers tick — customers like Jennifer's mom and the theme park visitors from Atlanta. Our goal was to develop a method to measure, reliably and accurately, the emotional connections between customers and the companies that serve them. The research program also sought to examine the relationship between soft attitudinal measures and crucial business performance metrics, including customer retention, cross-sell, share of wallet, frequency of purchase, profitability, and relationship growth. Coming up with a method for measuring customers' emotions is one thing, but proving that those emotional connections have tangible financial value is quite another.

Schneider and Bowen have argued for a more sophisticated view of the customer experience beyond mere conformance to functional requirements and an estimate of overall satisfaction. In their research, they analyzed hundreds of comments customers made about companies that either delighted or outraged them. They then classified those comments into groups with similar themes. Based on their analysis, Schneider and Bowen suggest that extreme expressions of customer delight and outrage can be characterized by whether companies meet — or fail to meet — a set of emotional requirements. These emotional requirements are organized, like Maslow's hierarchy of needs, from the basic to the complex. Their approach assumes that customers are people first and consumers second; it also assumes that people strive to satisfy a core set of needs in life at a level more fundamental and compelling than meeting their specific expectations as consumers.[2] This perspective, which is based on emotional needs, provides a useful foundation for developing a comprehensive measure of the customer side of the employee-customer encounter.

In his pioneering work, Abraham Maslow[3] classified human needs that energize, direct, and sustain existence into a hierarchy from the most basic to the most advanced. At the basic level, people have a set of physiological needs that are required to sustain them; they include oxygen, water, protein, rest, activity, appropriate temperature, and sex, among others. Only when these physiological needs have been met does a person's focus shift to meeting higher-order needs. Beyond these basic life-sustaining needs are needs for safety and security, love and belonging, enhancing self-esteem, and, ultimately, self-actualization, or the realization of one's individual potential and personal "completion."

We believe that in their relationships with the companies they do business with, customers have a hierarchy of needs similar in form to Maslow's. This hierarchy begins with the fulfillment of basic emotional needs and moves through the fulfillment of higher-order, aspirational ones. Gallup research has revealed that there is an underlying structure to this hierarchy of "emotional attachment" and that it's remarkably consistent from industry to industry. More importantly, its dimensions can be measured and managed.

AN EMOTIONAL INFRASTRUCTURE OF DELIGHT AND OUTRAGE

According to Schneider and Bowen, a customer's most basic emotional requirement is a sense of security: Will I be safe with this company? Feelings of security hinge on interrelated perceptions of orderliness, consistency, stability, and predictability. Customers generally dislike unpleasant surprises, and violations of security are almost universally met with extreme displeasure and outrage. So powerful is a customer's need for security that a thousand instances of meeting his or her needs can be undone by a single failure.

Assuming that a company meets a customer's security needs, his next set of emotional requirements focuses on a need for fairness and reciprocity: Will this company treat me fairly? At this level, customers and the companies with which they do business have an implicit social contract to treat each other fairly. Violations of this contract, like violations of security needs, are met with displeasure and outrage.

Ultimately, a customer has a strong need to enhance his self-esteem: Will I feel good about myself if I do business with this company? The need to enhance self-esteem, like the other needs for security and fairness, can take many forms. For example, customers feel better about themselves when they feel competent and in control. They value when their input is taken seriously and their voice is heard. And they appreciate it when they are treated as individuals with unique histories, experiences, and circumstances rather than as members of a "segment" or as a number.

TOWARD A MEASURE OF EMOTIONAL ATTACHMENT

To develop our new metric of emotional attachment, we pulled together an exhaustive set of candidate items drawn from prior surveys and from academic research into the psychology of human emotions. Customers in different product and service categories (for example, new car purchasers, recent travelers, and checking account customers) rated their current or most-often-used provider (of their car, airline, or bank) on a list of more than 60 candidate measures. Extensive analysis of these measures yielded a final list of eight emotional attachment items that showed strong linkages to attitudinal loyalty and key business performance metrics.

The final set consists of 11 customer engagement items, called the CE^{11}. These items are arranged into two distinct elements that parallel Adam Smith and Antonio Damasio's dual-process models. One element is arguably more rational, the L^3, and one emotional, the A^8.[4] Taken together, these items provide an assessment of how engaged a customer is with a particular company.[5] Each customer's CE^{11} score — a weighted average of the 11 items — allows us to classify him or her into one of four engagement groups that correspond to that customer's level of engagement with the company. We refer to customers at the highest levels of engagement as measured by the CE^{11} metric as *fully engaged* customers. These customers have a strong emotional bond with the company. They are more likely to be behaviorally loyal and are a company's most valuable and profitable customers. Those at the next engagement level — *engaged customers* — represent a company's opportunity segment. These customers haven't yet formed an enduring emotional connection with the company, but the foundation is in place to build stronger emotional connections with them.

Customers at the next level are referred to as *not engaged* customers; for most companies we work with, they make up the largest segment. Not engaged customers are attitudinally and emotionally neutral. They don't feel strongly one way or the other about the company. Their relationships with the companies they do business with are characterized by an ambivalent take-it-or-leave-it attitude; only switching costs and inertia keep them from leaving. The final engagement group — made up of the least engaged customers — we call the *actively disengaged*. These customers harbor substantial negative feelings toward the company. Most actively disengaged customers could be considered strong candidates for defection to a competitor. Yet many remain with the company — spreading their discontent to other customers or prospects along the way — because of either high switching costs or a sense that a competitor would be no better. Their motto is, "Better the devil I know than the devil I don't."

Our research reveals that across companies of different types, running the gamut from international cargo shippers to grocery shoppers, customers who are fully engaged represent an average 23% *premium* in terms of share of wallet, profitability, revenue, and relationship growth than the average customer. In stark contrast, actively disengaged customers represent a 13% *discount* in terms of share of wallet, profitability, revenue, and relationship growth than the average customer. At a local business unit level (a store, branch, sales team, or other local unit), those whose levels of customer engagement place them in the top 25% of comparable units within a company tend to outperform all other units on measures of profit contribution, sales, and growth by a factor of 2 to 1. Clearly, engaging customers on an emotional level has a significant financial benefit.

THE EMOTIONAL ATTACHMENT HIERARCHY

The eight individual emotional attachment items all show an ability to predict business results. But there are some important relationships among the items, and exploring them can enhance our understanding of how emotional connections are formed and sustained. Like Maslow's original framework and Schneider and Bowen's formulation, the A^8 measures can be divided into a hierarchy of emotional attachment. Its base represents the core requirement for any enduring relationship between a customer and a company, and its apex represents the highest achievement for any company: an irreplaceable position in the life of the customer.

Unlike Maslow's or Schneider and Bowen's hierarchies, however, our work suggests that there are actually four, not three, key dimensions to a customer's emotional attachment to a company. Each dimension represents a specific set of activities that meet customers' emotional needs. (See the graphic "Four Dimensions of Emotional Attachment.")

The first and foundational dimension of emotional attachment is *Confidence*. Is this company trustworthy? Can its employees be trusted do what they say they will do day in and day out? Confidence is the foundation on which higher levels of emotional attachment are built. But Confidence alone is not enough to build long-term, sustainable, and emotionally connected customer relationships.

FOUR DIMENSIONS OF
EMOTIONAL ATTACHMENT

Our work suggests that there are four key dimensions to a customer's emotional attachment to a company. Each dimension — Confidence, Integrity, Pride, and Passion — represents a specific set of activities intended to meet customers' emotional needs.

Can't imagine a world without
Perfect company for people like me

PASSION

Treats me with respect
Feel proud to be a customer

PRIDE

Fair resolution of any problems
Always treats me fairly

INTEGRITY

Always delivers on promise
Name I can always trust

CONFIDENCE

Beyond Confidence lies *Integrity*, the essential dimension of fair play. Does this company treat me the way I deserve to be treated? If something goes awry, can I count on this company to fix it quickly?

The next emotional requirement is *Pride*, a sense of positive association and identification with the company. Pride goes beyond simplistic notions of self-presentational, status, or "badge" qualities of association to deeper levels of shared values between the customer and the company. Customers who feel Pride are proud to be a customer not because of what their association with a company says to others, but more importantly, because of what it says to them about themselves. Customers' associations with companies not only convey information about them to others, but they also help define and sharpen their own self-concepts.

The fourth dimension, and the ultimate expression of emotional attachment, is *Passion*. A passionate customer describes his or her relationship with the company as irreplaceable and a perfect fit for him or her. Passionate customers are rare, but they represent the epitome of customer connectedness. They are customers for life and are worth their weight in gold.

CHAPTER **FIVE**
EMOTIONAL ATTACHMENT: CONFIDENCE AND INTEGRITY

"If I can't trust you . . . then I have no choice but to put you right back outside the circle. And once you're out, you're out. There's no coming back."
— Jack Byrnes (Robert De Niro)
Meet the Parents, Universal Pictures and DreamWorks SKG, 2000

CONFIDENCE

Many years ago, Sunkist used the fear of inconsistency to boost its brand with a cartoon commercial of a boy peeling open a no-name orange from which a monster emerged. "If it doesn't say Sunkist," the monster said, "you don't know what's inside."

In life, unless the potential rewards are significant, few of us like to take unnecessary chances. That's also the way people feel about the companies they choose to do business with. Do you want to take a chance that your next flight may not arrive on time? Would you care to risk staying at a hotel where the rooms sometimes aren't clean, or bank where your monthly statement is correct only occasionally?

The foundational dimension of emotional attachment — Confidence — is also the most basic. Is this company inside my circle of trust? Will it deliver on its promises, day in and day out? Has it figured out the basic costs of entry — the "table stakes" — to earn my business? One of the things people look for in a brand or a company is a promise of consistently high performance. Great companies *always* keep their promises. With a great company, customers always know what to expect, they feel secure dealing with the company, and they don't expect unpleasant surprises. Companies that keep their promises create trust — a sense that promises they make today the will keep in the future.

Always is a difficult standard to live up to, but it's the gold standard; customers expect nothing less. *Sometimes, usually,* or *occasionally* just won't cut it. If sometimes, usually, or occasionally is the best your company can muster, it will move you outside your customers' circle of trust, and there will be no going back.

Confidence is the bedrock upon which higher levels of emotional attachment are built. But Confidence alone is not enough to build long-term, sustainable, and emotionally connected customer relationships. It's only the starting point for an emotional connection.

A company's ability to engender confidence in its customers begins with its ability to consistently deliver a customer's basic requirements for that industry (such as clean hotel rooms or a perfect bank statement) and the more specific elements of the company's brand promise. Gallup's research has shown that companies that fail to build confidence have a much tougher time engaging customers than companies in which customer confidence is solid. For customers, the consistency between what a company promises and what it actually delivers is key to building Confidence. Unfortunately, in most companies today, what the company promises to its customers is rarely agreed upon at senior levels, let alone well understood among the company's rank-and-file employees. In fact, Gallup research has found that just 43% of customer-facing workers employed in a broad range of sales and service industries strongly agreed with the statement, "I know what my company stands for and what makes us different from our competitors." Although disturbing, this observation points to one immediate opportunity for increasing customer engagement: ensuring that your brand promise is known and understood at every touchpoint. Aligning your company's brand promise with consistent execution at all of its customer touchpoints is essential for building Confidence.

Examples of inconsistent delivery can illustrate the importance of building and sustaining perceptions of confidence. What if someone felt a company *only sometimes* or *rarely* delivered on what it promised? The bank might or might not credit your account properly. The produce at that grocery store may or may not be moldy. Your hotel room may or may not be ready on time. This sort of uncertainty and risk is unsettling to customers, and they will go out of their way to avoid it.

Some senior marketing executives at a major U.S. lodging chain brought to life the drive to avoid uncertainty and risk. One lamented the fact that guests visiting their hotels never knew exactly what to expect from one property to the next: "Once you've seen one of our hotels, well, you've seen one of our hotels."

Like accidental tourists, customers gravitate to the predictable to avoid unpleasant surprises.

INTEGRITY

Before he logged off his computer for the day, a businessman decided to visit the Web site of a well-known outdoor outfitter to order a few monogrammed shirts. While there, he also decided to buy a small pocketknife. According to the company's Web site, a customer could have his initials engraved on the knife, but the link to have this done did not work. The man decided to order the knife anyway, typing out a quick note to the company's "Contact us" e-mail link about his frustration with the engraving option.

Less than 30 minutes later, the man's cell phone rang. It was a representative from the outfitter. She apologized for the problem, got the information for the engraving, and told him she'd see that the shirts and knife were shipped without any delay. What really impressed him, though, was that he hadn't given the company his cell phone number. The service representative first called his home, reached the man's wife, and got the number to reach the customer quickly to resolve the problem.

What are a company's standards? What ethics does it live by? Will it treat all its customers fairly, following through on a promise even if doing so costs the firm money in the short term? Does it play by the rules? Does it treat me the way I want to be treated? How does it respond to product or service failures? If something goes awry, can I count on this company to fix it fast? These are some of the questions that illuminate the second level of emotional attachment: Integrity, the essential dimension of equitable treatment.

THREE TYPES OF FAIRNESS

But what constitutes fair treatment? Things get a bit complicated here because people apply different rules of fairness depending on their circumstances. Social psychological literature identifies at least three different types of fairness or justice: *distributive* fairness, which addresses how resources are distributed; *procedural* fairness, which covers the processes and systems that are used to determine how resources are allocated; and *interactional* fairness, which encompasses how people are treated at an individual level. All three types of fairness come into play at different times, and all are important. However, from a customer's perspective, distributive and procedural fairness carry the greatest weight because they represent chronic — or structural — issues. Customers' perceptions of transactional fairness, in contrast, can vary from interaction to interaction and therefore represent transient — or acute — issues.

Distributive fairness deals with how companies allocate resources among individuals. Do they allocate resources to me the way they allocate them to some, all, or no other customers? Procedural fairness covers the processes and systems companies use to distribute resources. Does the company follow the rules it has laid out for handling problems, processing returns and refunds, or addressing warranty claims? Are those rules reasonable and consistently executed? Is the company flexible or rigid in how it handles out-of-the-ordinary situations? Does it recognize that its customers' time is valuable, avoiding excessive wait times and providing help when needed? Last but not least, interactional fairness is up close and personal. It encompasses how a company's staff members interact with its customers: Do they treat customers with unwavering honesty, politeness, and respect in every interaction?

DISTRIBUTIVE FAIRNESS

Distributive fairness addresses how companies allocate resources among individuals. With distributive fairness, three different allocation methods or rules are possible: *equity*, *equality*, and *need*. People often apply these distribution rules inconsistently and sometimes combine them in internally incompatible ways.

Let's look at these three rules in Schneider and Bowen's terms. Fair treatment under the equity rule means that the company should reciprocate and distribute resources to me based on what I have invested in the relationship, or, as Schneider and Bowen might put it, "Treat me the way you treat *some*, but not all other, customers." In contrast, fair treatment under the equality rule means that a company should distribute resources equally among all customers, or, "Treat me the way you treat *all* other customers." Finally, fair treatment under the need rule means that the company should distribute resources to me based on my individual needs, or, "Treat me like *no other* customer."

In general, the equity rule comes into play when a customer has invested heavily in the relationship such as when frequent fliers expect preferential treatment based on the number of miles they have flown with the airline. In contrast, few customers employ the equity rule when they have little invested in the relationship. Instead, these customers will be more likely to employ the equality rule. The need rule is often invoked when a customer believes circumstances exist for special treatment. When it comes to fairness, the perennial challenge for companies is to find a balance among the three distribution rules.

To illustrate how these rules work in practice, consider the following scenario. You have been a subscriber to a financial services magazine for five years. While watching television one evening, you see a commercial offering a lower price to new subscribers. No offer has arrived in your mailbox for a special deal for loyal readers. Based on your application of the equity rule, you might question why the magazine is fawning over people who have never subscribed when you've been a long-time subscriber. As a loyal customer, you feel you should get equal, if not better, treatment than the nonsubscriber.

The equality rule works a bit differently. For example, a man buys a power drill from the local hardware store. The next day, the woman across the street tells him she bought the same drill on the same day at the same store — but for less money. "How did you get that price?" asks the man. "I told the guy helping me I wasn't sure," replied the woman. "He said he'd knock $10 off the price." That inequality would offend most customers. Though both customers bought the same drill from the same store, the man's sense of unfairness stems from the unequal treatment he received, with no equitable explanation given from the store for the unequal treatment.

The need rule works even differently. For example, a retailer sells small shelf units. One unit is set up for display; the rest are in boxes, unassembled. Store policy requires the units to be sold in boxes, and customers must assemble them at home. An elderly gentleman comes in, likes the shelf unit, but explains he would have great difficulty setting one up. Would it be OK, he asks, if he could buy the display unit? Applying the need rule, most people would feel that selling the elderly gentleman the display unit would be fair. Why? Because the special circumstances or needs of this individual provide an equitable explanation for the seemingly unequal treatment.

To demonstrate how all three rules can work in the same setting, consider the security screening line at your local airport. Frequent fliers (employing the equity rule) consider fair treatment to consist of special expedited lines reserved exclusively for them. Infrequent or leisure travelers (employing the equality rule) consider such treatment unfair to them; their sense is that everyone should wait in the same line they do. The person who is running late for his flight (employing the need rule) considers it completely fair to be moved immediately to the front of the security line lest he be delayed and miss his flight. Other passengers generally consider special treatment like this unfair — unless they, too, find themselves running late. Misunderstanding of the psychology of fairness needlessly contributes to the frustration customers experience every day.

PROCEDURAL FAIRNESS

Procedural fairness covers whether customers feel that your company's policies and procedures are fair and equitable. Is the game played according to the rules, and are the rules fair? When it comes to procedural fairness, it's important to understand that often the issue is not whether the customer followed all of the rules, because the fine print can make those rules difficult to follow. Customers, instead, want the process to be reasonable. Do your customers perceive your staffing levels as adequate to handle customer demand for checkout, check-in, assistance, or other services? Is your return policy overly restrictive in the eyes of your customers? Are customers required to pay a restocking fee or return shipping? Do you have the channels in place for customers to return goods easily? How long must customers wait for service either in person or over the phone? Is the only time a customer can make a service appointment during a weekday between 9 a.m. and 5 p.m.? The list could go on and on. Procedural fairness is the rationale behind express lanes in a grocery store: Those who have just a few items shouldn't have to wait for someone buying a week's worth of provisions.

One of the most egregious violations of the procedural fairness rule is unfortunately all too common. It happens when customers call a service center, only to hear this recording: "Your call is extremely important to us. Please hold and your call will be answered by the next available agent." As a customer, your immediate perception is that your call is *not* important, because if it were, the company would have enough staff to handle it without your having to wait. On top of that, telling you that you call is important, while you sit on hold awaiting a representative, simply adds insult to injury.

From the customer's perspective, any process or system whose primary purpose is to solve a business problem rather than a customer concern is unfair. We would argue that the search for customer centricity is really a search for procedural fairness. Anyone who designs products and services, interacts with customers, or prices products must keep in mind that customers want fair policies and procedures. A company that customers see as taking advantage of them or as designing policies and procedures that customers view as inequitable will quickly erode its customer engagement. Your business can take great strides toward authentic customer centricity and emotionally engaging your customers by reviewing its processes and systems from the customer's perspective and then evaluating them against your legitimate business needs. Often, minor changes to those processes and systems can make them appear fairer in your customers' eyes.

INTERACTIONAL FAIRNESS

The third rule is interactional fairness, which encompasses how a company treats people at an individual level. A company can excel at distributive and procedural fairness but still irk customers by the curt way in which it delivers those services. When your employees interact with customers, do they always treat them honestly and with respect? Are employees polite and courteous? Are they able to give customers their undivided attention, or are they multitasking? Interactional fairness matters in the trenches and up close and personal. You can think of it as the "bedside manner" portion of fairness. At issue is whether your employees make interacting with the company enjoyable.

Companies that ask their employees to focus on executing the functional steps of service delivery without also asking them to concentrate on and understand their customers' emotional needs are much like a new father who feeds and changes his infant but is puzzled when the baby continues to cry. Consider the following exchange between a mobile phone customer and the provider's service technician:

Customer: "I just purchased this phone, but I think there's something wrong with it. It keeps dropping calls."

Technician: "Are you sure?"

Customer: "Well, yeah. It just cut me off a minute ago, right before I walked in here."

Technician: "See, the reason I ask is that 90% of the problems we see here are due to user error. Are you sure you're using it right?"

Customer: [Now getting angry] "Yes, I'm using it right. This is not the first mobile phone I've owned. I'm sure there's a problem."

Technician: "OK, I'll take a look. But these are pretty good phones. I'm almost certain you're not using it right."

As it turned out, the phone was defective and ultimately was replaced, but not before the customer was insulted three times in this short conversation. This technician had a lot to learn about bedside manner, even though he executed the diagnostic script he had been given — one that emphasized checking for user knowledge and potential user error before examining the phone.

MOMENTS OF TRUTH: AN UNTAPPED OPPORTUNITY

The previous example also highlights another crucial facet that can help build Integrity: how a company responds to product or service failures. Though everyday policies and procedures can substantially affect customers' perceptions of a company's fairness, product or service failures — and how they are handled — can be critical moments in perceptions of Integrity.

Problems happen. It's an unfortunate but unavoidable fact of life. The steak you ordered at the restaurant is overdone. The telephone in your hotel room won't work. Your car wasn't fixed correctly the first time you took it to the garage. Your prized aisle seat has accidentally been given to another passenger. Companies that respond effectively to problems like these can actually maintain and build stronger emotional connections with customers.

Customers who experience a problem typically have significantly lower levels of emotional attachment with that company (often as little as one-half to one-third) than those who say they've had no problem with the company. The worst word-of-mouth stories about a company often start when a customer experiences a problem. On the other hand, customers who encounter a problem and are extremely happy with how the company *handled* the problem often have levels of emotional attachment equal to — and in some cases, exceeding — those who had no problem at all. Notice that the emphasis is on how the company *handled* the problem, not how it was *resolved*. Customers do not expect that a company will resolve all their problems to their liking, but they do expect the company to handle them in an exemplary way. This is because customers are far more sensitive to the process of service recovery than they are to its outcome. If the company handles the process courteously and fairly, customers more readily understand if the resolution is not to their liking. Companies who want to forge strong emotional connections with their customers should treat product and service failures as more than just problems they need to fix (or avoid or make disappear) — they are opportunities to engage their customers emotionally.

One characteristic of a great brand is the likelihood that if a customer experiences a problem, the company deals with it quickly and well. For example, you have a problem with a meal at a restaurant; the waiter apologizes, takes it back, returns with the meal properly prepared, and says, "Dessert's on the house." If the phone isn't working in your hotel room, a good hotel will fix it immediately or move you to a different room. If the dealership doesn't fix your car the first time, it apologizes for the inconvenience and gives you a free loaner until your car is fixed.

Now imagine if all a company does all of these things grudgingly. How engaged would you be with the restaurant if the waiter refused to take back the overdone steak, insisting the steak was cooked as you ordered? Or if the hotel clerk said that he or she couldn't get the phone in the room fixed until the next morning, and it was impossible for the hotel to move you to another room? Or if the auto repairperson insisted that it would be two weeks before the dealership could try fixing your car again?

If one of your customers has a problem, what's the best way to solve the problem and recover from it? There is no single behavior or script that will work in all situations. What's an acceptable solution for one customer may not be acceptable to another. One diner might be delighted with the free dessert, while another might prefer that the restaurant does not charge him for the dinner. One hotel guest might be satisfied with the hotel clerk's sincere apology and offer to move to another room; another guest might only be satisfied with a free stay.

What can you do when there's no single behavior that will satisfy all customers in every problem situation? First, you can use apply the three general rules of fairness, which can help you see the problem from the customer's point of view. You can also deploy a conciliatory strategy that Gallup has developed in its work with companies around the world. When a customer feels wronged, companies rarely take conciliatory measures. Why risk losing a customer when keeping him or her is well within your ability? Our six-step approach to problem resolution can help you avoid the destructive consequences of inaction. This method revolves around a simple yet profound act: an apology.

1. Acknowledge the problem. Too often, company representatives challenge a customer's concerns. Stonewalling or finger pointing is a common way in which companies avoid acknowledging a problem. For example, if a customer tries to return defective merchandise, some employees may respond — as the mobile technician did earlier — "Are you sure it doesn't work?" What the customer hears is "I don't believe you." When this happens, the company misses an opportunity to show respect and empathy by suggesting that the customer is not trustworthy.

   Customers want the company to hear their concerns. Are you their advocate or their adversary? If the customer thinks they have a problem, they have a problem. Affirming that you understand why they are upset or inconvenienced makes them feel they have someone on their side.

2. Apologize for the problem. This may seem obvious, but it rarely happens. There are many reasons why employees are often reluctant to apologize for a product or service failure. Sometimes, they are afraid the customer or their manager will hold them personally responsible for the problem; other times, they may fear that an apology represents a tacit acknowledgement of blame and acceptance of legal liability.

Don't confuse apologizing with accepting blame. A sincere apology communicates that you care about how the customer was treated. Offering apologies — even if it's not clear who was at fault — can go a long way toward helping repair the damage to your relationship with the customer.

But there is more to a sincere apology than just repairing a broken customer relationship. Gallup research also shows — and studies by psychology and sociology researchers confirm — that a genuine apology can actually strengthen a customer's emotional bond to your company, leaving him or her more psychologically and emotionally connected than customers who never experienced a problem. When Gallup surveyed a large group of U.S. retail banking customers, 26% of those who had not recently had a problem were fully engaged with the bank. But among those customers who had experienced a problem and were extremely satisfied with the way the bank handled it, 51% were now fully engaged with the bank.

To understand why apologizing works, you must realize that when a customer relationship goes awry, that customer feels isolated and vulnerable. If the company "owns" the problem, apologizes for it, and undertakes a remedy, this validates the customer's decision to trust the company in the first place, and it confirms his value to the company. Research done by Marti Hope Gonzales, a social psychologist at the University of Minnesota, has demonstrated that genuine remorse and expressions of regret are the key to a good apology, such as saying "I'm sorry, I feel awful about your problem" and then offering restitution.[1] If the employee who takes the complaint is not authorized to make restitution, the company should train him or her to say something like, "I'm not authorized to specify what the company can do to make this up to you, but I'm taking this to my manager, and we will make this right."

The late sociologist Erving Goffman[2], who devoted much of his career to researching the importance of "maintaining face" in social interactions, noted that apologies keep both parties' self-images intact: When the company accepts responsibility and helps to solve a customer's problem, the company looks good, and the customer's feelings are legitimized. When companies fail to acknowledge problems or to apologize, that's when lawsuits get rolling. Companies that resist apologizing out of fear that doing so will expose them to a lawsuit are often bringing on their own worst nightmare. That's because legal liability is not relevant to the myriad everyday snafus that erode customer engagement. The sooner you apologize, the less likely you are to hear from a customer's lawyer. After all, if an employee or manager apologizes and rebuilds the relationship, customers have little reason to pursue their grievances further.

Handling a problem that involves personal injury obviously does require legal advice. But, according to some recent research and legal cases,[3] apologizing may be a good idea even in those instances. In cases of medical malpractice, for example, research shows that patients are less likely to sue if their doctors make a heartfelt apology and work to alleviate the problem.[4] Since 2002, the hospitals in the University of Michigan Health System (UMHS) have been encouraging doctors to apologize for mistakes. According to Rick Boothman, a former trial attorney who launched the practice there, UMHS has seen the system's annual attorney fees drop from $3 million to $1 million, and filings of malpractice lawsuits and notices of intent to sue fell from 262 in to about 130 over the past few years. At the lawn mower company Toro, providing an apology as part of a revolutionary product integrity policy helped reduce legal costs per claim by 78%, from an average of $47,252 to $10,420, from 1992 to 2000. The average resolution amount for the period was reduced by 70%, from $68,368 for settlements and verdicts to $20,248. Several states have adopted or are considering legislation to shield physicians from legal liability when they offer an apology.[5]

So, if one of your customers encounters a problem, apologize. Your company has everything to gain — from boosting customer engagement to fending off an expensive lawsuit — from a prompt and sincere apology.

3. Take ownership of the problem and follow up, even if the problem is unresolved. Once a customer shares a complaint, the ball is in your court. You need to take responsibility for finding a solution. If you need to make a phone call, pick up the phone — don't make the customer call back. Even if you can't resolve the problem on the spot, the customer should feel that you're paying attention to the problem without him having to police it. Keep communicating with the customer while the problem is being fixed.

One effective approach to problem ownership is to promise to follow up by a specific date or time. A typical way to handle this is to say something like, "I'll let you know just as soon as I find something out." But this leaves the time frame open and may make customers feel they have to police the response. Instead, promise some form of contact by a specific date or time, even if you're unsure you'll have something to report. This accomplishes several things: First, when you do follow up as promised, you demonstrate to customers that you've taken their concerns seriously — and that you've kept the promise you made. Second, by getting back to them at a specified time or date, you free customers from having to follow up on their problem on their own. Having to recontact the company can further irritate and frustrate customers.

4. Handle problems on the spot. Customers hate to be handed off to someone else to address their problem or concern, whether they are being transferred to a different call center representative or being referred to a supervisor or manager for action. There are other good reasons to handle problems immediately. Besides meeting customers' needs, it often costs less to resolve a problem at the point of first contact, which can save the company money.

At a well-known hotel chain, for example, the standard practice was to refer guest complaints to the manager, who usually responded by offering one or more free overnight stays. In a pilot program, the hotel instructed all employees to apologize for complaints they received and offer a restitution they were authorized to provide. If a guest complained to a housekeeper about poor housekeeping, for instance, the housekeeper would apologize (even if he or she wasn't the person who had cleaned that room) and offer the guest a gift basket of toiletries, a complimentary bathrobe, or a small bouquet of flowers. If the guest was still fuming, the housekeeper referred him or her to the manager, who upped the restitution. The hotel's overall cost of handling complaints dropped dramatically while guest satisfaction with how their problems were handled increased — a win-win situation for the company *and* its customers.

5. If you can't resolve the problem immediately, quickly escalate the problem to a supervisor or manager. Delays cause frustration. The quicker the remedy is applied, the better the customer will receive it. Many companies have found that technology can be a real asset in problem resolution. For example, implementing a complaint logging system that automatically escalates problems to the next level of management if they remain unresolved for a predetermined period of time can help ensure that customer problems are resolved. But beware: You need to implement this kind of technology solution carefully. The last thing you want is for employees to think that their responsibility for resolving customer complaints ends with logging them into the system.

6. Leave the customer better off than before the problem. A customer's engagement level won't be as high as or higher than it was before the problem occurred unless he is better off after it. An agreeable resolution reassures customers that the company can see his needs and meet them — now and in the future.

When companies fail to resolve problems, frustrated customers begin to look for alternatives. They'll contact the competition.

They'll tell friends about their unfair treatment, making your company's poor service or shoddy products the star of their stories. They'll write a letter to a newspaper. Occasionally they sue. The negative effects of faulty problem handling can extend long after the customer's original problem.

A final note on Integrity: We have repeatedly found that a strong emotional attachment introduces a positive elasticity into customers' perceptions and interpretations of their experiences with a company. Customers who are fully engaged will grant that company a state of grace — or an unconditional pardon — when they encounter a problem because they apply a much more lenient definition of "service failure" than less engaged customers do. We've often heard of highly engaged customers who acknowledge their contributions to service failures ("I wonder what I might have done to cause this to happen?"). They're also more likely than less engaged customers to assume that a company's mistake was honest or unavoidable and forgive the company for making it.

To sustain that state of grace, companies should invite customers to speak up about any problems. Give them a complaint forum, such as a toll-free number, help desk, or Web site. And train your frontline workers to listen carefully so you learn about problems before they become the source of a customer's grudge. Customer problems will damage your company's reputation whether you hear about them or not — and you won't have a golden opportunity to say you're sorry if you don't hear about them.

CHAPTER **SIX**
EMOTIONAL ATTACHMENT: PRIDE AND PASSION

"One person with passion is better than forty people merely interested."
— E.M. Forster, English novelist (1879–1970)

PRIDE

The next dimension of emotional attachment is *Pride*, a sense of positive association and identification with a company. Pride goes well beyond basic notions of self-presentational, status, or badge qualities of association to deeper levels of shared values between the customer and the company, as well as feelings of competence and control. The most powerful relationships customers have with companies are those that make them feel good about themselves, and a key element of that feeling is when customers feel competent and in control.

Feelings of competence and control are largely based on predictability and past experience. It's easy to undermine these feelings by placing customers in a situation that is unfamiliar and difficult to navigate. Building perceptions of competence and control are one reason that retail banks invest so heavily in consistent branch and ATM design. The easier it is for a customer to understand a new branch layout or ATM keypad configuration, the more likely he or she will feel in control.

In contrast, one reason why airline customers are universally displeased with the industry is that almost every contact a traveler has with an airline is rife with ambiguity. Airlines routinely provide information about a particular flight's status, but when they do, it's often inaccurate or outdated. Often, the flight status information posted on video displays in the terminal doesn't match the information posted at the gate or online. The airline staff never seem to know — or seem unwilling to divulge — information about delays or changes. Ambiguities like these make customers feel incompetent and as if they lack control; this in turn makes them feel bad about themselves and even worse about the airline.

Customers also feel good about themselves when they believe that their decision to trust a company is well founded. No one likes to feel as though his or her faith in a company has been misplaced. When this happens, we also begin to question our judgment and our ability to make smart decisions. Customers prefer to do business with companies that make them feel smart about their decisions and don't make them second-guess their choices.

Customers' associations with companies not only convey information about them to others, but those associations also define, shape, and sharpen their own self-concepts. Customers who feel pride can say to themselves, "I'm proud to be a customer not just because of what my association with a company says about me to others. More importantly, I'm proud to be a customer because I'm proud to be associated with this company; it makes me feel good about myself."

CONSTRUCTING AND REINFORCING SELF-IMAGE

What you buy, what you wear, where you shop, where you stay, what you drive — all these purchases communicate something about you to others. The brands you buy and the companies you choose to do business with are often public expressions of who you think you are or who you wish to be; they reflect your current social status or the status to which you aspire. In certain categories, brands make statements that say to others, "This is who I am." Customers often identify in this way with the companies they do business with.

If you want customers to begin to feel a sense of pride in your brand, it's important to maintain a consistent experience. Your product, its packaging, the service you provide, the advertising, the pricing, and the location all must combine to meaningfully differentiate your brand from the competition to customers and prospects. Being identified with the company should make the customer feel special or unique. Before customers can feel a sense of pride, your brand must appeal to the individual's actual or aspirational self — to whom he is now or who he wants to be in the future. The brand must convey that it's perfect for you and people like you, but it's not for everyone. Our research has found that the degree to which people are proud to be your company's customers and the extent to which they view the company as an expression or an extension of who they are can determine your company's current and future success.

Social psychological research bears this out. People generally like to associate with winners, even when that association has little to do with them personally.[1] Social psychologists have labeled this phenomenon BIRGing — Basking In Reflected Glory. In a field study of BIRGing, Arizona State University professor Robert Cialdini and his colleagues had researchers position themselves at various locations on six university campuses the Monday following each of the schools' regular season football games. The observers' job was to count the number of university logo apparel items students wore as they walked across campus. Consistent with the BIRGing hypothesis, many more students donned logo apparel the Monday following a win than the Monday following a loss. Although few, if any, of the students observed walking across campus actually played on the football team — and therefore didn't contribute materially to the win or the loss — the pride of associating with a winner apparently encouraged them to don their school colors. In follow-up conversations with these undergraduates, students were also more likely to use the pronoun *we* to refer to their university after a victory than after a loss.

Just like the BIRGing students in the study, being associated with a company can make a customer feel smarter, better informed, or more innovative, or it can confer upon them a higher level of status. There is, however, a reverse side to BIRGing called CORFing or Cutting Off Reflected Failure, in which people actively try to distance themselves from entities that would reflect badly on them.

Being proud to be a customer carries with it a necessary precondition — respectful treatment. Treating customers with respect, whether in face-to-face interactions or in advertising and other messages, reinforces customers' pride in associating with a brand. Respectful treatment validates their choice and helps them feel that the company values them as patrons. Though there are the few cases where disrespectful treatment represents an integral part of the customer experience — for example, a New Yorker's pride in being a Peter Luger Steak House customer hinges in part on the fact that the waiters there are gruff — these cases are the exceptions that tend to prove the general rule.

As it turns out, pride is not always attached to the largest selling brands, the most prestigious companies, or the luxury end of the continuum. Many people take pride in their association with small or virtually unknown companies that excel at delivering on a particular promise that appeals to relatively few consumers. Association with companies like these may appeal to the customer's identity as a rebel or a nonconformist. And let's not forget the companies that serve a specific niche in the market.

KNOW THYSELF

Pride functions on multiple levels. Though my associations with the brands I buy or the companies I choose to do business with communicates, "This is who I am" or "This is who I want to be" to other people, these associations also communicate the same powerful messages to myself. A transplanted couple on the East Coast, for example, may retain their Wells Fargo checking account because they like the connection to the American West. The power of the Pride dimension is not just what doing business with a particular company tells others about me — it's what being a customer tells me about *me*.

In the 1970s, Stanford University social psychologist Daryl Bem described this dynamic in his self-perception theory.[2] Bem argued that people come to know who they are and what they believe by observing their own behavior. When Bem first proposed the theory, the prevailing attitude theories at that time suggested that human behavior arises in response to internally held attitudes and beliefs, rather than the other way around. In other words, traditional views of the self held that people have self-knowledge or attitudes ("I like ice cream."), and that self-knowledge guides their behavior ("I will go get some ice cream."). In contrast, Bem argued that people learn about themselves by observing their own behavior ("I am eating ice cream, therefore I must like ice cream."), much as we learn about others by observing their behavior and drawing inferences based on what we observe. Though no single theoretical approach can account for all the observed differences in human behavior, Bem's theory of self-perception accounts for an important subset of situations in which we acquire self-knowledge. The self-perception theory, along with other subsequent theoretical advances, provides a powerful mechanism that can help us better understand customer behavior.

Several years ago, then University of Texas psychologist Robert Wicklund and student Peter Gollwitzer[3] developed a theoretical approach that can help us understand how our choices of companies construct and reinforce our self-concepts. In their theory of symbolic self-completion, Wicklund and Gollwitzer noted that few, if any, of us are "complete" in our own eyes or the eyes of others. Instead, we all aspire to something more and have some desired self-definition, or sense of self, that we would like to achieve. Often, however, our "actual selves" fall short of this desired definition, and the discrepancy between who we really are and who we'd like to be is psychologically uncomfortable. Because of this discomfort, people are motivated to close the gap and reduce the discrepancy. Good examples of this motivation are a person who wants to see himself as a runner but has not yet developed the stamina to run more than a few yards, or a graduate student who fervently desires to be a professor but still has a ways to go to obtain the academic credentials necessary for such a position.

When people realize that they aren't quite what they'd like to be, they gather the trappings or symbols of the "completed self" around them (the source of the term "symbolic self-completion") to psychologically fill in the missing pieces. In other words, to bridge the gap between desire and reality — or in lieu of actually achieving their desired self-image — people embrace the symbols that reflect the self or status they want to achieve. The aspiring runner buys expensive running shoes and a flashy tracksuit and immediately subscribes to *Runner's World* magazine. The aspiring skier buys the newest skies and skiwear. The budding academic dons wire-rimmed glasses and tweed with leather elbow patches. In this way, they psychologically lay claim to their desired self-image.

According to Wicklund and Gollwitzer, this attitude is summarized in a Japanese aphorism: *Nō aru taka wa tsume o kakusu* or "The strong falcon hides its claws." This expression suggests that people who have actually earned status or achieved a desired self-image have no need to drape themselves in its symbols. Only those who are incomplete need do so.

We believe that people embrace the brands they buy and the companies they do business with as symbols that help them define and sharpen their own senses of who they are. Some people are proud to be Wal-Mart customers because it reinforces their identification as value-oriented, everyday people. Others are proud to be Nordstrom customers because they identify with the chain's upscale image and aspire to that status. Because all of us feel less than complete in some aspect of our lives, there are limitless opportunities for customers to connect with brands and companies as a means to building their desired self-identity.[4] The relationships we build with the companies we choose to patronize profoundly affect how we construct and sharpen our self-concepts.

PASSION

The fourth dimension — Passion — represents the ultimate expression of emotional attachment. A passionate customer uses expressions like "It's irreplaceable" and "It's a perfect fit for me!" to describe his or her relationship with your company. For these customers, the number of potential alternatives they'd consider using is zero. If the grocery store is out of their favorite brand of toothpaste, for example, they'll visit three other stores in search of it or wring the tube dry rather than use a different brand. They can no more imagine their lives without your company than they could imagine life without air or water or sunshine. This is important because some psychological research shows that the harder it is for people to imagine a situation or an event, the less likely they think it is to occur.[5]

Passionate customers look to your company to set the standard for other companies to follow. These customers are relatively rare — they make up only 18% of all customers in Gallup's customer database — but they represent the zenith of customer connectedness. They are customers for life and are a significant financial resource and annuity for companies. Passionate customers of one luxury retailer, for instance, spent 44% more annually on average than non-passionate customers. For an international credit card provider, passionate customers used their cards 45% more often and spent 78% more using their cards each month, revolving significantly larger balances in the process, than non-passionate customers did. Within the business-to-business arena, passionate customers of a global cargo shipper gave them 39% of their total business compared to 22% among non-passionate customers, an 80% larger share.

Passionate customers may strike us as somewhat odd because the company figures more prominently in their day-to-day lives — mentally, emotionally, and physically — than it does in the lives of many of your senior executives and certainly more prominently than it does in the day-to-day lives of most of your employees. Yet it's highly worthwhile to get to know your most passionate customers on a one-on-one basis. Not only are they truly committed "ambassadors" for your brand, but they hold the keys to building greater levels of passion throughout your customer population.

THE SELF-FULFILLING NATURE OF CUSTOMER ENGAGEMENT — AND DISENGAGEMENT

In Greek mythology, Pygmalion, king of Cyprus, created a statue of a young woman so beautiful that he fell in love with it, adorning it with jewelry and robes and bringing it to his bed at night. Aphrodite, feeling pity for poor Pygmalion, enchanted the statue and brought it to life so Pygmalion would no longer have to pine for a flesh-and-blood version of his alabaster beauty.

The Pygmalion myth is a metaphor for the conventional wisdom that strongly held beliefs, wishes, and desires can actually create the conditions that will make those beliefs, wishes, and desires come true. Throughout the years, the Pygmalion myth has been the subject of books, plays, and an extraordinary amount of academic research. In George Bernard Shaw's play *Pygmalion*, for example, Henry Higgins turns a Cockney street urchin named Eliza Doolittle into a refined society woman by sheer determination. Higgins' beliefs in the arbitrariness of class distinctions and the power of the human transformed a lowly flower girl into a cultured member of society. In the academic world, sociologist Robert Merton coined the term "self-fulfilling prophecy" in a 1948 *Antioch Review* article in which he described how initially false rumors that the Last National Bank was on the verge of insolvency eventually led to a run on the bank that ultimately forced it into bankruptcy.[6]

People's beliefs and desires have tremendous power to shape the world around them in ways that make those beliefs and desires come true. The self-fulfilling prophecy is one of the most thoroughly researched phenomena in the world, and hundreds of research studies have documented it in contexts as varied as schools[7] and businesses,[8] and from expectations as varied as mental illness[9] to physical attractiveness.[10] These and other observations suggest that when your company creates strong emotional connections with your customers, they internalize a self-fulfilling prophecy that leads them to interpret all aspects of your business more positively.

These perceptions, in turn, reinforce their already strong connections and help to make them even stronger. This process, however, can also work against you: Customers who harbor negative and antagonistic feelings toward your company also internalize a self-fulfilling prophecy that leads them to interpret all aspects of your business more negatively, which reinforces their already strong negative feelings. Emotionally engaging your customers initiates an upward spiral of positivity that becomes self-reinforcing. Failing to engage them, however, initiates a downward spiral that can be difficult to counteract.

THE EMOTIONAL ECONOMY AND CUSTOMER ENGAGEMENT

One of the crucial goals of our initial customer engagement research program was to scientifically document the relationship between the CE^{11} metric and many business performance metrics such as customer retention, cross-sell, share of wallet, frequency of purchase, total sales, profitability, and relationship growth, among others.

The following representative examples build the economic case for customer engagement. We have chosen examples from various industries in countries around the world to illustrate its broad applicability. Our goal is to demonstrate that the CE^{11} metric has a direct relationship to business performance measures at multiple levels within the company:

- The individual customer: The customer's engagement level determines how profitable that customer is.

- The work unit: How well employee groups engage their customers determines the economic success of the store, branch, or team.

- At the enterprise level: How well companies successfully engage customers throughout the enterprise determines the economic success of the company.

ENGAGEMENT ECONOMICS FOR THE INDIVIDUAL CUSTOMER

Our combined research reveals that across different companies, fully engaged customers represent an average 23% premium when compared to the average customer, while actively disengaged customers represent a 13% discount. This generalized finding is based on analyses of thousands of customers' CE[11] ratings and how those ratings are related to the customers' subsequent behavior toward the company. Relating individual levels of customer engagement to customers' subsequent behavior is an essential requirement for any metric used to evaluate the health of a company's customer relationships.

Here is a sampling of the powerful — and consistent — relationship between customer engagement and business outcomes at the individual customer level:

- Fully engaged customers of a super-regional consumer bank have total banking relationships that are 26% larger and generate revenues that are 13% higher than actively disengaged customers.

- Fully engaged clients of a European private bank grow their assets at twice the rate of actively disengaged clients.

- Fully engaged guests of an Asian hotel chain give the chain twice as much of their annual lodging expenditures as actively disengaged guests.

- Fully engaged customers of a U.S. grocery retailer visit the store 20% more often and give the company almost twice as much business as actively disengaged customers.

- Fully engaged viewers of a cable television channel watch that channel twice as much as actively disengaged viewers and are twice as likely to pay attention to the commercials that air on the channel.

The economic benefits of customer engagement play out just as dramatically in the business-to-business sphere. Fully engaged customers of a specialty chemicals supplier give the company twice the amount of business as actively disengaged customers and 50% more business than customers who are emotionally neutral. Even in businesses as esoteric as meatpacking, fully engaged customers also give the company twice the amount of business as actively disengaged customers and more than 30% more business than customers who are emotionally neutral. In fact, we see this 2-to-1 ratio in business performance between fully engaged and actively disengaged customers in almost all of the business-to-business customer relationships we've analyzed.

ENGAGEMENT ECONOMICS FOR THE LOCAL UNIT

If individual customers who are highly engaged deliver greater value to the company, then local units that engage their customers at higher levels should also deliver significantly enhanced financial results. Our research bears this out. For example, Bank W is a community bank in the eastern United States with more than \$3 billion in assets and 70,000 customers served by approximately 30 branches. Bank W measures customer engagement at the branch level twice each year by surveying customers from each of its branches. When we analyzed the economic impact of customer engagement for this bank, we found that branches that effectively engaged their customers (the top-performing 50% of branches) had roughly 10 times the account growth on a percentage basis than branches that didn't engage their customers. Also, they had more than 10 times the deposit growth and three times the loan growth on a year-on-year basis than branches that were ineffective at engaging their customers (the bottom 50% of branches).

Bank A is multinational consumer bank with branches in several Asian, South Asian, and Middle Eastern countries. Its India operation includes approximately 15 branches located primarily in large urban areas. Bank A measures customer engagement at a branch level, surveying customers from each of its branches. Our analysis revealed that branches that effectively engaged their customers — the top-performing 50% — generated almost 70% greater revenue, 40% greater revenue growth, and 16% greater revenue *per account* than the bottom 50% of branches.

Finally, Retailer S is a regional grocery chain with approximately 80 stores in the Northeast United States. Retailer S regularly measures customer engagement at the store level, surveying customers from each of its stores. The results showed that for Retailer S, the top-performing 50% of stores generated 18% greater annual sales (controlling for store size), four times greater annual sales increases per store, and 12% greater sales *per customer* than the bottom 50% of stores.

ENGAGEMENT ECONOMICS FOR THE ENTERPRISE:
STRESS-RESISTANT CUSTOMER RELATIONSHIPS

Companies that forge strong emotional bonds with their customers reap benefits from the emotional economy beyond those attributable to individual customers or local business unit performance. The stock values of companies that successfully engage their customers appear to be better insulated from the impact of severe economic fluctuations, whereas in companies whose customers are less emotionally invested, stock values appear more fragile when the market becomes volatile. The result is that companies whose products, processes, and people deliver excellence at every customer touchpoint are less vulnerable in the marketplace. These companies are more resilient, and this "stress resistance" helps them not only to withstand transient economic downturns but also to maintain consistent levels of market capitalization in the longer term.

To examine this issue, Gallup researchers conducted two separate studies, the first across multiple industries and the second focusing on retail banking in the United States. In August 2000, we collected and analyzed the customer engagement scores for 17 companies in different industries using a nationwide random sample. These companies represent major national players that compete in five different industries — airlines, automotive, mass retail, consumer electronics retail, and online retail. We compared each company's CE[11] scores to the change in the company's stock price from its closing values on Sept. 10, 2001, to its closing value after the market close on Sept. 17, 2001, (the first full day of trading following the Sept. 11 terrorist attacks).

The results of this analysis were astonishing. CE[11] scores captured from customer surveys conducted one year earlier (during August 2000) proved to be powerful predictors of each company's vulnerability to this significant market event. The higher the company's August 2000 CE[11] score compared to Gallup's database, the smaller the percentage decline in the company's stock price on the day the markets reopened. In fact, the correlation between CE[11] percentile scores and stock price change on Sept. 17, 2001, was 0.70.

For example, Southwest Airlines, whose CE[11] percentile score of 61 topped the airline industry in Gallup's research, suffered a 24% reduction in its stock value when the markets reopened on Sept. 17. In contrast, United Airlines, whose CE[11] percentile score of 3 was the lowest of any company measured in Gallup's research, suffered a 43% reduction in its stock value — double that of Southwest — on Sept. 17. Lest we be too quick to conclude that the magnitude of United's stock decline was simply the result of it being one of the two airlines (along with American) directly involved in the Sept. 11 attacks, it's worth noting that neither United nor American suffered the greatest percentage stock losses among the major U.S. carriers. Other airlines (including Delta Airlines) posted declines that were as large as or larger than either American's or United's. For example, Delta Airlines, whose CE[11] percentile score of 22 was also among the lowest of the companies measured in Gallup's research, suffered a 44% reduction in its stock value on Sept. 17.

Interestingly, the damage done to Southwest's stock on Sept. 17 was about half of what its seven largest competitors suffered, whose stock declines ranged from roughly 37% to 65% and averaged 47%. Moreover, Southwest remained profitable and did not have to reduce its schedule or its workforce as all of the other major U.S. carriers were forced to do. It's also worth noting that since 2001, only American and Southwest (of the airlines measured in our research) have avoided bankruptcy protection.

Subsequent analysis revealed that this effect wasn't simply due to the negative impact of terrorist attacks on airline stocks. When airlines were removed from the analysis, the strong effect, though somewhat attenuated, still emerged for automotive and various retail companies (correlation = 0.42). And when we examined historical as well as forward-looking stock performance, CE[11] scores were significant predictors of stock price changes stretching as far back as September 2000 and as far forward as August 2006.

When we performed the exact same analysis on the same companies using scores from the American Customer Satisfaction Index (ACSI; http://www.theacsi.org) for the comparable time period, we found that the higher the company's ACSI score, the *larger* the percentage decline in the company's stock price on the day the markets reopened. In other words, the more satisfied customers were with the various companies included in this analysis, the more their stock prices suffered immediately following the events of Sept. 11. The correlation between ACSI scores and stock decline was a significant -0.49.

For those who are skeptics, all this analysis, though intriguing, could simply be written off as a one-time anomaly without additional verification. However, a second independent study of U.S. retail banks found exactly the same relationship between CE^{11} percentile ranking and stock decline after Sept. 11. In that study, we collected and analyzed the customer engagement scores for eight retail banks, this time in April 2001, as part of a national study of the industry. Our research again compared each company's CE^{11} scores to the change in the company's stock price from its closing values on Sept. 10, 2001, to its closing value after the market close on Sept. 17, 2001. Just as in the industry study, the higher the retail bank's CE^{11} score compared to Gallup's database, the smaller the percentage decline in the bank's stock price on the day the markets reopened. The correlation between CE^{11} percentile scores and stock price change in this study was 0.59.

THE CUSTOMER SPEAKS. ARE YOU LISTENING?

Do a company's customers ultimately control the fate of the company's stock? Yes and no. Whether a company engages its customers or leaves them ambivalent — or, in some cases, antagonistic — certainly helps determine whether those customers will continue to patronize the company, give it the lion's share of their business, and do so more profitably. That has a clear and direct impact on the company's bottom line.

But there is more to the story. Customers' expressed emotional connections to the companies they do business with represent an important reality check on the true health of the brand. These emotional responses measure how well each company delivers on its most basic promises and reflects the extent to which it's building long-term relationships with its customers. Customer perceptions are thus an essential bellwether of future company performance. Some would say that emotional reactions drive markets. Gallup's research suggests that emotional reactions drive customers, too. Companies would be wise to pay close heed.

SIX PRINCIPLES AND THREE CRITERIA

Over the past 50 years, Gallup has conducted more than 10 million interviews with customers. What have we learned about the nature of customers' connections to the companies with whom they do business? We can summarize the main points in these six basic principles:

- Satisfying customers is not enough. Focusing on creating satisfied customers is a one-way ticket to mediocrity and poor business results. In today's competitive and fast-moving marketplace, customer satisfaction is the cost of entry. It will not differentiate the good from the great.

- Emotion frames the relationship. Customers aren't strictly rational in their judgments and behavior. Your most valuable and profitable customers have strong emotional bonds with your company. You must honor and strengthen those bonds.

- Engagement = health. *Customer engagement* describes the health of the relationship between your customers and your company. The quality of this emotional relationship ultimately determines your long-term financial success with your customers.

- You never step into the same river twice. Every time your company interacts with customers, they become a little more engaged or a little less engaged. No interaction produces a neutral result.

- Variance hurts your business. Though most companies strive to create a consistent customer experience from location to location, no company we have worked with actually does. There is as much variability in the quality of the customer experience from unit to unit within your company as there is between your company and its competitors.

- "All politics is local." When former Speaker of the U.S. House of Representatives Thomas "Tip" O'Neill said this, he was referring to the world of politics, but he could just as easily have been talking about organizational management. Organizations can't dictate strong customer relationships from the top; people and work units create them, and companies must manage them locally.

Organizations that seek breakthrough improvements in customer retention, profitability, and growth must fully engage their customers. Engaging customers means effectively addressing their functional requirements *and* their emotional needs.

Based on the accumulated research evidence, we believe that any metric companies use to assess the customer side of the employee-customer encounter must meet three criteria:

- It must incorporate a way to assess the rational *and* the non-rational or emotional dimensions of the customer relationship.

- It must provide reliable and demonstrable links to financial performance outcomes.

- It must readily lend itself to meaningful improvement efforts at the local *and* enterprise levels.

Customer engagement meets all these requirements. And, as we'll see in the next chapter, it does so organically, right in the middle of our brains.

CHAPTER **SEVEN**
WIN THEIR BRAINS AND THEIR HEARTS WILL FOLLOW

*"From the brain and the brain alone arise our pleasures, joys,
laughter, and jests, as well as our sorrows, pains, griefs, and tears."*
— Hippocrates

Until just a few years ago, Read Montague was haunted by a paradox. Ever since seeing the original "Pepsi Challenge" commercials as a youngster in the 1970s, Montague, a neuroscientist and director of the Human Neuroimaging Laboratory at Baylor College of Medicine, had been perplexed by the finding that in spite of Pepsi's apparent superiority in blind taste tests, more people actually claimed to prefer Coca-Cola. How on earth could this be, he puzzled? So after earning a doctorate in biophysics from the School of Medicine at the University of Alabama at Birmingham, Montague decided to find out.

Montague and his colleagues recruited research subjects to re-create the original Pepsi Challenge, but this time the taste testers did so while a functional magnetic resonance imaging machine (fMRI) scanned their brains. An fMRI machine measures the flow of oxygenated blood to various parts of the brain on the assumption that greater activity in a particular brain area increases the need for oxygen in that area. Because they tend to show up as bright colors on the resulting brain scan images, the areas with enhanced blood flow are often described as "lighting up." Areas that light up are experiencing intense neural activity.

In Montague's research, the brains of subjects blindly sampling Pepsi lit up in the *ventral putamen*, a region thought to process feelings of reward. When compared to results for those sampling Coke, the activity in that area was five times greater for Pepsi than for Coke. This matched the results of the original Pepsi Challenge, which showed in blind taste tests that people prefer the taste of Pepsi to Coke. But Montague didn't stop there. He had other subjects do the taste test thinking the sample was Coke or Pepsi and something surprising happened. Subjects who were told the sample was Coke showed enhanced activity in the *medial prefrontal cortex*, an area believed to be involved in higher-level thinking. The medial prefrontal cortex of subjects who were told their sample was Pepsi, on the other hand, did not light up in the same way. Apparently, believing the sample was Coke allowed subjects — almost all of whom claimed to prefer Coke anyway — to override their brain's more energetic reward response to Pepsi's taste.[1] There, right in front of him, was neural evidence for the profound effect of branding on consumer perceptions.[2]

WHERE IN THE BRAIN? THE NEUROANATOMY OF CUSTOMER ENGAGEMENT

Montague and his colleagues aren't alone in their quest to better understand the inner workings of the human brain. Scientists have conducted an enormous amount of research in recent years into how the inner workings of the brain relate to different behaviors from moral judgments[3] to brand preferences[4] and intense romantic love[5] to different kinds of decision making. What is most astounding is that much of what we have learned about the human brain was discovered in the past 15 years: We have learned more about the human brain since 1990 than in the entire previous history of the human race.[6]

So imagine that you could peek inside the heads of your customers as they think about your company or your products, services, or brands. What would you see? Would the brain activity of customers with a strong emotional connection to your company vary from that of customers who are indifferent? Would strongly connected customers' brains light up in different ways from customers who were not connected? Intrigued by the question, we set out to find an answer.[7] In collaboration with colleagues at Nihon University School of Medicine in Tokyo, we used fMRI to examine real-time brain activity in customers of a Japanese luxury retailer, referred to here as Luxury Retailer I.

Approximately six months before the study, we attempted to contact more than 2,000 households by telephone using outbound random digit dialing (RDD) from a pool of 14,800 eligible households within train commuting distance of the section of downtown Tokyo where Luxury Retailer I is located. After screening for conflicts such as employment at a department store or in any industry related to any aspect of this study, participants were asked to evaluate the retailer and their main bank (the institution where they conduct the majority of their banking) using Gallup's CE[11] metric; they also agreed to be contacted for follow-up studies. From this larger group of survey respondents, we identified and recruited three different groups to participate in the fMRI scanning portion of the research based on how engaged they were with the luxury retailer. One group of four participants was highly engaged, one group of seven was moderately engaged, and a third group of five was disengaged from the retailer. The 16 women[8] who met the full range of selection criteria for inclusion in the study were invited to the laboratory for an hour-long brain scanning procedure.

After being positioned inside a research fMRI machine,[9] participants in each group were presented with 32 simple yes or no statements about Luxury Retailer I, including Gallup's CE[11] items, while the machine scanned their brain activity. The women were also asked the same set of questions about their main bank, as well as a set of neutral questions about daily life, and they were given a rest period between testing sessions. Each statement was presented in Japanese on an overhead video monitor. After reading each statement, the woman answered yes or no using a hand-held device.

Our hypothesis was simple. Our main objective was to explore whether our metrics of emotional attachment and customer engagement actually related to customers' emotional responses to the companies they do business with in general and to Luxury Retailer I in particular. So we expected to find significantly heightened neural activity in brain regions associated with processing of emotional material among the women who were highly engaged with Luxury Retailer I compared to those who were less engaged. The brain region typically implicated in emotional processing is the limbic system, which includes the *amygdalae, anterior cingulate,* and *orbitofrontal cortex.*[10] Thus, our initial hypothesis was that these three areas would light up among highly engaged participants.

NOT SO FAST

One of the initial findings to come from this research seemed unrelated to brain activity per se. Participants who were disengaged from Luxury Retailer I took longer to respond to the stimulus statements with a yes or no than did participants who were more emotionally engaged.[11] We found that interesting for two reasons. First, faster reaction times are associated with things that we think about more often or that are more "top of mind" or salient — in social science jargon, they are *accessible*.[12] Many research studies have used reaction time as a proxy for attitude accessibility. Faster reaction times to the statements about Luxury Retailer I strongly suggest that it is easier to bring to mind and therefore plays a more prominent role for highly engaged customers than for those who are less engaged. Second, another way that attitudes become top of mind is when they are associated with strong emotion.[13] Some researchers have suggested that one reason for this increased access to strongly felt attitudes is that they engage and activate portions of the limbic system — the amygdalae and orbitofrontal cortex.[14]

WHERE DO THEY LIGHT UP?

When we analyzed the results of the brain scans, we found that the brains of customers who were highly engaged with the retailer were more active while they were thinking about Luxury Retailer I than were the brains of customers with lower levels of engagement.

As we expected, that increased activity was concentrated in the orbitofrontal cortex, a part of the limbic system associated with the processes involved in making decisions and carrying them out. The orbitofrontal cortex has also been implicated in integrating the thinking and feeling (the cognitive and emotional) systems.

But some of the findings were unexpected. Two other areas of the brain showed greater activity among highly engaged participants: the *fusiform gyrus* and the right *temporal pole,* which are located in the temporal lobe. Though there is still some debate about the specific functions of the fusiform gyrus, most researchers agree that one of the functions of this area is facial recognition. Researchers also believe the right temporal pole is involved in facial recognition and facial memory[15] in addition to verbal memory. Finding elevated activity in these two regions suggested that the highly engaged participants were remembering their prior experiences at Luxury Retailer I, including interactions with employees whose faces they were probably bringing to mind. This is all the more plausible because Luxury Retailer I only sells merchandise face to face. Recent research reveals that virtually the same brain region — the *fusiform face area* — lights up when people actually see faces and when they imagine or recall them.[16] These findings underscore an employee's key role in building strong customer engagement in each employee-customer encounter.

PASSION REALLY LIGHTS THE WAY

When we began to look deeper, however, the relationship between brain function and customer engagement became clearer. After we analyzed the brain scan data to look for differences related to the emotional attachment dimension of Passion, we found that the brains of customers who were most passionate about the retailer were considerably more active while thinking about Luxury Retailer I than were the brains of customers with lower levels of Passion. We also discovered that the elevated activity was concentrated in the same three brain regions as with highly engaged customers: the orbitofrontal cortex, fusiform gyrus, and right temporal pole. For highly passionate customers, two other brain areas lit up that are directly related to emotional processing within the limbic system: the right *amygdala* and the *anterior cingulate cortex (ACC)*.

The amygdalae are almond-shaped groups of neurons located within the temporal lobes. Research has demonstrated that the amygdalae perform a major role in processing and remembering emotional reactions, primarily by helping to form and store memories associated with emotional events. Intense emotional experiences activate the amygdalae, which in turn direct neural signals through the ACC on their way to the orbitofrontal cortex.

One function the ACC may perform is that of a lens that focuses complex neural signals; some researchers have even suggested that it serves as a gateway for "good or bad" reactions and that it's aware of good or bad outcomes before the awareness of those outcomes enters our consciousness.[17] The ACC is also active during demanding tasks requiring judgment and discrimination; examples include when you detect errors or experience intense feelings such as love, anger, or lust. Researchers have also found that the ACC is active in brain imaging studies when mothers hear a baby crying.[18] These results underscore the ACC's presumed role in social sensitivity.

So the answer to our rhetorical question about what you might see if you could peek inside the heads of your customers as they think about your company is "Yes, the brain activity of customers with a strong emotional connection to your company is remarkably different." When they think about a company, customers who are highly engaged and the subset of those customers who are strongly passionate about the company engage a specific set of brain regions associated with emotional processing and storing emotional memories, as well as areas related to facial recognition and facial memory. This provides strong evidence that the emotional centers of the brain — as evidenced by neural activity — play a crucial role in building and sustaining customer engagement.

But there is more to the story. Although Gallup's CE^{11} metric showed a strong relationship to enhanced neural activity in the emotional parts of the brain, this was driven primarily by the emotional attachment component of the measure. In fact, we found many of the same patterns of enhanced neural activity (i.e., the orbitofrontal cortex, temporal pole, and fusiform gyrus) when we analyzed the A^8 or emotional attachment subscale data separately. Recall that the CE^{11} metric consists of two pieces, one that assesses the more rational dimension of the customer experience (the L^3) and another that addresses the emotional dimension (the A^8). Exploring the brain scan data further, we found that the traditional, and arguably more rational, component of the metric — the L^3 — did not relate to *any* enhanced brain activity. Just being highly satisfied or highly likely to recommend Luxury Retailer I was insufficient to produce differential neural activity in the emotional processing regions of the brain. Only high scores on the A^8, or emotional items, were related to enhanced brain activity. This lends additional credibility to our contention that CE[11] provides an integrated metric to assess the rational *and* emotional dimensions of customers' relationships with a company.

The enhanced brain activity we observed in the fMRI study was company specific. Customers who were strongly attached to Luxury Retailer I but not to their primary bank did not show the same enhanced levels of neural activity when thinking about their bank. People don't appear to be hard-wired to become emotionally attached to every brand they encounter. Instead, the emotional connections appear to be selective and only apply to certain companies.

Finally, customer engagement and emotional attachment were strongly related to actual customer behavior. Highly engaged participants reported spending four times as much at Luxury Retailer I, both in the total amount spent per year and share of their discretionary spending, than did participants who were less engaged.[19]

What is most striking about these results is that a simple and easily collected attitude measure — one that was administered six months earlier — was able to reliably distinguish customers whose thinking/feeling systems were actively involved in their evaluations of the company from those whose thinking/feeling systems were not engaged. The extremely strong relationship between customer engagement, emotional attachment, and self-reported actual spending and share of total department store spending was even more striking.[20]

In an ideal world, all our organizational vital signs — as measured by the performance metrics we deploy — would be validated against an empirical relationship to both neural processing and future behavior. How do your company's performance metrics measure up? Do they assess the things that actually matter? How well is your company engaging your customers' emotions and lighting up their brains?

CHAPTER **EIGHT**
EMPLOYEE ENGAGEMENT

*"No problem can be solved from the same consciousness
that created it. We must learn to see the world anew."*

— Albert Einstein

It was 1968, and though he seemed to have everything, Robert Noyce was not happy at work. The pride of Grinnell, Iowa, had earned a doctorate from MIT, co-invented the integrated circuit, made several other groundbreaking research contributions in solid-state physics, and risen to an executive position at Fairchild Camera and Instrument, a profitable maker of semiconductors and technical instrumentation — and he had accomplished all this before the age of 40. Even by his own high standards of success, Bob Noyce was a very successful man. So why did he feel miserable?

As a pioneering researcher into semiconductors, Noyce already had a crucial role in ushering in the electronic age and had risen through a succession of roles to become general manager of Fairchild's semiconductor division. This was an interesting time for Noyce; he was not naturally inclined to dictate orders or give direction to people. He preferred the collaborative, personal approach he had learned in the lab, in part because he grew up in a small town where everyone knew each other.

Noyce particularly hated the top-down approach to management, secrecy, and mind games he had experienced in an earlier job.[1] As the son of a Congregationalist minister, Noyce also felt that doing the "ethically right" things for employees would result in improved business performance.[2] He said that "The job of the manager is an enabling, not a directive job. . . . Coaching, and not direction, is the first quality of leadership now. Get the barriers out of the way to let people do the things they do well."[3] He was interested in finding an "anthropological approach" to building Fairchild's organization.[4]

Noyce's expectations were ahead of their time. He was typically prescient in describing the benefits of a positive, engaging workplace. In the 1960s, most organizations weren't conducive to building the culture he sought. This was certainly the case at Fairchild, where Noyce was in charge of the most profitable division. In his new leadership role, Noyce realized that Fairchild didn't sufficiently appreciate the Semiconductor division's contributions to the bottom line and that senior management didn't seem to know what they were doing. As time went on, Noyce began to run into problems with Fairchild's board more often, and his most talented employees began a rapid exodus to other firms that would appreciate them.

> By the late 1960s, Noyce not only was alienated from his bosses, he also was out of touch with the innovative, technical side of Semiconductor in which he had taken such pride a decade before. . . . He missed doing science, and . . . even after it had

been years since he sat at a lab bench, Noyce would tell his family that he was 'going to the lab' when he left for work each day.[5]

Around this time, Noyce began to think about leaving Fairchild to start his own company. He thought that an opportunity existed for a company making semiconductor memory devices — a view that turned out to be prophetic. But Noyce's main reason for leaving Fairchild centered on his growing dislike of his current job. His letter of resignation noted, "as [the company] has grown larger and larger, I have enjoyed my daily work less and less." He continued that he wanted to start a small company where he could "get close to advanced technology again," and have "more personal creative work in building a new product, a new technology, and a new organization."[6]

Noyce was also able to convince coworker Gordon Moore to join him in his new venture. This enabled Noyce and Moore to continue their productive partnership, in which Noyce played the part of the big, strategic thinker and Moore filled in the details. Noyce threw himself into his new venture with a passion he had not exhibited in years, developing business plans, securing financing, and, most importantly, recruiting talented scientists and engineers to join him and Moore. It's a tribute to Noyce and Moore's genius and determination that they were able to do this at all; it's even more remarkable that their efforts established a template for a high-tech startup that many still follow today. Did their venture work? As a matter of fact, the little company they founded — christened "Intel" — has gone on to spectacular success.

All of this depended, however, on Noyce leaving Fairchild in the first place — something that we, blessed with the benefit of hindsight, might find inevitable but seemed less obvious then. What finally motivated him to leave was that Noyce found continued employment at Fairchild unendurable. The deciding factor was his desire for a strong, positive work environment in which he could make a significant contribution in a way that reinforced his view of himself. Not surprisingly, these are the very things that every employee desires from his or her workplace.

THE LEV OBSERVATION

As we discussed in Chapter 1, New York University Professor Baruch Lev has written extensively about intangible assets and how to account for their contributions to company market value. His research has found that intangible assets contribute much of the value in most firms and that the earnings generated by intangible assets are a better predictor of stock market returns than either accounting earnings or cash flows. If his findings are correct, a portfolio of stocks with high intangible assets should perform better than a portfolio with fewer intangible assets. When Lev tested this, he found that companies with high intangible assets did indeed have higher financial returns.

In our research, we have found that engaged employees are the main source of much of these intangible assets. When employees are *engaged* — or emotionally and psychologically committed to the firm — businesses perform more efficiently, and when businesses perform more efficiently, employees become even more engaged. Engaged employees feel a stronger sense of ownership of the firm's successes and failures and want to contribute to its improved performance. As most organizations become more successful, they invest more in their people, creating an increased sense of pride or ownership. We see this reciprocal relationship as a dynamic that should be present in healthy organizations.

We are frequently asked the question, which comes first, employee engagement or higher performance? In an attempt to answer this question definitively, we recently completed a study of 2,178 business units from 10 companies in six industries.[7] What we found was that engagement predicts performance in key areas — including customer engagement, employee retention, sales, and profit — better than performance predicts engagement. In the search for a good measure of the source of Lev's intangible assets, one needs to look no further than the engagement of the firm's employees.

ENGAGING YOUR EMPLOYEES

Our interviews with executives reveal that they know engagement increases performance, but they don't feel like there's anything that they can do about it. For many, it's either easier to give in to this feeling of helplessness or to pretend that the problem doesn't exist. And who can blame them? Until recently, there has been limited research on applicable approaches that truly transform organizational culture, and much of what existed came from the Terminator School of Management.

Just how long has the Terminator School of Management been around? Henry Ford may have been the first to ask so bluntly, "Why is it that I always get the whole person when what I really want is a pair of hands?" — but he wasn't the first business leader to have this attitude. This mode of thinking goes back much further than Ford; it germinated from seeds planted in the Industrial Revolution as more mechanized forms of production began to disrupt previous generations' reliance on skilled craftspeople to produce goods and services.

THE PAPERMAKER'S DILEMMA

The increasing demand for quality paper in 18th century France provides a good example of this disruption.[8] Though paper mills varied in the quality and type of paper produced, most used similar organizational structures. A few entrepreneurs owned the majority of the mills — often a family — but independent journeymen paper workers controlled most of the work. These paper workers closely guarded their methods and worked according to rules largely of their own choosing. They were also an itinerant society, moving from town to town whenever it suited them. This was somewhat due to the seasonal nature of papermaking, as it was dependent on the weather and the volume of water running through the rivers and streams that powered the mills. But even in areas with year-round production, skilled paper workers tended to move frequently. This made it very difficult for the mill owners to control the quality and quantity of the mill's output.

The Montgolfier family (later famous for inventing the first practical hot air balloon) owned one of the largest and most prosperous papermaking firms. They had long considered innovation to be the main reason for their success and ultimately decided it was time to make their production processes more modern.[9] Their drive for innovation was partly a response to increased competition from Dutch paper producers. But they were also motivated by a profound belief in a scientific approach to papermaking — a heritage of their Enlightenment era education in science and natural philosophy. This scientific, innovative approach contrasted sharply with the traditions that drove paper workers' activities. Their traditional practices made it extremely difficult for the Montgolfiers to experiment with different modes of production or to implement the superior technologies that they already knew.

The Montgolfiers, therefore, "intended to unravel the fabric of acquaintance, experience, kinship, skill, and work itself"[10] that the papermaking society had knitted together. They locked the journeymen out of their mills and recruited new workers that they could train in new ways of papermaking. Their goal was to transform each mill into a "temple of rational technology rich in skilled, malleable workers."[11] Their belief in the ability of a carefully designed environment to turn out better paper and develop superior workers illustrated the focus on "Reason" during the Enlightenment era. In their way, the Montgolfiers were trying nothing less ambitious than the creation of a new type of worker — a blank slate on which they could script their own instructions, not unlike how one would program a computer today.

This last point is important. The line of thinking that culminates in Henry Ford's lament — "Why is it that I always get the whole person when what I really want is a pair of hands?" — begins here. The Montgolfiers wanted to gain more control over paper production by creating a new work environment where workers functioned as interchangeable employees rather than temporary migrant workers. Their thinking was that these employees would recognize that their interests were aligned with those of their employer, as opposed to the journeyman paper worker who answered to no one but himself. They also saw this as a better system for innovating because it would not rigidly tie their new employees to old ways of doing things; instead, the system would steep employees in all facets of papermaking and a family known for its scientific and technological abilities would govern it.

Because this occurred before the invention of the papermaking machine in 1799, the unskilled human automatons that later peopled sweatshops did not populate the Montgolfiers' mills. But the efforts of the Montgolfiers and others like them to create a new, more malleable employee lived on in others who would try to take their efforts one step further. With the advent of mass-production methods in the 19th century, many companies would try to make machines of men, as Henry Ford longed to do.

We are still living with this legacy today. Employers have been wrestling with the problem of how best to organize employees' work lives for a long time. Now that we've described the problem in some detail, it's time to focus on a solution.

"EMPLOYEES: WHAT ARE THEY GOOD FOR?"

If we were to ask this question in a Gallup Poll, we would probably get an answer like this: "Companies need employees to get the job done and to meet the demands of the job with excellence." So it follows that without "the job," there would be no need for employees. Fair enough. Where there is an employee, there is a need for some job function that companies cannot have performed more efficiently any other way.

When it comes to understanding human behavior in the workplace, one of the most notable discoveries occurred in the mid-1990s when we discovered that no organization — large or small — has a single culture. Instead, it has as many cultures as it has workgroups, managers, or supervisors. The locus of culture is at the local level, where 5, 10, or more people work together every day. Although many of you may be nodding in agreement at this notion, it was a dramatic shift in how leaders perceived corporate culture and how to manage it. Leaders have long understood that they have very little control over the culture that exists at the local level, but this discovery made it imperative that they find the best managers and supervisors to build a high-performing culture one employee, or one conversation, at a time. Executives cannot legislate culture with mission or vision statements or through values clarification; it must also grow organically one workgroup at a time.

CULTURING CULTURE

Having a high-performing business culture is a competitive advantage today. Most companies expect every employee to be a builder because every employee through his or her actions either makes the culture stronger or weakens it. Employees, in turn, want to be proud of their organizations and local teams. And, in many countries today, the *employer needs the employee* more than the other way around. As the world shifts from an industrial to a knowledge-based economy — and as employees are increasingly valued for what they know as much as for what they produce — the employer's power has diminished or evaporated. So, how do we manage people for success and high levels of productivity in the new economy? Too many organizations build management models on the assumption that managers and leaders have the power in the company/employee relationship, but that's no longer always the case. The answer is *employee engagement* or the ability to capture the heads, hearts, and souls of your employees to instill an intrinsic desire and passion for excellence. Engaged employees want their organization to succeed because they feel connected emotionally, socially, and even spiritually to its mission, vision, and purpose.

Just as engaged customers are among a company's most profitable patrons and passionate advocates, engaged employees are a company's most productive and efficient workers. Others have argued that employees join companies but leave managers.[12] Employees may choose to work for a company for several reasons — the high-minded and the practical. They may be attracted to its mission and purpose and its stature in the marketplace or by a belief that by working there they can make a difference in the world. They may also be attracted by the promise of a regular income, reasonable working hours, and good benefits. Whatever their motivation for joining the company, their local work environment either energizes and nourishes them and fosters their learning and growth or starves them and frustrates their development. When this happens, they will leave the company or — even worse — hang around doing the minimum needed until it's time for retirement. Engaged employees, in contrast, are involved and enthusiastic about what is happening in their local work environment.

Among the many variables that discriminate these two types of workplaces is the quality of the local workplace manager and his or her ability to successfully meet a core set of employees' emotional requirements. (See the graphic "Four Dimensions of Employee Engagement.")

FOUR DIMENSIONS OF EMPLOYEE ENGAGEMENT

Among the many variables that discriminate between highly productive workplaces and those that are unproductive is the quality of the local workplace manager and his or her ability to meet a core set of employees' emotional requirements. Work units that meet these conditions of engagement perform at a much higher level than work units that fail to meet them.

Opportunities to learn and grow
Progress in last six months

HOW CAN WE GROW?

Best friend
Coworkers committed to quality
Mission/Purpose of company
My opinions count

DO I BELONG?

Encourages development
Supervisor/Someone at work cares
Recognition last seven days
Do what I do best every day

WHAT DO I GIVE?

Materials and equipment
I know what is expected of me at work

WHAT DO I GET?

Copyright © 1993-1998 Gallup, Inc.

Work units that meet these conditions of engagement perform at a much higher level than work units that fail to meet them.[13] Primary within these conditions are emotional elements that reveal our basic human needs: to be recognized as individuals and to contribute. At a local level, managers can influence employees' most basic needs by setting clear expectations and providing needed resources. More than this, they can energize their employees by showing them that they care personally and professionally:

- Personally managers can create meaningful relationships within workgroups and position employees so that they can do what they do best.

- Professionally managers can provide challenging work and opportunities to learn, grow, and make significant contributions.

Some hard-core graduates of the Terminator School of Management have suggested that all this talk about positivity in the workplace is nothing more than a bunch of fluff with little real application in the cutthroat world of business. Our research strongly suggests otherwise: When human needs are met, the positive emotions that result encourage employees to look beyond the work in front of them and to care about the overall welfare of the business. More importantly, it's hard to create passionate, engaged customers without passionate, engaged employees.

Psychologists such as Barbara Fredrickson at the University of North Carolina have done considerable research into the way to use positive experiences to build social and psychological resources such as optimism, resiliency, friendships, social support networks, and creativity.[14] And, these resources are more long lasting than the positive emotions that helped build them. The friends we make in good times are with us in bad times, and, similarly, the creativity we nurture when we are feeling confident is likely to be there for us when we are under stress. There are significant physical payoffs, as well. For example, a study of elderly nuns showed that those who had expressed the most positive emotion in early adulthood lived up to 10 years longer than those who expressed the least positive emotion.[15]

THE 12 ELEMENTS

Gallup has developed a 12-item survey instrument — the Q^{12} — designed to measure engagement levels of a given group of employees. (See the graphic "Four Dimensions of Employee Engagement.") When Gallup began the research that culminated in the Q^{12}, we had interviewed more than a million employees over 25 years, asking them hundreds of different questions. From this rich vein of data, Gallup delved to find the best questions — those that most consistently and reliably discriminated top-performing workgroups from their poorer-performing peers. After a comprehensive review of all the workplace studies we had conducted up to that time, the final 12 emerged as the items that had the strongest linkages to high performance and did the best job of measuring how well companies were meeting employees' core requirements on the job.[16]

At this time, we have administered the Q^{12} to more than 10 million people in 51 languages and 144 different countries for 736 organizations. We have tested it in many cultures and among employees of all ages and education levels and it has proven to be an accurate reflection of whether our core requirements as employees are being met in the workplace. It gets at the common issues we have in the workplace as living, breathing, *feeling* human beings through a serious and scientific study into what differentiates productive workgroups from their less productive peers. What we found was that high scores on these 12 items reflected an underlying emotional engagement in the employees who took the survey, an engagement that results in improved business outcomes, including increased levels of productivity, profitability, and employee retention.

BASIC NEEDS: WHAT DO I GET?

The Q^{12} begins with the most basic needs in the workplace — clear expectations and the materials required to do the job. An organization that does not meet these needs has no credibility with its employees who will essentially stall until it remedies the situation. In all the mumbo jumbo surrounding management initiatives during the past two decades, organizations have largely ignored these most basic human needs. In our rush to build self-directed work teams, *Kaizen* disciples, personal development and leadership training, Six Sigma black belts, and a host of other initiatives, we have lost sight of the costs of entry in the workplace: clear expectations and basic tools. It doesn't get much simpler than that.

INDIVIDUAL CONTRIBUTION: WHAT DO I GIVE?

Once companies arm employees with expectations and equipment, they need to experience success in their performance. A key to their success is the degree to which the job fits their talents, skills, and preferences. Employees perform best in activities they inherently enjoy and for which they have a well-developed predisposition.

It's also crucial that employees feel that they are contributing to the organization and that those contributions are valued. Honest feedback is essential to an accurate assessment of performance, but more than that, it provides the kind of data our minds need to learn and eventually master new tasks and demands. Frequent and immediate recognition for good work also creates beneficial positive emotions that broaden our perspectives and stimulate creative thinking about how we can do more. The right recognition reinforces authentic successes by cementing the memory of what the employee did right and encoding that memory with positive emotions that make it more powerful and meaningful. It must be the "right" kind of recognition, however, because we have found significant individual differences in how employees prefer to receive recognition. Great managers understand this, and by providing individualized recognition, they show that they know their employees and care about them. Giving individual recognition is one of the most powerful ways managers connect the needs of the employee to the needs of the organization.

TEAMWORK: DO I BELONG?

Employees have a need to belong to something bigger than themselves. This sense of belonging starts with the social membership benefits we expect from the groups to which we belong: Do I have any friends here? Does anyone listen to me or care what I have to say? On one level, the need to have friends and to belong seems obvious — who wants to spend all his time with strangers? Yet this aspect of employee engagement is the one that tends to generate the most resistance from managers and executives. We have heard some of the more ardent supporters of Terminator Management say that if employees are working hard, they won't have time for friendships. Others have resisted the idea that employees' opinions have some merit. Yet those same executives expect all their employees to commit themselves body and soul to the organization and to the highest standards of quality in job performance without offering them anything in return.

The best leaders realize that employees won't commit body and soul to any endeavor that doesn't seem to be worth the risk. As

Maslow's work and our research into customers' emotional attachment to the companies they do business with demonstrates, people have an innate need for security in their lives, including their work lives. Following the thinking of Anthony Giddens,[17] making an emotional and psychological commitment requires:

- Continuity in your social and material conditions — a sense of the reliability of people and things.

- Confidence in your place in society and your right to be yourself.

- Faith that you can achieve your maximum "you-ness" — or, in the words of the U.S. Army slogan, to "Be all you can be."

UNLEASHING INNOVATION

When employees feel that these three conditions have been met, they feel a sense of safety and security that breeds autonomy and self-direction. The result is a happier and more productive employee who treats customers well and has a stake in the company's continued financial growth. It also engenders the kind of psychological commitment from employees that encourages them to be active, creative agents rather than just another robotic Terminator. Active, creative employees like these hold the key to the spirit of innovation that today's companies are desperate to unleash.[18] The challenge of unleashing innovation in businesses today is not just about having the right structures, processes, systems, or policies in place to foster creativity and innovation, although programs such as GE's "Imagination Breakthroughs" and IBM's EBO model can certainly help. No, it's also about unlocking the potential that already exists within your organization. Even the best processes and systems are only as effective as the people driving them. The secret to unleashing innovation in any company is as simple as engaging every employee.[19]

ORGANIC GROWTH: HOW CAN WE GROW?

A psychologically committed employee in an engaging work environment is primed for innovation and growth. Employees who have the opportunity to discuss their progress develop a deeper emotional commitment to the organization. Once this longer-term commitment is formed, the employee naturally raises the question of where am I going from here? Questions like this signal that the employee is beginning to build part of her identity around her role.

This process of positive association and identification with the company is akin to the dimension of customer Pride discussed in Chapter 6. As an employee begins to include her job in her self-concept — and if she likes what that says about her — she begins to develop a deeper psychological affiliation with her job. We can measure this affiliation in several ways. For starters, she is much less likely to quit. On average, an engaged employee is only half as likely to leave the organization at a given point in time as an employee who is not engaged. This is significant because we are all going to leave our current employer eventually. Like death and taxes, turnover is inevitable — we don't live forever — so it's really just a question of "when" rather than "if." In an increasingly tight market for talented employees, firms must engage their best employees if they hope to retain them as long as possible.

There is, however, a subtle form of turnover that occurs when employees are physically present but psychologically absent. Borrowing from the military, Curt Coffman, the coauthor of *First, Break All the Rules*, calls these employees "ROAD warriors" — workers who are Retired On Active Duty. ROAD warriors are an insidious source of lost productivity because the company is paying them for work they are not doing or doing at the minimum level to stay employed. What's worse, they are taking up space that a more productive employee could occupy. Engaged employees are much less likely to become ROAD warriors.

Once an employee has begun to think about her growth and development in her job, she begins to make discretionary contributions to the organization and to think more creatively about how to improve the workplace.

SHOW ME THE MONEY

Baruch Lev and others have demonstrated the large contributions of intangible assets to companies' financial growth and, by extension, to the continuing prosperity of the world's most vibrant economies. If you are interested in knowing whether your organization is building its intangible assets, look to your employees' engagement.

Our work with employee engagement has revealed that engaged workgroups deliver higher levels of productivity and profitability; greater attendance and retention; and increased safety, including the reduced exposure to insurance and worker's compensation claims that come as a result of improved safety.[20] Engaged workgroups are also more effective at engaging the customers they serve.

We have been studying the core concepts that differentiate successful organizations from those that are less successful since 1997. Our sixth and most recent meta-analysis included data from 681,799 employee responses in 23,910 independent business units in 125 companies from all over the world.[21] This study confirmed previous findings that showed that in comparison to disengaged workgroups, engaged workgroups are:

- 18% more productive

- 12% more profitable

- 12% better at engaging customers

- 51% less likely to leave the organization (low-turnover companies)

- 31% less likely to leave the organization (high-turnover companies)

- 62% less likely to be involved in an accident on the job

- 27% less prone to absenteeism

- 51% less likely to be a source of inventory shrinkage

We also have significant evidence that employee engagement leads to enhanced business performance from our study of organizational performance over time, including evidence that the average company that grows its employee engagement experiences significant gains in financial performance.[22] In our recent analysis of company stock market performance, companies with high employee engagement significantly outperformed their peers in earnings per share (EPS). We reviewed the data for 89 publicly traded companies for which we had employee engagement data on the entire employee population collected over multiple time periods.[23] We collected employee engagement data from 2002 to 2004 and then compared each company to its actual competitors (so as not to bias the results by comparing software companies to pharmaceutical companies, for example). On average, comparable data were available for 7.3 competitors per organization. We also looked at financial performance in 2004 to 2005 relative to a base-line previous three-year average from 2001 to 2003.

Relative to their competition, high-engagement organizations exhibited an upward trend, with EPS in 2004 to 2005 that was 18% higher than their competitors' EPS. This also represented an increase of 15.6 percentage points from baseline. Low-engagement organizations fared worse, with EPS in 2004 to 2005 that was only 3% above their industry equivalent for a net increase of six percentage points above baseline.

Taken together, the growth rate of high-engagement companies was 2.6 times the growth rate of the low-engagement companies. This difference represents a tangible example of how engaging employees builds intangible assets. These results, along with our ongoing research, show conclusively that engaged employees drive the most successful firms and the most productive business units within those firms to succeed.

CHAPTER **NINE**
ENGAGING YOUR EMPLOYEES

> *"The following sentence is false.*
> *The preceding sentence is true."*
> — Douglas R. Hofstadter, *Gödel, Escher, Bach: An eternal golden braid*

It's one thing to know that more engaged employees are more productive. It's another thing to make an employee more engaged. You may be wondering if that's even possible. Fortunately, the answer is *yes*.

Our understanding of the concepts of employee and customer engagement grew from our recognition that rational-functional models of human decision making and behavior don't reflect the complexity of actual employee and customer behavior. By systematically examining the interdependent motivations, needs, and traits of employees in decades of research, we discovered key insights into employee behavior that help explain why the rational-functional model was so wrong. We have also learned that companies can change and focus employees' behavior in more positive directions by engaging employees' hearts and minds. A careful look at more than 10 million interviews with employees have led us to four core principles of employee engagement that, when combined with the key principles of customer engagement, begin to sketch out a road map that we will use to navigate the terrain of HumanSigma:

- Manage by outcomes not behaviors. Great organizations and managers view excellence within a role as achieving the right outcomes, not just conforming and executing the steps of the job the right way.

- Liberate don't legislate. The most dramatic increases in productivity occur when companies allow workgroups to choose their own initiatives and focus on them. Anything that makes employees passive viewers instead of active participants in the employee-customer encounter — such as tight scripts that attempt to squash spontaneity out of employee behavior — is counterproductive.

- Engagement is for everyone. Almost every employee can become more engaged. We're not saying that it's easy to accomplish this — only that it's possible.

- All politics is local. This holds true for customer and employee engagement. Like customer engagement, companies can't dictate employee engagement from on high; they must manage engagement locally. Everyone from the boardroom to the mailroom is responsible for the quality of his or her workplace.

MANAGE OUTCOMES, NOT BEHAVIORS

When executives and managers respond negatively to employee behaviors, employees become fearful and defensive. The result is a JDS mind-set that inhibits creativity and gradually ossifies the culture into a frozen parody of itself:

- It does this by inculcating a form of "learned helplessness" among employees.

- It introduces a high degree of rigidity into organizational structures, thus making them less adaptable in the face of changing circumstances.

- Also, it instills a bias in favor of procedural or structural remedies to organizational challenges.

Many organizations assume that the human resource department is responsible for orienting new employees to their roles. And — for the sake of consistency and scalability — firms have emphasized the steps of "how to do the job" over the outcomes that will result from "a job well done." Usually, these organizations create a list of the right steps by studying best practices and then teaching everyone to follow those steps in an attempt to imitate the same behaviors as those exhibited by the most successful employees. This seems simple and rational. In *The Terminator*, cyborgs were created for the same reason: to provide a predictable, reliable replacement for human beings.

But this basic assumption is flawed. First, as Socrates noted in Plato's *Republic*, the best performers in a role don't all do it in exactly the same way; instead, they use unique behaviors and talents to achieve their goals. It's also difficult for people to learn, adopt, and sustain a regimented set of behaviors that don't come naturally to them. For example, people can learn to walk or talk differently, but when they stop thinking about those behaviors, they fall back into their natural ways of walking and talking. Similarly, they can take courses on how to be empathic or how to think strategically, but if those talents don't come naturally to them, the tips and techniques they learn won't necessarily stick. Ultimately, they will return to who and what they were to begin with. Finally, organizations have defined success based on how well an individual has learned and can execute the steps of his or her role. Great organizations and managers, in contrast, don't do this — rather than legislating behavior or steps, they legislate the right outcomes and then consistently communicate those expectations to all employees. In doing so, they capitalize on Heider's concept of *equifinality* by allowing each employee to find his or her own path to success.

LIBERATE, DON'T LEGISLATE

When you manage by outcomes rather than behaviors, you begin with the assumption that employees are equipped with minds and the ability to think for themselves and are best off finding their own way to meet their objectives. In some of the companies we've worked with, this assumption has been controversial, perhaps because managers and executives find it difficult to trust employees to this degree.

As we noted earlier, firms with superior intangible assets have enjoyed superior financial performance over the past decade or so, and this trend shows every indication of accelerating. But where did these intangible assets come from? In every example we have found, they have resulted from stoking the creative furnaces of the firm's employees. This, in turn, has generated sustainable productivity increases that are different from the diminishing returns we see from the incremental productivity improvements achieved through a typical quality management approach. These productivity improvements manifest themselves in various ways. In some business units, the greatest gains come from improved customer relationships or documented increases in employee creativity, while other groups achieve gains simply because employees show up to work more often. Improvements are often the result of a combination of these and other things.

The most dramatic increases commonly occur in groups that companies allow to focus on initiatives they choose. Companies that have liberated their managers and employees in this way have discovered that this often makes workgroups more financially productive in ways that the executives could not have foreseen. But this sort of divergent thinking is the very essence of creativity; most research agrees that two of the necessary conditions for creativity are divergent thinking and mastery of the domain in which creativity is desired. In other words, for creativity to occur, employees need to know enough about their work environment to be able to experiment with it. They need to be capable of the kind of divergent thinking that enables envisioning a structure or solution other than the current one, and they need freedom to try some of the divergent alternatives they develop.

Although some people are more prone to be creative and are better at it than others are, most people are capable of creativity to some degree. Sadly, however, many organizations are designed to stifle creativity by limiting opportunities to experiment on the job or by legislating so many performance steps into a role that employees must spend most of their time and energy complying with routine instead of creating more profitable and productive alternatives.

For those executives or managers who remain unconvinced, it's worth noting that this management approach — defining the right outcomes and then allowing employees to find the best way to achieve those outcomes — is consistent with the best research on human development and behavior. For example, brain research shows that creativity is enhanced through experience; our minds use an accumulation of repeated experiences to build simple, situation-specific rules to guide our actions.[1] Typically, the more experiences a person has, the better he or she becomes at recognizing the best way to respond. This kind of learning, however, requires an engaged mind. Employees who are hemmed in by Terminator Management systems that interfere with their perceptions and learning systems won't have the opportunity to experiment with how they respond to different situations and will miss the opportunity to develop optimal ways to respond.

Engaged employees have a better understanding of the long- and short-term goals of the employee-customer encounter and how their roles help to achieve them. They are also far more likely to care about whether customers' needs are met, are more motivated to learn how to apply themselves, and likelier to know when they can stretch business rules — and how far — if the situation warrants it.

One way to speed the building of employees' intuitive reasoning[2] is to ask them to consciously imagine the possible consequences of likely actions, much as elite athletes have learned visualization skills as a means to prepare for competition. These mental simulations[3] prime a future set of best guess responses that employees later can try on real customers and coworkers. Tight scripts and overly detailed attempts to squash variability in employee behavior rigidly limit the behaviors available to employees, making it difficult if not impossible for them to experiment with responses that could lead to performance improvement at the local level. Just like learning any new behavior, the secret to improving employee-customer encounters isn't really a secret at all. It comes from:

(1) knowing what's expected

(2) practicing or visualizing how to respond to customers

(3) actually responding to customer requests or needs

(4) evaluating the results using customer data, recognition, and other feedback

(5) repeating steps 1 through 4

Without goals, however, the creative impulse is rudderless. That's why the first item of Gallup's employee engagement metric, the Q^{12}, is "I know what is expected of me at work."

Most companies try to remove uncertainty by attempting to foresee every possible outcome and then scripting behavior for all these contingencies. Of course, this assumes that the customers will know their lines and behave predictably when employees are running the scripts. It's much more realistic for organizations to accept that customers have different needs and will behave in unpredictable ways then to give employees the knowledge, tools, and permission they require to meet those needs. Instead of making employees try to fit the customers to the script, let employees use their knowledge, experience, and creativity to listen to customers, observe their behaviors, and respond appropriately to customer needs.

Anything that makes employees passive rather than active participants in the employee-customer encounter is counterproductive. Too many rules and tightly scripted responses can make employees lazy or confuse, demoralize, or mislead them by subverting the learning process and by denying employees the real-time feedback they need to learn and improve. To help employees learn, great managers provide them with accurate information about the goals they are expected to reach and how well they are doing in meeting them. Great managers also help employees learn by watching them in action and coaching them in the moment. These tactics — information and coaching combined with recognition and frequent customer feedback — help reinforce learning and lock it in.

Research shows that brain development is "use it or lose it"[4] — or, as neuroscientists put it, "experience dependent." Our experiences not only shape the information that enters our minds through our perceptual systems, but they also influence the way in which the mind develops the ability to process that information. Experience stimulates capacity for specific forms of information processing. Once an employee becomes accustomed to ignoring customer comments or behaviors because they don't conform to the steps in the script the employee is required to follow in a given situation, employees will be primed to ignore customers in all situations.

This kind of learned helplessness[5] can be very dangerous for sales and service organizations because frontline associates play an essential role in building or destroying customer engagement.

Every interaction an employee has with a customer represents an opportunity to build and reinforce that customer's emotional connection to the company or to diminish it. Although employee interactions are not the only means that companies employ to create strong emotional connections with customers, they frequently represent a largely untapped resource for building those relationships. Yet in most companies, the lowest paid and least appreciated employees are generally those who interact directly with customers, including cashiers, tellers, sales clerks, and customer service representatives. Ensuring that employees are engaged in their work is the best way to ensure that they will engage the customers they serve.

ENGAGEMENT IS FOR EVERYONE

It's crucial to understand that almost every employee can become more engaged. It might not be easy to engage them, but it's possible.

Personality psychologists like to discuss this potential in terms of "trait versus state." *Traits* are defined as the enduring characteristics that make us who we are as individuals — whether we are introspective or outgoing, for example, or cheerful or given to melancholy. A *state* is defined as our attitudes and behaviors that change according to circumstance.

What we have learned is that the trait portion of engagement is not dominant. In other words, a person's engagement level is not predetermined, and almost anyone can become engaged in the right circumstances. We say "almost" as a precaution because there are likely some employees with who will never be engaged at work, no matter what work they do or where they do it — but these exceptions are rare. The vast majority of employees can be engaged, productive workers if they find a role that fits who they are.

Companies can gain significant increases in individual, work-group, and organizational performance by increasing employee engagement at these levels. The research evidence demonstrates that engagement is not only valuable, but also quite attainable by workgroups that choose to improve their management approach in this way. We have seen bitter and negative workforces execute a profound turnaround and become engaged and committed to the success of their organization. Given the potential for such profound turnarounds, there really is no excuse for not trying.

ALL POLITICS IS LOCAL

One of the most significant findings from our employee engagement research is that contrary to popular wisdom, engagement is primarily a local phenomenon. There is as much variation in engagement levels within companies as there is among companies. On average, most companies we have studied have some of the most engaged workgroups we have seen, as well as some of the least engaged. This contradicts much of the management research conducted at the overall company level. In part, this is because that, although strong company leadership is necessary for building engagement and productivity, the real work occurs at the local level. The hard work of engaging employees begins with one employee at a time in workgroups shepherded by managers who pay careful attention to each of the engagement dimensions the Q^{12} measures. The best companies we have studied often are distinguished because they simply have more of these managers. When leadership is committed to engaging employees top-down throughout the organization, engagement is more likely to cascade through all levels. When managers at the highest levels make sure their employees are engaged, those employees are more likely to do the same with the employees who report to them. This cascade effect mirrors the way almost all company initiatives are filtered from the leadership level to local environments. In this way, the Q^{12} metric reflects how well organizations adapt to changing conditions; companies with the most engaged employees are also often the most nimble in response to changes imposed either from above or from the marketplace.

The benefits of an engaged workforce are not limited to superior reactions to stress. The greatest long-term benefits accrue from the intangible assets created by engaged employees who are given the trust and independence required to produce innovative approaches and strategies. Robert Noyce was an extraordinarily innovative man who found his creative output limited in a disengaging environment. He needed to re-engage in his work to attain his highest levels of innovation and creativity.

If the secret to sustained organic growth is engaged employees and the intangible assets they create, then it follows that organizations should do everything in their power to mobilize the creative energies of every employee. History provides many examples of the lone inventor struggling to create stupendous leaps in science and technology, but, in reality, few of those inventors achieved their advances in utter isolation. Most scientific, technological, and commercial advances are the product of the technology transfer and diffusion of ideas that happens when a critical mass of talented people are working toward the same objectives. In the language of economics, there are significant "externalities" produced when talented people interact. They are mostly likely to occur in relatively small groups where the talents and traits that make us unique are best channeled into productive use.

Another way to encourage creativity among employees is to encourage strong relationships among employees and between managers and the employees they supervise. Attachment research[6] provides clues to how managers can accomplish this in their workgroups. This research shows that the best predictor of a child's attachment to his or her parents is the way parents narrate their own recollections of their childhood experiences, particularly when those memories are laden with emotional content — how their experiences made parents feel. So the structure of parents' narratives — *how* memories are recalled, not just *what* is recalled — powerfully predicts the strength of the parent-child relationship. The employee-manager relationship is similar in that conversations between managers and employees — and among coworkers — can help strengthen these relationships; managers can even strengthen the employee's emotional connection to the organization. The primary ingredient of these secure attachment experiences is the pattern of emotional communication among employees.

Research in the neurosciences has helped explain that these social interactions are how the mind establishes meaning. "Meaning" and "interpersonal experience" appear to be mediated by the same neural circuits responsible for initiating emotional processes,[7] making emotion central to creating subjective and interpersonal experiences. Our fMRI study of customers showed evidence of how this process works in a commercial context. In the study, the brains of customers who had the strongest levels of emotional attachment to the retailer were significantly more active while thinking about the retailer when compared to customers with lower levels of attachment. That increased brain activity was concentrated in five specific regions related to emotion, emotional-cognitive processing, and memory.

Of course, there is more to boosting employee engagement than simply encouraging coworkers to get to know each other and structuring a workplace to take maximum advantage of a team's collective strengths. Human beings are complex creatures and are motivated by more than just self-development. We need to be motivated — and we need to coordinate our activities — to accomplish anything significant. First, there must be some form of reciprocity among people for cooperation to exist. We have already discussed reciprocity regarding engaging customers, and its principles are largely the same among employees, although the stakes are much higher. In the context of the workplace, *reciprocity* means that rewards should be commensurate with perceived effort. Without appropriate rewards, workers experience emotional conflict, which activates their biological stress mechanisms.

It's very important for the typical employee to feel some sense of control over his or her circumstances and feel that he or she has opportunities to participate fully in the social life of the workplace. A lack of recognition and rewards implies a lack of participation in that social life. Rewards are not limited to tangible things such as pay and benefits; they can also include intangibles such as praise and recognition, increased responsibility or autonomy in the role, or self-esteem enhancement. This is not the kind of self-esteem parodied by many, where "Everyone's a winner!" Instead, we are talking about the authentic psychological well-being that results from concrete examples of personal success. These "concrete examples" are important because without data to back up perceptions of performance, employees can get seriously off course. Research has shown that the average person when asked to rate his performance will say that it is above average.[8] This is a mathematical impossibility — not everyone can be above average — which illustrates how poor most of us are at judging our own performance. This reinforces how crucial it is to have trusting relationships with coworkers; it can help each member of a team be accountable to an objective standard and help them maintain a focus on the right outcomes.

An environment that meets these psychological needs reinforces that the employee is a valued contributor and provides a buffer against situations that can lead to stress. Just as receiving an inoculation can create immunity to disease, engaging employees can thus provide immunity from future workplace afflictions.

LESSONS LEARNED

Improving employee engagement starts with addressing some of the most basic human needs by fashioning a workplace environment to reinforce elemental psychological needs and aspirations. The principles described in this chapter are not "nice-to-have" items that are based on an ideal image of how we wished the world would work; rather, they are fundamental needs that workplaces must meet if their employees are to flourish as human beings and workers. These emotional requirements are rooted in social and biological adaptations that have accumulated over thousands of years of human history, and help us to know when we belong, are valued, and provide benefits to a group.

These expectations do not reside in our minds as some sort of checklist; rather, they exist as a subjective set of responses to situations or relationships with significant emotional content. Think of the people who are closest to you: Are you close to them because of the objective benefits you gain from them? Or are you close to them because of who they are and how they make you feel? Employees engage with their work environment in much the same way; their evaluation is heavily dependent on how their work makes them feel. Though they can provide a list of the objective benefits their job provides — pay, health insurance, paid vacation, and a convenient location are examples — each person filters these benefits through his or her unique emotional expectations for himself or herself, which affects engagement.

Creating the kind of workplace that meets employee needs is a challenge, but it can be done. Our research shows that business units that figure this out have demonstrably higher performance, while those that don't lag financially and leave no lasting positive impressions on customers. We see this pattern clearly when we first administer an employee engagement survey in an organization: Almost always there are workgroups with exceedingly high engagement levels and correspondingly excellent financial performance, while there are also workgroups with abysmal engagement levels that are underperforming financially — and under-serving their customers. Our research with companies in the United States reveals that only about one in three workers can strongly agree that they are in a job that gives them the opportunity to do what they do best every day,[9] and that percentage is generally lower in other countries. The fact that so many employees feel stifled in their current role is an indictment of the quality of their management. That's the bad news. The good news is that companies can change this dynamic by gaining a better understanding of every employees' talents and repositioning them, or reconfiguring their roles, so employees can thrive.

Employee engagement provides a starting point for improving organizational performance. Like politics, "all performance is local," and it varies from location to location and team to team within the same organization. Addressing that variation and its impact on overall organizational health is the key to managing your organization's HumanSigma.

CHAPTER **TEN**
THE SCOURGE OF LOCAL VARIATION

"Think globally, act locally."
— Rene Dubos

As advisor to the U.N. Conference on the Human Environment, Rene Dubos believed that global environmental concerns could be addressed only by considering the cultural, economic, and ecological conditions that exist within the local environment. Sustainable global environmental change, he argued, couldn't be achieved by focusing action at a global level, but would result only from the cumulative impact of thousands upon thousands of local changes. His phrase "Think globally, act locally" summarizes this bottom-up change philosophy.[1] Dubos' focus on and call to local action has considerable relevance for business leaders who aspire to drive consistency and create sustainable change within their organizations. It's surprising, however, how few of those leaders heed this sage advice.

But what does "Think globally, act locally" really mean in business? The answer lies in how we examine and use the very metrics that many of us deploy to manage our businesses every day. Take these claims, for example: A major airline touts itself as an industry leader in on-time performance and has the flight departure and arrival data to prove it. An apparel retailer claims to be an industry leader in customer satisfaction, citing an independent study of customers in the category. A retail bank announces that it has won an award for being one of the country's best places to work for the fifth year in a row. These "summary" claims may be legitimate, but even a quick review of the on-time performance of specific flights, candid conversations with customers who shop in the store's different locations, or visits to different bank branches will inevitably reveal a considerable range in the quality of the customer and employee experiences hidden behind those averages. Within the same airline, some flights are never on time; some always are. Within the same retailer, one store delivers exceptional service; another struggles to drag customers through the door. Within the bank, some branches are exceptional places to work; others are awful.

HIGH-LEVEL PERFORMANCE SUMMARIES ARE NOT ENOUGH

High-level summaries (averages) of our companies' vital signs may make potentially useful marketing claims and may even make executives and managers feel better about their overall performance in the marketplace. But because these summaries obscure the staggering range of performance from location to location within the company, they are inadequate to provide managers and executives with the information and tools they need to manage effectively and improve their performance.

This pattern of local variability reveals several key insights. First, the variation in local performance within a company is vast. In fact, the variability *within* a company easily dwarfs the differences *between* competitors. We can bring inconsistency within a retail chain to life by creating a frequency histogram of the chain's 1,100 stores' performance on their key customer metric.[2] (See the graphic "Performance Varies By Location.") Each bar represents the number of stores that fall into one of a number of discrete performance bands, with poorly performing stores on the left and exceptional performers on the right. In this particular case, the best performer's performance is 3.5 times as strong as the poorest performer's. If you had to choose one of this retailer's stores to shop in, which one would you choose?

PERFORMANCE VARIES BY LOCATION

The variability *within* a company easily dwarfs the differences *between* competitors. Data from a retail chain illustrates the wide variation in customer engagement that exists within the chain's 1,100 stores based on how these locations performed on the company's key customer metric. Each bar represents the number of stores that fall into one of a number of discrete performance bands, with the poorest-performing stores on the left and the exceptional performers on the right. In this case, the best performer's performance is 3.5 times as strong as that of the poorest performer's.

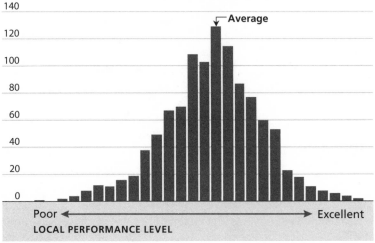

NUMBER OF STORES (per performance band, 1,100 stores total)

Source: Gallup

Second, because the histogram produces the familiar bell-shaped curve, the pattern of performance approximates a normal distribution, suggesting that variability from location to location is largely unmanaged. From the customer's perspective, this is critical because customers experience variation not averages. Customers are sensitive to the consistency (or a lack thereof) of a company's products or services. Spotty and uneven performance characterizes poorly performing companies. World-class companies, in contrast, are characterized by not only the high quality of their offerings but also by how consistently they deliver that quality time after time from location to location. For sales and service organizations with a high degree of direct employee-customer interaction, substantial variability in the customer and employee experiences they create represents a significant threat to the sustainability of the enterprise.

The existence of a broad range of performance variability within a company suggests that the only way to manage that variability and improve local performance is to provide performance feedback at the level within the organization where it originates. In practice, this means the store, the bank branch, the local office, or the sales team — the local level where customer interactions occur and where the customer experience is created. Because most managers' spheres of influence are circumscribed and local, the customer metrics they rely on to manage must also be focused locally.

Suppose that instead of assessing your heart rate, your physician substituted the average heart rate for your town in your medical chart. It seems absurd, but in many companies, something very akin to this happens every day. The vital signs of the employee-customer encounter are often assessed at the wrong level to be practically useful and manageable. What does your apparel retailer's claim that it is an "industry leader in customer satisfaction" mean to you as a customer if you are routinely confronted with subpar service at the local store? And what does the fact that your employer is identified as "one of the country's best places to work" mean to you as an employee if your local workplace is miserable and depressing? Because these vital signs are often measured at too high a level, they fail to provide insight at the levels within the company where real improvement can be made.

The vital signs of the employee-customer encounter are only useful when measured at the appropriate level within the organization. For sales and service organizations, the right level is the local "unit" level where customer interactions occur and where employees spend almost all of their time. When the effectiveness of the employee-customer encounter is assessed at the right level within the company, a fascinating new perspective emerges.

Consider this example from Telecom R, a major long-distance telephone service provider. To assess how well it meets customer requirements, Telecom R regularly measures the customer experience at the total-company level by surveying a random sample of customers who have recently called the customer service call centers. Telecom R also conducts an annual employee survey with a selected sample of its employees across the company.

Now imagine that you are a manager for Telecom R. When you receive your copy of the company's quarterly customer satisfaction scorecard, it indicates that 88% of customers who contacted one of the company's call centers were satisfied with the service they received. The report from the annual employee survey reveals that just 40% of Telecom R's employees company-wide feel the company adequately compensates them. But, as a local manager, what exactly does this information tell you? As anyone who has tried to use this type of information can attest, it doesn't tell you very much. To truly understand the totality of the employee-customer encounter, you must deploy your metrics much deeper into the organization. When you do, you'll make some startling discoveries.

Now consider the experience of a large grocery store chain, Grocer C. Grocer C regularly assesses the customer perspective by surveying a random sample of customers, producing national, regional, and even district-level scorecards. It also measures the effectiveness of the customer experience at the individual store level by surveying a random sample of customers who have shopped at each store. One of its districts includes two stores located just a few miles apart. Customer performance metrics at one of these stores are routinely very high. At the other store — reputed to be among the worst local places to shop for groceries — these same metrics are exceedingly low. Though it's the same chain, these locations are very different places to shop. Because Grocer C measured at the correct level, it discovered that within a region or even a district, a vast range of performance exists that is invisible to assessments performed at too high a level. Armed with this detailed knowledge, managers at Grocer C were in a position to take appropriate action in the stores that needed the most change.

Next, consider the experience of Bank T. Some time ago, company leaders recognized that the bank's employees play a vital role in the company's profitability in two key ways. We might describe the first way as *direct cost-efficiency*. Productive and committed employees generate greater output at a higher level of quality than unproductive and uncommitted employees do. Moreover, they stay longer with the firm, reducing training and replacement expense. These efficiencies translate into bottom-line cost reductions and contribute to enhanced profitability. The second is *indirect customer outcomes*. Productive and committed employees generate stronger connections with their customers, which lead to higher levels of customer retention, profitability, and growth. Employees who build and nurture strong customer relationships have an indirect impact on corporate financial health.

Early in Bank T's efforts to understand how to boost employee productivity and enhance organizational commitment, the bank routinely assessed its employees' opinions by surveying a random sample of employees and asking their opinions on an exhaustive and detailed range of issues. Company leaders hoped that the survey would help identify a key set of employee issues that, if improved, would make employees happier and more productive. The results were disappointing. Because Bank T measured at the overall company level, its efforts to take meaningful action to improve employee satisfaction and productivity proved largely ineffective.

It was not until Bank T began to understand its employees' attitudes at the local workgroup level — each bank branch — that company leaders fully understood the challenges and opportunities each location faced in trying to improve employee productivity and morale. Within their organization, leaders discovered a striking range of employee attitudes that ran the gamut from extreme delight to outright disgust with the workplace. Bank T also discovered a vast range of performance within the organization: some local workgroups epitomized the highest standards of excellence and world-class performance, while others were extremely demoralized.

LOCAL VARIATION IS THE SCOURGE OF HIGH PERFORMANCE

Understanding local performance variation is crucial to improving the effectiveness of the employee-customer encounter. About two decades ago, W. Edwards Deming and Joseph Juran noted that the presence of variability on critical performance metrics is a threat to the vitality of an enterprise because it's prima facie evidence that the business is not being managed effectively.[3] And, intuitively, the greater the range of performance on critical measures, the more costly — in terms of actual operating expenses *and* revenue loss (such as customer defection) — the business is to operate.

Inconsistency like this is the scourge of organizations that aspire to high performance. And though it's the nature of performance distributions to show variation, the magnitude of that variability is itself a critical measure of organizational health. Unfortunately, in most organizations, this variation in the effectiveness of the employee-customer encounter goes largely undiagnosed. Customer and employee metrics are often focused on too broad an overview of the organization. When this is the case, they fail to reveal the true range of performance variability that actually exists within the organization and to provide the level of local detail that line managers need to use this information productively. As a result, variability remains large and mostly undetected, bleeding off revenues, profits, and growth and resulting in anemic growth.

The three preceding examples illustrate one of our most consistent findings: When it comes to the effectiveness of the employee-customer encounter, there is a vast range of performance from location to location within companies. That extensive range of local performance variation begs to be managed. What's more, it suggests that there is no such thing as a single corporate culture or consistent branded customer experience.

Interestingly, companies spend millions of dollars each year in efforts to create a consistent, coherent brand image and position. Our research suggests that companies squander much of this investment. The extensive variability in the customer experience from location to location means that each location — and each touchpoint — creates a different and inconsistent version of the brand with some that bear little or no resemblance to the brand that executives back at headquarters believe they are building. In short, there are often as many different "brands" as there are local units and customer touchpoints.

But where does inconsistency come from? The patterns of performance outcomes described in the examples above are not limited to call centers, grocery stores, or banks. They play themselves out every day in companies of all types, large and small, and in different industries around the globe. In the face of this kind of performance variability, it's tempting for managers to hypothesize that it can be explained primarily by immutable factors that either can't be changed or are constant across the enterprise and must be managed centrally. Our research, however, reveals that these patterns cannot be traced back entirely to static or immutable differences from location to location or from team to team. Within a chain of retail stores, for example, controlling for immutable factors such as store age, location, store size, local market demographics, and the presence or absence of competition accounts for only a portion of the variation that exists among stores on customer metrics. Even after the effects of these factors have been removed, performance variation in the customer experience still persists. A similar argument can be made for employee metrics.

This presents something of a paradox. If we assume that the traditional arsenal of marketing weaponry (the "four Ps" of Product, Price, Promotion, and Place, plus Processes and Policies) remains relatively constant within the same company, then these variables can't explain the observed inconsistency in the customer experience. These factors, which often play a key role in driving and sustaining customer engagement, must be managed centrally. Improvement methodologies such as Six Sigma are ideally suited for managing these kinds of factors.

Ruling out the six Ps as causes of local variability leaves us with just one set of factors to explain local inconsistency: local management, as well as differences among the local employees who interact with customers. In short, the problem exists within the employee-customer encounter itself. For example, if a local sample of customers perceives subpar performance on local processes or policies, the process or policy itself can't be the root cause because these don't differ from location to location. Instead, the search for a root cause must focus on how processes and policies are *implemented* at a local level.

The successful implementation of standardized processes, policies, and other drivers of customer engagement that should be more or less constant across the enterprise brings us back to a consideration of exactly who is doing the implementing and how that implementation is being managed. For this reason, businesses must focus on reducing variability in local "people" processes (the "who" and "how" of implementation). The power of an approach focusing on reducing local performance variability lies in its simplicity and flexibility, allowing each unit to identify and correct its own causes for disengagement. Any location can optimize its performance, regardless of its starting point. The lesson from our research is not that a business unit in a "C" market can necessarily be as profitable as one in an "A" market, but rather that the "C" *and* "A" locations can improve considerably if they adapt to meeting the requirements of their customers and employees. Nothing in our research suggests that the local conditions can be so bad that a given business unit cannot improve — or so good that a local unit cannot fail.

This brings us to the third new rule of HumanSigma management:

Rule 3: Think globally, measure act locally: You must measure and manage the employee-customer encounter locally.

Do your current performance metrics go deep enough into your organization to provide local managers with the information they need to manage effectively?

CHAPTER **ELEVEN**
HUMANSIGMA

"To predict is difficult — especially the future."
— Danish proverb

R Buckminster Fuller, the noted futurist, philosopher, archi-
tect, and inventor, is credited with popularizing the term
synergy. In his landmark book *Operating Manual for Spaceship
Earth,* Fuller writes:

> Synergy is the only word in our language that means [the] be-
> havior of whole systems unpredicted by the separately observed
> behaviors of any of the system's separate parts or any subassem-
> bly of the system's parts. There is nothing in the chemistry of a
> toenail that predicts the existence of a human being. [1]

Fuller was describing one of the central concepts within his
general systems theory, but examples of synergy reveal themselves
in areas as diverse as chemistry, metallurgy, and interpersonal
collaboration. For example, the analgesic effects of codeine can
be enhanced or potentiated by adding acetaminophen (Tylenol),
producing levels of pain relief that are greater than those provided

by either compound taken separately — and more than just the additive effects of the two drugs. Similarly, the individual HIV-fighting properties of various drugs can be potentiated when they are combined in a drug "cocktail." Again, the combined effect of the drugs is greater than the sum of the individual parts. Though often maligned for being overused, the concept of synergy is the essence of HumanSigma.

We have described a comprehensive set of tools that can help your company evaluate and more effectively manage the health of the separate elements of the employee-customer encounter. If you think about these two human systems as discrete functions, however, you will fail to realize their potential to drive sustainable organizational change and growth. The real benefit of HumanSigma comes when organizations approach the employee-customer encounter as an interdependent and synergistic system. When your company manages employee and customer engagement using a HumanSigma approach, they can potentiate, strengthen, and drive your organization's financial vitality.

PUTTING THE PIECES TOGETHER

Conventional views of the relationships among employee attitudes, customer requirements, and financial performance have emphasized their sequential nature. You can think of these variables as successive links in a chain, in which each variable affects the next to drive some ultimate outcome. This perspective suggests that engaged employees create engaged customers who foster organizational success by delivering positive financial outcomes. Though this perspective has some validity, we believe that it fails to convey the true multidimensional nature of the inter-dependencies among employee and customer engagement and overall organizational financial performance.

Employee engagement does have a direct and measurable relationship to and impact on customer engagement.[2] But, like the ways in which heart rate and respiration interact to speed life-giving oxygen to all parts of the human body, the ways in which these organizational functions interact to enhance a company's financial vigor are more complex than a simple linear chain of factors. Integrating the vital signs of employee and customer engagement into a single performance construct supported by a single performance measure — the HumanSigma metric — provides a comprehensive means to capture and understand this dynamic system. This is because the combined impact of a company's human systems taken together is substantially greater than the effects of the individual systems separately.

OPTIMIZE

Our first experience with the power of this dynamic interaction of employee and customer engagement arose quite by accident. Several years ago, we were working with a large retailer to measure and improve its customer and employee relationships. As part of this process, we collected metrics on employee and customer engagement for each store in the chain. Not surprisingly, our analysis found strong linkages to financial performance for each separate measure. Within the stores, these two performance indicators were reported and acted on independently of one another because, as with most such measurement programs, different functional groups within the company owned the individual parts. The corporate human resources department owned the employee engagement initiative, while store operations owned the customer measurement initiative. As you might expect, there was no formalized interaction between or integration of the two teams responsible for these programs. They rarely, if ever, communicated with one another.

One day, however, the corporate owner of the employee engagement program ran into his counterpart on the customer side at lunch in the company cafeteria. A lively discussion about the two programs ensued. It became clear that the top-performing stores were using some best practices that could be transferred to stores where employee and customer engagement were gaining considerably less traction. With the best principles of the service-profit chain in mind, the two program owners decided that it might be interesting to compare notes on which stores were the best on each performance indicator. After all, if the sequential service-profit chain model was correct, we would expect there to be considerable overlap between the two groups of best performing stores.

To perform the analysis, we first identified the 10 highest and 10 lowest performing stores based on their success in engaging employees. We then identified the 10 highest and 10 lowest performing stores based on their success in creating customer engagement. Our working assumption, given the demonstrated statistical linkages between employee and customer engagement, was that some of the top performers in creating employee engagement would also be among the group of top performers in developing engaged customers. Unfortunately, we were wrong:

Just *one* store appeared on both lists. Somewhat nonplussed, we went back to the data in search of an explanation.

As we began to work through the implications of these findings, we made an intriguing discovery. Stores that performed well (those that scored in the top 50% of all stores on the measure) in employee *and* customer engagement — even though they may not have had the highest scores on either metric — tended to deliver considerably better financial results than those that scored poorly on the two measures. Furthermore, stores that performed well on both measures also outperformed those that scored high on one but not the other of these metrics.

Just as respiration and heart rate combine to efficiently and effectively deliver life-giving oxygen and nutrients to the entire human body, customer and employee engagement interact to promote an enhanced level of financial vigor throughout the organization. This relationship is depicted graphically by plotting individual stores' scores on these metrics along two axes representing local employee and customer engagement scores, with each dot representing an individual store in the chain. (See the graphic "Optimized.") By looking at the "scatter" of the points, it's easy to see the considerable variation in performance on employee and customer engagement at the local level.

Our subsequent research has confirmed that this pattern holds true not just for the large, multi-store retailer in this example, but also for companies of different sizes and in various industries. When viewed from the perspective of local business unit performance, customer and employee engagement — like codeine and acetaminophen — potentiate one another, creating the opportunity for accelerated improvement and growth of overall financial performance.

OPTIMIZED

Customer and employee engagement interact to promote an enhanced level of financial vigor throughout the organization. This relationship is depicted graphically by plotting individual stores' scores on these metrics along two axes representing local employee and customer engagement scores, with each dot representing an individual store in the chain. By looking at the "scatter" of the points, it's easy to see the considerable variation in performance on employee and customer engagement at the local level.

SCATTER PLOT OF INDIVIDUAL STORES' SCORES
(customer engagement vs. employee engagement)

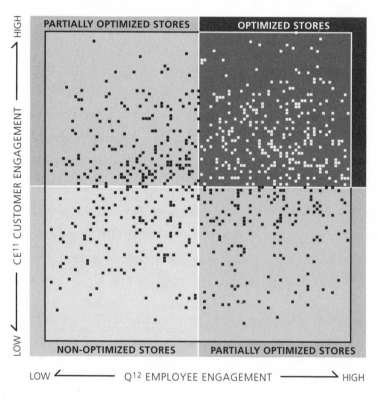

Source: Gallup

HUMANSIGMA META-ANALYSIS

As our body of HumanSigma case studies has grown, so has our ability to look for relationships across companies of different types, sizes, and geographical locations. Using these data, we have been able to probe the relationships among employee engagement, customer engagement, and financial indicators across a number of companies and business units using a statistical technique called meta-analysis. Meta-analysis allows us to integrate data accumulated from many studies of companies that use different financial indicators. This technique provides uniquely powerful information because it controls for measurement and sampling errors, as well as other idiosyncrasies that can distort the results of individual studies. A meta-analysis eliminates biases and provides an estimate of the true validity or true relationship between two or more variables.

Statistics typically calculated during meta-analyses also allow researchers to explore the presence or absence of factors that moderate relationships. Countless meta-analyses have been conducted in the psychological, educational, behavioral, medical, and personnel selection fields. The research literature in the behavioral and social sciences includes many individual studies with apparently conflicting conclusions. Meta-analysis, however, allows researchers to estimate the average or typical relationship between variables and make corrections for different sources of variation in findings across studies. It provides a method by which we can determine whether validities and relationships generalize across various situations (for example, across firms or geographical locations).[3]

Our HumanSigma meta-analysis of engagement and financial performance includes 1,979 business units in 10 different companies in the financial services, professional services, retail, and sales industries.[4] (See the graphic "Impact Coefficients for HumanSigma Quadrants.") It reveals that local business units that score above the database median on employee *and* customer engagement metrics — what we refer to as "optimized" HumanSigma units — are, on average, 3.4 times more effective financially than units that rank in the bottom half on both measures. They are also about twice as effective financially as units that are high performers on one but not both of these critical vital signs.[5]

From our analysis, the impact coefficients for each HumanSigma quadrant indicate the average net gain per business unit associated with each quadrant. The impact coefficients have been standardized to account for the uniqueness of company-specific measures; they reflect the differences observed between the quadrants, with a base value of 1 for the non-optimized or lower-left quadrant. A business unit that moves from the non-optimized quadrant to the optimized one will see 3.4 times the gain in performance compared to a unit that stays in the non-optimized quadrant.

This seems impressive on paper, but how does it look in the real world? In one high-end retail chain, we found that optimized HumanSigma stores generated $21 more in earnings *per square foot of retail space* on average than all other stores combined — a difference that translated into more than $32 million in additional annual profits for the entire chain. Within a U.S. community bank, optimized HumanSigma branches grew their number of accounts, total deposits, and total loans at twice the rate of the remaining branches, a difference that translated into more than $162,000 in additional profit growth for the bank each month.

IMPACT COEFFICIENTS FOR HUMANSIGMA QUADRANTS

Our meta-analysis of engagement and financial performance includes 1,979 business units in 10 different companies in the financial services, professional services, retail, and sales industries. It reveals that local business units that score above the database median on employee and customer engagement metrics are, on average, 3.4 times more effective financially than units that rank in the bottom half on both measures. They are also about twice as effective financially as units that are high performers on one but not both of these critical vital signs.

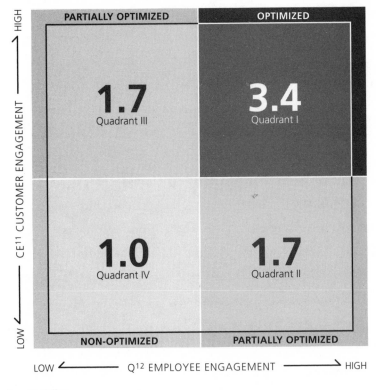

Source: Gallup

As we refined the HumanSigma concept, we formulated a relatively simple way to combine employee and customer engagement scores at the local unit level to yield a single HumanSigma score. The single score summarizes the overall effectiveness of the employee-customer encounter that is reliably related to that unit's overall financial vitality. This HumanSigma score ranges from 1 to 6 and allows us to classify units into six broad performance bands. (See the graphic "HumanSigma Performance Bands.")

Units at HumanSigma level 1 and level 2 (HS1 and HS2) perform significantly below par on employee or customer engagement metrics and are in dire need of significant intervention and improvement activities. These two performance bands account for a little more than one-third of all local units according to our database. Units that fall within HS1 and HS2 performance bands are failing to meet their financial obligations and require immediate and intensive care. The HS1 and HS2 bands include business units with poor performance on employee *and* customer metrics. It is not too surprising that those who fail on both metrics also fail financially. But a closer look at the shape of the performance bands also reveals that the HS1 and HS2 bands have long "tails" in the top-left and bottom-right quadrants. This extreme and unbalanced performance on the two metrics — very high on one but very low on the other — is also associated with relatively poor financial performance. This is a crucial point because it underscores that to attain optimum performance units need to approach the employee-customer encounter in a balanced way rather than trying to excel at just one part of it.

HUMANSIGMA PERFORMANCE BANDS

As we refined the HumanSigma concept, we formulated a relatively simple way to combine employee and customer engagement scores at the local unit level to yield a single HumanSigma score. The single score summarizes the overall effectiveness of the employee-customer encounter that is reliably related to that unit's overall financial vitality. It ranges from 1 to 6 and allows us to classify units into six broad performance bands. Business units with moderately high levels of employee *and* customer engagement are more effective than units that excel at only one of these measures. Even extremely high performance on only one measure results in little financial gain if performance on the other measure is low.

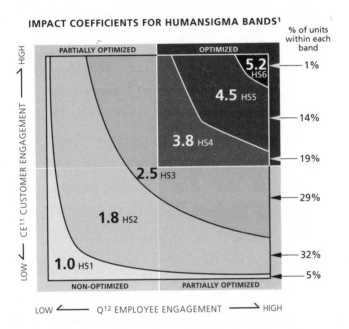

IMPACT COEFFICIENTS FOR HUMANSIGMA BANDS[1]

Note: [1]Impact coefficient represents the relative levels of revenue growth within the six bands of HumanSigma performance. Business units in HS6, for example, have 5.2 times the revenue growth of units in HS1, on average.
Source: Gallup

Units at HumanSigma level 3 (HS3) account for slightly less than 30% of all units in our database. These units are frequently out of balance, ranking high on one vital sign but poorly on the other. Units that engage their employees without engaging their customers suffer from *omphaloskepsis* — they are too inwardly focused and have lost their direction. In contrast, those that engage their customers without engaging their employees are living on borrowed time, providing their customers with excellent service by sheer force of will or plain dumb luck. Over the long term, customer engagement in these units will tend to erode and a lack of employee engagement will eat away at productivity.

Of the three remaining HumanSigma levels that appear in the optimized quadrant, units in HumanSigma level 4 (HS4) are "emerging optimized" performers. They have established balance in the vital signs of the employee-customer encounter, but they can gain substantial improvement by strengthening these signs. Units at HumanSigma levels 5 and 6 (HS5 and HS6) have hit their stride and are extremely healthy performers. These "super optimized" performers often make a disproportionate contribution to total company financial performance. These HS5 and HS6 units tend to deliver financial results that are about 3.5 times as good as HS1 and HS2 units' results. If replicable best practices are to be found within the organization, they will be found within these units.

We contend that sales and service companies should strive to become high-performing HumanSigma organizations by moving as many of their local units as possible into the HS5 and HS6 performance bands and keeping them there. To accomplish this, organizations must reduce local performance variability and increase overall performance in a balanced and deliberate way. Improving HumanSigma performance is critical because our research has shown that when units move into successively higher HS bands, there is a high potential return on investment because most of the financial gains are organically grown from ongoing operations and carry less risk than many other potential investments.

At one large U.S. specialty retailer, for example, stores that improved by at least one HumanSigma level or remained in levels 5 or 6 across successive measurement waves grew their same-quarter sales by more than $86,000 or about 3.7%; they also improved their gross margins by more than $38,000 per store. In stark contrast, stores that remained stagnant at levels 1 through 4 or declined by at least one HumanSigma level from wave to wave saw their same-quarter sales and gross margins decline slightly. Stores that were already high and sustained HumanSigma performers or those that improved their HumanSigma position by at least one level accounted for all the same quarter sales and margin growth for the entire chain. It's also worth noting that in the first year of measurement, 42% of stores were in HS5 or HS6, while 17% were in HS1 or HS2. By the second year, however, an additional 22% of stores had moved into the top two HumanSigma levels, while just 8% remained in the bottom two levels.

We found similar results at a large U.S. regional consumer bank. Branches that improved by at least one HumanSigma level or remained in levels 5 or 6 across successive measurement waves accounted for more than 99% of the bank's year-over-year profit increase. Just as with the specialty retailer, branches that were already high HumanSigma performers or that improved their HumanSigma position accounted for virtually all the year-over-year profit growth for the entire regional bank. Unlike the specialty retailer, this bank initially had fewer high-performing HumanSigma branches. In the first year of measurement, 18% of branches were in HS5 or HS6, while 21% were in HS1 or HS2. By the second year, however, an additional 11% of branches had moved into the top two HumanSigma levels, while just 9% remained in the bottom levels.

Finally, at a major European private bank, branches that improved by at least one HumanSigma level across successive measurement waves grew their same-quarter assets under management, revenue, and profit at nearly twice the rate of branches that remained stagnant from wave to wave. This is particularly significant because in the first year of measurement, no branches were in HS5 or HS6; in fact, except for the one branch in HS1, all of the bank's branches were in HS2. By the second year, however, more than half of the branches had moved into HS3 and none remained in the lowest level.

These results underscore a pair of important points. First, though upward movement from lower to higher HumanSigma levels is strongly associated with enhanced financial vitality, so too is high performance. Improvement from lower levels *and* maintenance at higher levels are crucial for sustainable organizational profitability and growth. Second, in sharp contrast to traditional customer and employee measurement initiatives that often fail to show meaningful improvements over time, dramatic improvements in HumanSigma performance in relatively short periods of time are not only possible but also likely.

What is striking about the impact coefficients for the HumanSigma quadrants and levels is that they approximate a complex nonlinear function commonly referred to as the "phi" function,[6] which has broad application in fields as diverse as sculpture, architecture, biology, fractal geometry, and physics.[7] The relationship of the phi function to unit-level financial performance is intriguing because the phi function is directly related to the well-known "golden ratio" of 1.618034 (rounded). We believe the phi function provides a fitting mathematical representation of how improvements in HumanSigma performance result in organically generated financial gains.[8]

Physicist Stephen Wolfram has argued[9] that nature uses simple programs, such as those based on phi, to generate complexity, and it turns out that nature loves the kind of growth HumanSigma exemplifies. Just look at the logarithmic spiral pattern of growth sunflowers and nautilus shells, the rise and fall of stock markets, or the growth of a rabbit population in a new environment exhibit, and you will see these principles in action. This is the same growth pattern we have observed within a number of companies: The performance gains from HumanSigma improvements tend to come from innumerable small gains in everyday performance that accumulate at the local level, rather than in large, identifiable chunks. The myriad small improvements made by the engaged work teams result in an exponential increase in output.

CUT YOUR EMPLOYEES' STRINGS

HumanSigma is designed to measure and aid in reducing local *performance* variability. But this is not accomplished by reducing the variability in how that performance is achieved, but rather by allowing and encouraging variability that meets important employee and customer outcomes. In other words, variability in performance *outcomes* is bad and must be reduced, but variability in how those outcomes are achieved is good and even essential to success.

The employee-customer encounter does not lend itself to a strict set of expected behaviors and interactions. There is not a single, best way to do things, but rather a single, best emotional outcome. Employees tend to behave in different ways, even though they have the same basic emotional expectations. This is why traditional process-improvement methods such as Six Sigma not only don't work in these situations, but they may be exactly the wrong thing to do. In most employee-customer encounters, the best resource is between the ears of that employee — so specifying a scripted response for that employee to follow, rather than letting her find her own best way to the optimal outcome, is the wrong approach.

Some of the things that are common to us as human beings — our most basic needs, instincts, and desires — are also the things that define us as individuals. These needs aren't likely to change much once we mature, so a manager's goal should be to work with human nature, rather than against it, as much as possible. Don't try to change the things that are difficult or even impossible to change; instead, use each person's unique talents to maximum effect. Or as the maxim says, "Never try to teach a pig to sing; it wastes your time and annoys the pig." Allowing people to find their own best way to an outcome may feel messy, but it's the path to maximum performance.

To a large extent our emotions drive our unique predispositions. We are not, like the Terminator, completely rational and calculating in our actions. As research by Daniel Kahneman and others has demonstrated, people don't examine all the pertinent, observable factors and weigh the likely outcomes of following each potential choice when making decisions. For one thing, our brains simply don't have the computational capacity; furthermore, we always miss a considerable amount of information about our situation, and research has shown that even when we are presented with additional information, we tend not to use it anyway.[10]

Our brains tend to be more primitive than the omniscient rational maximizer that classical economics assumes it to be.[11] We prefer intuitive or dogmatic responses, and specific emotional triggers tend to dominate our actions. Our brains are better at recognizing patterns than they are at applying rules, which makes us poor substitutes for computers. These traits are common to all human beings regardless of culture or society, and we should respect those traits precisely because they kept us alive through several ice ages into the present. The logical, deductive reasoning exemplified by the Terminator is a comparatively recent product of civilization, and it must work hard to be heard over the hubbub of our primitive brain as it efficiently directs most of our daily activities. This is as it should be because that primitive brain is more reliable in many circumstances, including the everyday employee-customer encounter.[12]

STACK 'EM HIGH AND SELL 'EM CHEAP

The Nobel laureate in economics Herbert Simon[13] noted that in environments with randomly distributed food, organisms can get by with simple food search strategies. Many businesses use a similar approach to finding and keeping customers. If you assume a random distribution of potential customers in the population — or, equivalently, that your employees can't tell the difference between high- and low-potential customers — then a simple sales strategy like "stack 'em high and sell 'em cheap" will work fairly well. But what if customer behavior presents clues that employees can use? What if employees can observe or gather many of these clues by having conversations with potential customers? Let's assume that your employees are capable of doing this and learning from it. Then the best sales strategy is to encourage employees to learn from experience on how to address customers' individual needs.

To make this individualized approach work, though, employees need accurate feedback on their effectiveness. That is why HumanSigma measurement systems are needed. HumanSigma provides the accurate measurements required so employees can learn valid performance improvement strategies. And because people are generally poor at knowing when they are bad — and, conversely, knowing when they're good — at something, accurate feedback systems are even more crucial to success.[14]

The uncomfortable truth here is that left on their own, employees *will* develop their own strategies for interacting with their customers and their fellow employees, whether you play a constructive part in that process or not. So why not involve yourself in that process from the beginning? Your involvement will be more effective if you follow a few simple guidelines from the literature on cognition that explains the conditions necessary for employees to learn new, valid strategies. [15]

LEARNING NEW STRATEGIES

The table "Learning New Strategies" shows the two key variables necessary for learning to occur: the quality of the feedback provided to employees and the consequences of employee errors.[16] Poor quality or "noisy" feedback makes strategy formation an uphill climb. As we have seen with traditional customer and employee satisfaction programs, measurement systems that fail to address our core emotional requirements are unlikely to result in significant improvement because they don't focus on the right things and are therefore too noisy to be helpful. Organizations that have adopted HumanSigma measurement systems, however, have outperformed their largest peers by 26% in gross margin and 85% in sales growth over a prior one-year period. But measurement is only half of the solution. If the company isn't organized to take advantage of this superior feedback — if the consequences of errors are small due to lack of accountability or genuine senior-level commitment — there is insufficient pressure for real improvement.

Organizations will achieve significant performance improvements only if they provide high-quality feedback to employees who are motivated to use it. As the table shows, both conditions are necessary for employees to develop productive strategies for dealing with customers and for working as a well-oiled team.

LEARNING NEW STRATEGIES

Employees learn when they are provided with clear feedback and when they are held accountable for their mistakes. If errors have no consequences, bad strategies survive as easily as good ones. And if the feedback provided to employees is unclear, it is possible for them to act on the wrong message.

FEEDBACK AND CONSEQUENCES

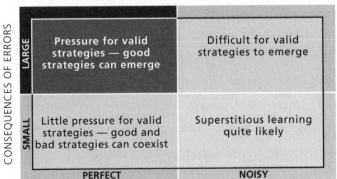

	PERFECT	NOISY
LARGE (CONSEQUENCES OF ERRORS)	Pressure for valid strategies — good strategies can emerge	Difficult for valid strategies to emerge
SMALL (CONSEQUENCES OF ERRORS)	Little pressure for valid strategies — good and bad strategies can coexist	Superstitious learning quite likely

QUALITY OF FEEDBACK

Source: G. Gigerenzer & R. Selten (Eds.), *Bounded rationality: The adaptive toolbox.* Cambridge, MA: MIT Press, 2001.

BIRDS DO IT, BEES DO IT

At this point, skeptics may still be wondering whether employees — engaged or not — are capable of making their own decisions. Recall the CEO from the Introduction who didn't trust his employees enough to deviate from standard operating protocols: He perceived every employee action as an opportunity for something to go wrong. We encounter this attitude all too frequently among the senior executives of sales and service organizations, and it continues to mystify us.

When you study excellence, you tend to find exceptional performance in many places. We are consistently amazed by the innovation and creativity people contribute in all manner of occupations and situations, often in spite of their work environment. Excellence is all around us if we would only pay attention. For instance, consider the junior high science teacher who individualizes his instruction to students of wildly varying interests and abilities and Johnny the bagger, an employee at a local grocery store whose simple thoughts for the day inspire his customers and coworkers alike.[17] Or consider Ronald Ruiz, the Bronx bus driver who delights his passengers by decorating his bus for the holidays and knows more than 100 of his regular riders by name[18] and the coffeehouse worker who knows hundreds of customers and their drink preferences. Finally, consider the red-jacketed Traveler's Aid volunteer at Newark Liberty International Airport who not only provides information and directions with an infectious smile, but also sings in a wonderful baritone voice while he does it. More to the point, when companies make the transition to a more engaging and trusting relationship with their employees, we have seen quantifiable evidence of the benefits, some of which we've shared in this book.

The following example from the animal kingdom provides a good metaphor for the benefits of cutting your employees' strings and letting them make some decisions for themselves.

Insect colonies operate with a decentralized form of control; centralization requires a considerable amount of communication, which no insect has evolved the brainpower to use. One fascinating example of insects' decentralized decision-making process is the system honeybees use to select a site for a new colony.[19] When a honeybee hive outgrows its existing home, reconnaissance bees fly off in many directions to find a suitable place to build a new one. When these recon bees come back, they describe their observations by means of a "waggle dance." Over a couple of days, the bees hammer out a consensus (well, "waggle out," actually), and a new site is chosen. Just how do they do this?

The bees choose a new site by a process of elimination. Individual bees gradually stop dancing until only one waggle dance survives. It seems that the bees who encounter a particularly good site are the ones that tend to dance the longest and hardest for it, so this method generally results in a good choice. The hard rules of evolution wouldn't have it any other way. The quality of the outcome — a good home — is what counts, not whether the bees who argued for it are better looking or whether they followed the proper dance steps.

Think about this for a moment, because it's astonishing. Most bees only visit one location, yet the swarm is able to evaluate all the possibilities with a high degree of accuracy by "listening" to what each scout bee has to say. Ultimately, the bees choose the site with the greatest "buzz" (we couldn't help ourselves), even though few bees actually saw it.

Even though a swarm is composed of bees with limited brainpower, the swarm can make sophisticated and accurate decisions. This is possible because:

- The swarm distributes the evaluation of potential sites among many bees.

- The swarm distributes the task of identifying and deciding upon the best site to the bees that actually saw the sites.

If honeybees can be trusted to make complex decisions, why are so many customer-facing employees constrained in their dealings with customers by executives and managers? Each employee has a brain infinitely more powerful than that of a honeybee, and an engaged group of employees is far more competent than a swarm. A group of engaged employees can handle situations together that the most competent individuals among them couldn't handle on their own. They do this by distributing memory, computations, and skills among the team, and by bringing a diversity of experiences and talents to a situation that none of them possesses alone. If the queen bee can allow the kind of distributed decision making needed for her swarm to prosper, we think it's worth the risk to allow your employees the same freedom. Ultimately, this is exactly the kind of synergy Buckminster Fuller had in mind when he wrote the *Operating Manual for Spaceship Earth*.

THE ECONOMIC IMPERATIVE

Organizations whose leaders are afraid to unleash the skills and talents of their employees are likely to wind up in history's dustbin. There is good evidence of the superior performance attained by companies that embrace HumanSigma principles, and many of them have only scratched the surface of the available benefits.

Think about the variability and risk inherent in any business planning and how little control organizations have over most of it. These include:

- macroeconomic conditions
- currency fluctuations
- product cycles
- new market entrants or departures
- local demographic shifts
- weather
- variable productivity across employees
- variable profitability among customers

Can your business reduce its exposure to any of these forms of risk? Sure, to varying degrees; for instance, it can mitigate the consequences by buying insurance, participating in hedge funds, making contingency plans, and so forth. But can you see into the future to predict changes in the world economy? Not really. Can you prevent new competitors from entering your market? Not legally. Can you reduce the variability in output by your employees? *Yes.* Can you improve your customer relationships while also increasing margins? *Yes.*

This brings us to the next rule of HumanSigma management:

Rule 4: There is one number you need to know: We can quantify and summarize the effectiveness of the employee-customer encounter in a single performance metric — the HumanSigma metric — that is powerfully related to financial performance.

Are your current performance measurements integrated into a simple and powerful system that gives managers the essential feedback they need to generate financial growth?

Earlier efforts to reduce variability in employee performance erred by focusing on the people themselves, and not what they do. Employees are not like pigeons in Skinner boxes that can be conditioned to behave according to the dictates of a paternalistic command and control regime. If they were, Kim Jong-Il would have the world's fastest-growing economy. So treat your employees as if they were Pinocchio — cut their strings and let them be real live girls and boys. As famed U.S. Army General George S. Patton noted, "Never tell people how to do things. Tell them what to do and they will surprise you with their ingenuity." Our next chapter will show you some ways to cut employees' strings and some ways to redefine your relationships with your customers.

CHAPTER **TWELVE**
THE STRATEGY AND TACTICS OF HUMANSIGMA:
EVALUATE, INTERVENE, AND ENCOURAGE

"Well begun is half done."
— Aristotle, Greek philosopher, 384 B.C.–324 B.C.

ollowing his annual physical exam, Grant's doctor tells him
that he should be concerned about his cholesterol levels.
They are quite high — much higher than recommended to avoid
the increased risk of heart disease associated with elevated
cholesterol levels. So every six months, Grant dutifully fasts for
12 hours and submits to a new blood test with lipid screen. Each
time, he receives the same disheartening news — his cholesterol
levels have not gone down. After several rounds of testing with
no improvement, Grant visits his doctor demanding to know why
— in spite of his diligent commitment to having his cholesterol
levels checked — his cholesterol remains high. His doctor asks
whether he has started an exercise program. Grant has not. Has
he altered his diet? No. Has he taken any of the medications that
he prescribed for him? No, he has not. He never got around to
getting those prescriptions filled. Grant's doctor's reaction is
predictable and identical to the one that almost every one of us

would have. He looks at Grant in utter disbelief. "If you haven't done anything to reduce your cholesterol, why would you expect it to be any lower?" he asks. Grant's reply to his doctor: "Well, I've been getting it checked regularly. Isn't that enough?"

It's hard to believe that anyone would behave as Grant did. After all, we all know that you can't lower your cholesterol simply by having it checked on a regular basis. That's just common sense. Measuring your cholesterol is one thing, but taking steps to reduce it by changing your behavior or making healthier choices is something else entirely. But as strange as it may sound, we have seen many companies behave in much the same way when it comes to their customer and employee measurement systems. Like Grant, far too many companies treat their customer and employee metrics as ends unto themselves rather than as a means to a higher end. They dutifully measure wave after wave, checking off the "voice of the employee" and "voice of the customer" boxes on the corporate to do list and then expect their scores to improve magically as a result. They emphasize the measurement itself, staring transfixed at the resulting performance scorecards, data printouts, and fancy reports, but fail to use this information to make real changes within their organizations. Like Grant, when their scores don't improve, they are dumbfounded. And, just like Grant, they begin to look for someone to blame. We call this process "the 18-month rule."

THE 18-MONTH RULE

Ask supply-side professionals about their experiences with most traditional customer and employee measurement and management programs and, if they are being honest, they will describe something very similar to the 18-month rule. Simply put, this rule states that most traditional customer and employee programs tend to flatline after a brief and modest initial improvement. We call it the 18-month rule because 18 months is about how long it takes before the performance results flatline and the client calls to demand a face-to-face meeting to discuss "the future of the program." Invariably, the focus of this meeting is on why their company's performance over time more closely resembles the EKG of a dead person than that of a healthy and continuously improving organization.

Like Grant's physician, we typically discover that the company hasn't taken any meaningful steps to create change within the organization, believing, like Grant, that regular measurement should be enough.

"WELL BEGUN IS HALF DONE"

Though many interpret Aristotle's pithy aphorism to mean that a strong beginning is essential for success, it also suggests that a strong beginning is just the first of many steps and that disciplined follow-through is essential for success. What happens after the measurement phase concludes is more important to the overall success of an initiative than the measurement itself. In other words, if you pray for potatoes, you better grab a hoe. The effective implementation of an organizational change and improvement process — grabbing the right hoe — can mean the difference between HumanSigma efforts that are a one-off event or that become integral to your company's business strategy and processes. In this chapter, we'll begin to put some flesh on the bones of HumanSigma, and we'll answer the question: "OK, now that I know about this, what do I do with it?"

For our purposes, we'll assume that you currently have some sort of customer and employee measurement system in place, preferably one that incorporates many of the ideas and discoveries on customer and employee engagement that we discussed in earlier chapters. (If you don't have a measurement system in place, we strongly suggest that you consider creating one. It's difficult to create change without accurate and timely performance metrics.) We'll also assume that you and your company don't really want to be like Grant and instead want to create real and sustainable organizational change. That kind of disciplined change program will need to incorporate two distinct types of interventions, which we call *transactional* and *transformational* intervention activities. We'll describe their characteristics a little later in this chapter. First, we need to think more broadly about how to prepare your company to become a HumanSigma organization.

HUMANSIGMA AS A STRATEGY

HumanSigma is a strategic approach that is supported by tactics for driving improvement and organizational change. One of the reasons Six Sigma has been so successful and has outlasted other management initiatives is that it was embraced as a corporate strategy. It galvanized management, particularly at senior levels, making them partners in and owners of the Six Sigma philosophy. Senior-level involvement and support is crucial because without it, any initiative, strategic or otherwise, is doomed to failure — including HumanSigma.

On a strategic level, HumanSigma should be considered an enterprise-wide initiative intended to drive business performance by optimizing the human systems that are vital to your organization's success. Like all strategic initiatives, HumanSigma is also a management *philosophy*. This philosophy recognizes that by optimizing your company's human systems, it can achieve a sustainable competitive advantage that is not easily copied. This can differentiate your company from its competitors in a marketplace where the traditional marketing weaponry — the "four Ps" (Product, Promotion, Price, and Place) — is rapidly becoming commoditized, if it isn't already. HumanSigma can make your human systems a true competitive advantage.

So-called "Six Sigma companies" such as Motorola, GE, and Bank of America receive that moniker because they are committed to Six Sigma as a strategic tool and way of doing business. These companies have thoroughly embraced the Six Sigma philosophy, and its methodology permeates their culture and is part of the ongoing management dialogue. Six Sigma black belts have status within the company not afforded to other mere mortals.

HumanSigma companies demonstrate a similar commitment to HumanSigma as a management philosophy — as a strategic initiative *and* a way of doing business. A focus on optimizing the human dimensions of business performance permeates those cultures and is part of the ongoing management dialogue.

ALIGNING ORGANIZATIONAL STRUCTURES: HUMAN SYSTEMS MANAGEMENT

Recall from Chapter 8 that Intel cofounder Bob Noyce wanted an anthropological approach[1] to running an organization. He understood all too well that for any major organizational endeavor to succeed, creating the right organizational infrastructure is key.

Most companies are still organized by function, such as operations, human resources, sales and marketing, and finance, and often working in isolation from each other. These functional "silos" can hobble an organization's ability to create real, sustainable change. Because they are inwardly focused, it's possible for the business objectives of one functional area to be at odds with another. This can create drag, inefficiency, waste, or even more dire consequences.

A former marketing services executive of a now-defunct U.S. airline shared a particularly telling example of this sort of "at odds" structure with us. The airline was urgently trying to increase revenue and passenger share while aggressively managing costs and achieving identified operational targets such as on-time percentage. The advertising function, which was separate from the marketing services function and reported to a different senior executive, was given the objective of increasing passenger volume. Increasing passenger volume, in turn, became a key performance indicator for the head of advertising, one on which a portion of his compensation and that of his team's was based. The group set out to achieve its objective with an ambitious advertising and promotional campaign designed to fill seats, which turned out to be successful beyond their wildest dreams. The campaign hinged on the claim that, beginning immediately, the airline was "new and improved" with service enhancements, including friendlier flight attendants, better food, and faster lines at the airport. Even after adjusting for normal advertising hype, any reasonable observer would have expected to experience significant improvements in product and service quality.

This campaign's launch came as a complete surprise to the airline's in-flight and ground operations employees; they received no advance notice, additional training, funding, or resources to achieve the promised results. Reaction from frontline employees was understandably negative — it was yet another misguided management initiative for which they would have to withstand the worst of complaints.

Ground operations, catering, and in-flight services, however, were tasked with aggressively managing costs, which they attempted to do with ruthless efficiency. These employees were already feeling stressed to meet existing standards, and still the new campaign promised more benefits to the traveling public that the employees were neither equipped nor motivated to provide. Airport employees were being measured based on on-time departures, which could be negatively affected by trying to meet the new layer of service expectations the campaign created. In most cases, flight attendants did not have the time or resources on board the aircraft to provide the additional enhancements as promised. What's more, the airline didn't offer incentives or other activities to generate the expected changes in employee behavior.

Unfortunately, not only were these functional silos' objectives at odds, but they also failed to communicate with one another. The result was an increase in the already considerable gap between campaign promises and service delivery. The sudden increase in passengers resulted in a fiasco — unusually full aircraft with inadequate ground staff to handle the surging volume, severely underestimated catering requirements, and insufficiently staffed crews. It all culminated in a horrific experience for travelers, many of whom were trying the airline for the very first time. Instead of guaranteeing a new and improved airline, the airline sealed its fate by frustrating and alienating the thousands of new customers they had worked so hard to acquire.

A key assumption of the Six Sigma methodology is that customers do not experience your company through a series of corporate functions; instead, they experience it through a series of processes. A *process* is defined as "a series of steps or activities that take inputs, add value, and produce an output."[2] These processes may intersect with one or more functional areas within the organization. So a crucial component of the Six Sigma strategy is defining the processes within the organization and appointing a *process owner* for each. Process owners are then tasked with identifying and collecting the key performance measures for their specific process. Because each process has its own customers, process owners must determine what the specific requirements of the process are from the perspective of their customers. Once the requirements and metrics have been identified, process owners are responsible for improving the parts of the process that are most important to customers or in the greatest need of repair. This seems simple enough, but when all is said and done, Six Sigma efforts rely all too often on generating centralized fixes to identified quality issues. This is one reason why it has been difficult to apply Six Sigma principles to the issue of local variability in performance.

With respect to HumanSigma, it's unlikely that many organizations will be willing, at least initially, to blow up their traditional, function-based organizational structures. Most will want to have proof that such a re-alignment makes sense and will help them better achieve their strategic goals. Although some organizations will cling to their traditional structure, those that want to become "HumanSigma companies" may ultimately evolve away from strict functional areas. Without this change, it can be difficult to balance the sometimes-competing demands of the employee and customer systems.

Though the specific business processes within an enterprise differ from company to company, the human systems are relatively fixed, comprising two key human constituencies — your customers and employees. And although Six Sigma's strategic objective is to optimize a company's critical business processes, HumanSigma's strategic objective is to optimize the vital signs of your company's human systems.

CHIEF HUMANSIGMA OFFICER

HumanSigma optimizes these vital signs by focusing on performance and change on two levels within the company: the enterprise level ("think globally") and the local level ("act locally"). This two-pronged approach requires a *system owner* for each of the critical human systems — employees and customers — paired with an effective change mechanism that can be driven down to the team level where the employee-customer encounter occurs and where real, sustainable change actually happens. These system owners should be coordinated by and partnered with a corporate HumanSigma champion charged with ensuring that these two dynamic systems are energized and optimized. Human systems do not conform to strict functional silos or traditional organizational lines. This is most evident within the employee system where employees affect every facet of organizational performance from marketing to operations not just human resources. Likewise, the health of your company's customer system is not exclusively the domain of marketing, operations, or quality. Embracing HumanSigma as a business strategy may require you to revamp your organizational structure to align your human systems with your strategic business objectives more closely.[3]

What might this revamped structure look like? You could start by consolidating responsibility for managing your company's human systems under an executive champion — a "Chief HumanSigma Officer" — who has corporate support for broad-based change initiatives to improve HumanSigma performance. This individual must have a span of control that, at a minimum, extends to the customer and employee domains. He or she must be able to fund the required activities and mandate action in response to identified opportunities. This champion should also be someone who can effectively straddle the multiple functions that intersect with your company's human systems, including the crucial areas of human resources, marketing, and operations. Not every identified improvement opportunity will reside at the local level; for example, shared services, centralized delivery or procurement channels, and product development. The Chief HumanSigma Officer should also be charged with addressing these enterprise-level issues.

In Chapter 1, we suggested an even more aggressive approach. This would be to consolidate responsibility for marketing *and* human resources under a single executive. Other configurations are possible. But, to manage and leverage your company's human systems effectively to drive productivity, profitability, and growth, responsibility for customer and employee outcomes — and the employee-customer encounter itself — should be housed within a single entity with broad authority and resources to promote organizational change.

THE TACTICS OF HUMANSIGMA: EVALUATE, INTERVENE, AND ENCOURAGE

Having covered the steps needed to align your corporate structure to support HumanSigma, we can now turn to the tactical activities that can help shape and improve your HumanSigma performance. Achieving and maintaining excellence in human systems' performance demands regular attention to three interrelated activities: *evaluation, intervention,* and *encouragement.* To meet the demand for *evaluation,* company leaders and managers need objective data to provide an accurate assessment of current performance and set realistic short-range and long-term goals. To address the demand for *intervention,* specific activities should target identified areas for improvement and capitalize on identified strengths at the local team level and the enterprise level. Those activities must be appropriate for each team's current level of performance, embracing a "meet them where they are" philosophy. Finally, to address the demand for *encouragement,* recognition and reward programs should provide incentive for continued improvement. Meeting all of these demands, but particularly the demand for intervention, requires attention to a combination of *transactional* and *transformational* activities.

Transactional activities are those that recur regularly, but they tend to be more topical and short-term in focus. Typical transactional interventions include activities such as periodic measurement, internal assessments and audits, education and training, brainstorming sessions, and action planning. Transformational activities, in contrast, result in fundamental changes in the company's human ecosystem. They address questions such as do we have the right people in the right roles? Are our compensation and reward systems properly aligned with our strategic objectives? Are we organized to effectively drive successively higher levels of HumanSigma performance?

With that, we arrive at the fifth and final new rule of HumanSigma management:

Rule 5: If you pray for potatoes, you better grab the right hoe. Improvement in local HumanSigma performance requires deliberate and active intervention through attention to a combination of transactional and transformational intervention activities.

Has your company "grabbed the right hoe"? What kinds of actions is your organization taking in response to opportunities identified by measurement data? Are you building an organizational structure that supports your HumanSigma efforts?

CHAPTER **THIRTEEN**
THE DEMAND FOR EVALUATION

"You cannot manage what you cannot measure."
— Unknown

In Chapters 3 through 9, we described two long-term research programs at Gallup that identified metrics to assess the health of your organization's customer and employee relationships. In Chapter 11, we described how to bring those metrics together to assess HumanSigma performance in your company, illustrating how HumanSigma performance is directly and powerfully related to overall financial performance and business success.

A credible effort to improve your company's HumanSigma performance begins with installing the systems necessary to evaluate how well you are meeting your employees' and customers' fundamental emotional requirements. In previous chapters, we've described key performance metrics for assessing these outcomes. Once organizations implement these, they need to establish the internal teams responsible for the initiatives, construct an appropriate measurement and reporting system, and identify if they need additional survey items to evaluate the more functional elements of the customer and employee experience. Typically, these items are added to identify elements of the customer and employee experience that have a direct impact on creating customer or employee engagement.[1]

GRAB A HOE

Throughout this book, we have emphasized that our research and ideas are founded on how humans actually behave as customers and employees. That's because they are people first and customers and employees second. Apostles of the Terminator School of Management would have you believe that human behavior can be parsed into discrete chunks of activity, not unlike a software subroutine, and that a deep scrutiny of these chunks will provide some means of dampening our most irritating human instincts and quirks. We believe the evidence shows quite the opposite: Our fundamental human nature dominates our attitudes and behaviors so much that it's best to understand us as we are and then learn to make the most of it.

One place where this point of view clashes with that of the Terminator School is in how to use employee and customer engagement data. In our work with dozens of large, sophisticated organizations, we have encountered many executives who believe that the act of collecting data constitutes a transformational intervention on its own. In other words, like a software program provided with better input, employees armed with better data should be able to transform an organization automatically. Though improvement is not so simple, we regularly encounter this belief. Our point here is that evaluation is a transactional activity; it supports interventions large and small, but it's rarely a transformational endeavor on its own. We've all heard the maxim that "measurement improves performance." Well, that's only partly true. Measurement only improves performance when it's acted upon. Measurement is a necessary step, but it's only the first step toward meaningful organizational change.

TRANSACTIONAL ACTIVITIES: EVALUATION

Engaging employees and customers — and driving HumanSigma performance — requires a year-round focus on changing behaviors, processes, and systems to meet and anticipate these constituencies' needs. This requires a total commitment from the leadership team down to frontline units and employees. To implement the right changes, a rigorous process of monitoring engagement and defining appropriate support and activities is needed. Local units must be held accountable for their engagement levels, their successes should be celebrated, and they should receive the support they need to increase engagement.

Measurement Logistics. Once you've established the overall goals of your HumanSigma program, it's time to identify how often you should measure, how to build a measurement plan, and how to conduct the measurement. Ideally, employee engagement measurement should be conducted twice a year with all employees. This provides the best picture of the employee experience. Every employee should have a voice in the process. Our experience has shown that taking follow-up actions on the feedback of a subset of employees can be counterproductive; unless all employees are included, some will feel disenfranchised from the process. Only when the voice of every employee is included can the process be truly effective.

Choosing the right frequency of measuring customer engagement at a local level depends on a number of factors. First, the right frequency hinges on your organization's ability to assimilate the information and take action to create change. But real, sustainable change does not happen overnight. If measurement happens too often, it can be frustrating and counterproductive to local teams because they may not see the fruits of their improvement efforts before the next measurement results are delivered. How many diets have been derailed by an apparent lack of progress as reflected by too frequent weigh-ins? Conversely, if measurement doesn't happen often enough, the process will lose its urgency and become a one-off event rather than an ongoing dialogue. Our experience suggests that quarterly customer measurement often works best. It's frequent enough to remain "top of mind," but allows enough time between measurement waves for improvement to occur.

Finally, each customer-facing unit in the company should receive customer and employee feedback from samples of its customers and a census of its employees. This ensures that the results are seen as indicative of the unit and not discounted because the team's results are lumped in with a larger organizational grouping. Providing this level of local detail also allows managers to observe the degree of variability that exists at all levels within the organization, often for the very first time.

Analysis. Analysis of the data is one of the most important steps in the HumanSigma methodology. This is true for two reasons: First, it helps leaders identify enterprise-level opportunities and prioritize actions at a macro level. Second, it encourages managers and workgroups to identify specific opportunities to respond to unique local issues.

The Terminator School of Management places a great deal of emphasis on this step, but it does this for all the wrong reasons. Many organizations torment their employees and customers with unbearably long surveys, attempting to reduce any activity to its discrete parts. The survey responses are then exhaustively analyzed for gleaning the secrets to improving relations with the survey's target audience. This "deconstructionist" approach is an unfortunate legacy of business process re-engineering methodologies that have been repurposed to address human systems' management. Although this approach sounds perfectly logical, it is often quite flawed — and it leads to the unfounded belief that specific improvement actions can be clearly and unambiguously derived from survey responses (the oft-cited quest for actionability). Having examined data from hundreds of customer and employee surveys and from millions of customers and employees, we can say without question that actionability does not come from crafting a better and more precise survey item. True actionability comes from using survey data to identify areas of opportunity and then supplementing those data-driven insights with deep conversations with employees and customers to arrive at a set of local solutions. It's hard work, and there are no shortcuts or silver bullets.

First, the idea that an analytical process like this can produce a handful of discrete "management levers" feeds the illusion of centralized control of the employee-customer encounter that we discussed in Chapter 1. Second, asking your employees or customers a laundry list of questions gives them the impression that you don't know very much about them and that you are grasping at straws. Third, the data that are accumulated in these surveys are often much more complex than the methods used to analyze them — methods that can oversimplify findings and lead to generalizations with scant empirical foundation.

Analytical efforts are important, but they are often done incorrectly and wrongly treated as ends in and of themselves. One reason for conducting these analyses is to identify the aspects of employee or customer engagement that apply across the enterprise and the causal factors that drive employee and customer engagement enterprise wide. But don't consider these enterprise-wide findings the end of the story. One of the best uses of the data is to inform local change management efforts by encouraging discussions about local performance and unique local issues. Analytical efforts shouldn't be used to generate a list of answers; they should be used to generate better questions or hypotheses to feed an adaptive change management process that drives improvement.

Identifying Performance Zones. Enduring success in an organization demands ongoing assessment and progressive change to achieve and then maintain the highest levels of performance. But all too often, change activities are regulated under a single organizational policy. A single initiative works well for workgroups that have attained a certain performance level, but not for others who are past that point, or for those who have yet to reach it. These other groups fail to reach their full potential for improvement because too little is expected of high performers, and those at the lower level are often left straggling behind never able to fully catch up. There is a better way to take every team to its highest performing level: Meet them where they are, not where you wish they would be.

The most dramatic and enduring change happens when the activities are appropriate to the unit's current level of performance.[2] Teams that are already high performing — typically those in HS4 through HS6 — should be allowed to continue to do what already works for them. They have made the correct decisions and undertaken the right interventions and education initiatives to improve, and they should be allowed to continue on their own paths to further growth. This growth should be guided, supported, and encouraged, but not co-opted. On the other hand, units that are underperforming require a firmer hand and significantly more guidance. Corporate champions and representatives of best performing sister units in the organization should provide this support. By assimilating better strategies for developing customer and employee engagement, poor performing units gain the confidence and the tools they need to begin directing their own improvement activities. Control of their own destiny is a target *and* a reward. One-size-fits-all programs, which are appropriate when new initiatives are introduced or single issues are mandated for action, don't work as well when there isn't a single optimal strategy or action plan that works for all organizational units. In such situations, a flexible approach and delivery will bring the greatest reward at the lowest cost.

By identifying performance zones and tailoring interventions to current performance — a process we call *adaptive intervention* — organizations can apply solution strategies that best fit a team's current performance level. As progress is made, the solutions adapt. Strategies that were effective at one performance level are replaced by solutions more effective at the next. This approach eliminates two of the strongest barriers to enduring change: habituation and a phenomenon that social scientists call "learned helplessness."[3] For example, teams often lose enthusiasm for change when the same approaches and messages are repeated, even when those approaches and methods are otherwise effective. An adaptive approach to intervention bypasses the danger of change habituation and encourages continued progress over time. Likewise, when faced with performance expectations that are perceived to be outside of their ability to accomplish, poor performers tend to give up and become helpless, undermining the objectives of the initiative at the outset.

The Way Forward. Once organizations have received baseline performance data, it's important for them to develop a road map spanning a three-year period. Why three years? To some extent, the time frame is arbitrary, but we have found that anything shorter than three years tends to be viewed as a one-off or stand-alone event, while anything farther out than three years seems too long given the rapid pace of change in today's business environment. This three-year road map establishes enterprise-wide and team-level performance targets. The road map is a key activity because it defines the scale of the change required and the expected successes.

Our typical approach is to use baseline performance data as the starting point for the road map and then define an aspirational target as its destination, dividing the target into achievable "chunks" based on the number of years in the time frame. A typical goal might be to move all units up by at least one HumanSigma level within a year. Or it may be more complex, such as asking top-performing units to maintain their HS5 or HS6 performance while moving HS2, HS3, and HS4 units up by one level within a year. Units in HS1 should, at a minimum, be expected to move into HS3 within one year's time. Whatever the target, the organization should paint a clear and compelling picture of where it expects workgroups to be at the end of the three-year period, and the Chief HumanSigma Officer must aggressively communicate these targets.

There is no single path to success that works for every organization. All are at different points on the road to excellence: Some are closer, while some are further; some have smoother paths, while others more difficult terrain. All organizations and workgroups, however, have a common need to know where they stand and the distance between them and their targets. Having a plan of how to progress and knowing what to expect year by year or month by month is crucial. We need support and control to keep us on the right path and the motivation to keep us moving ahead. To achieve the objective of all-around excellence in an organization, we need to adapt change processes to fit the current state of every unit; in other words, we need to "meet them where they are." We'll now turn to some general types of intervention activities that successful companies have used to drive change within their organizations.

CHAPTER **FOURTEEN**
THE DEMAND FOR INTERVENTION

"It is common sense to take a method and try it. If it fails, admit it frankly and try another. But above all, try something."
— Franklin D. Roosevelt, 32nd president of the United States

All things considered, a new evaluation system is relatively easy for local workgroups to adapt to because it can be a largely passive experience for them. Of course, the stated intentions of performance management systems are not generally discussed in terms of compliance, but that is often the end result. Typically, someone else decided how to measure their performance, how often this will occur, and what to do if the performance is lacking. That's because the legacy of many measurement systems is simple compliance checks: Local managers are essentially treated like children who are asked to clean up their rooms or do their homework. It's equally difficult for employees to respond positively to a system that treats them like toddlers, so a passive resistance or grudging compliance on their part is a perfectly natural response. To gain the employees' commitment to improvement, they need to be involved in that effort and not just told how to do it.

The evaluation strategies we described in Chapter 13 are intended to be much more than just another surveillance system. Instead, these are the precise evaluation activities that will best serve efforts to improve local performance. For the most part, these will *not* be compliance efforts but will rely on the active participation, initiative, and creativity of local work teams. This kind of involvement requires building effective relationships with employees and communication lines that work in both directions and not just from the top down. So the intervention stage is where the organization's commitment to HumanSigma principles is tested, and it's arguably the most difficult. But the intervention stage is also where the seeds of dramatic organizational change are planted. An effective HumanSigma intervention process begins with orienting employees toward the need for and benefits of change, as well as the reasons for selecting a particular intervention activity instead of others.

Communication and Orientation. Organizational change initiatives sometimes fail because the rationale for and benefits of the initiative are not communicated to all the parties involved. We have seen many situations where the business case and rationale for an initiative are well-known by senior management but remain relatively opaque to the rank and file who must make the desired changes. It's hard for employees to embrace an organizational change initiative if they aren't sure why it's being done or how it will benefit them.

Consequently, communication and orientation activities are essential elements of any effective organizational improvement initiative. Orientation activities play two key roles: At the beginning of an organizational change program, employees need to know what engagement is and how it will benefit everyone involved. Organizations also need to provide a process and language to help employees begin to implement actions in response to local performance measurement. These activities, however, should be targeted toward workgroups that are ready to receive and implement these educational objectives.

TRANSACTIONAL ACTIVITIES IN INTERVENTION

As initial orientation efforts trickle down through the organization, companies need to avoid two extremes regarding how they are applied: dumbing down the activities to a series of apparently meaningless actions or orders or providing too much information with little direction on how to use it. We have often seen both of these errors, though the first is much more common at the local level. The key to success here is adapting the activities or information to a group's ability to manage on its own. This is probably why we see so much dumbed down content — it's aimed at the lowest performers rather than tailored for the different abilities of local teams.

Brand Promise Alignment. If you believe, as we do, that your frontline employees play a crucial role as brand ambassadors and are truly the face of your brand in the marketplace, then an obvious place to begin an intervention process is with the brand promise itself. What is your company's brand promise? And how well-known is it throughout the company — from the executive suite to the frontline customer service representatives?

A few years ago, we conducted a simple exercise with the leadership team of a large, multi-site specialty retailer. During a daylong off-site meeting, we asked each team member — including the CEO — to write down the company's brand promise to its customers and its employees. These responses were then collected and displayed anonymously on a whiteboard. Of the 12 members of the company's executive team, no two members agreed on the company's brand promise to its customers or its employees. In our experience, this result is not unusual. Most members of leadership teams have a hard time articulating their company's brand promise, but you can find the foundation for building customer and employee engagement in this essential, but overlooked, element of your company's strategic plan.

If the senior leaders of a company have a hard time articulating the brand promise, how likely is it that the promise will be known — and importantly, lived — by anyone else in the company, especially employees with a high degree of customer contact? It's not very likely, and some recent research by Gallup bears this out. In a recent survey of employees in a wide range of sales and service industries, slightly more than 4 out of every 10 customer-facing employees strongly agreed with the statement "I know what my company stands for and what makes us different from our competitors." In hospitality and retail banking, the numbers were closer to 3 out of every 10 employees. Perhaps more disturbing is that 1 in every 14 employees with direct customer contact had absolutely no idea what their company stands for or what makes them different.

For these reasons, one of the first transactional intervention activities should be a brand promise alignment exercise. An essential first step to building engagement is to infuse the brand promise for customers and employees into every aspect of the business, from associate on-boarding to annual reviews to continuing employee education.

In our experience, The Ritz-Carlton Hotel Company provides one of the best examples of brand promise alignment. Not only are the elements of the employee and guest promise clearly articulated, but they are also printed on a wallet card that every one of Ritz-Carlton's "ladies and gentlemen" carries with them at all times. How well-articulated, known, and lived are your company's employee and customer promises?

Action Planning. One of the most common, but poorly executed, transactional activities used today is action planning. Our experience suggests that for action planning to be effective, it must be completed in a timely manner, usually within one month of receiving local HumanSigma performance feedback. We believe that the specific elements of local unit-level action planning are often best left to the local unit for two reasons: First, on reviewing its performance feedback, the local unit is in the best position to identify the specific actions that are most likely to be productive in its own local environment. Second, engaging all members of the local team in developing specific improvement actions helps ensure that the team owns those actions and will execute them. But we have also found that some units are better able to handle this kind of laissez faire approach to action planning than are others. Therefore, the freedom that a unit is given to decide its own action planning should be determined by its level of performance. Consistent with the "meet them where they are" philosophy we described earlier, top performers should be allowed a great deal of autonomy and encouraged to create their own action plan with minimal interference or oversight. Their high performance indicates that they have taken appropriate steps in the past and can be trusted to continue on their proven trajectory. Managers of these workgroups should also be recruited to take on roles as coaches and mentors to the poorest performers.

In contrast to the top performers, struggling units have demonstrated their inability to succeed. It's unlikely that, if left alone, their actions will meet with much success. Our own data support this observation. In one company, for example, 80% of units that either had not completed the action-planning process or made tangible progress toward their agreed-upon goals after the first measurement wave remained in HS1 or HS2 or dropped into that zone from higher levels after the second wave of measurement. We recommend that poor-performing units like these receive a clear and specific set of actions to focus on, rather than choosing actions for themselves.

Performers in HS3 should be given a mix of mandated actions and a small range of discretionary activities to choose from along with coaching to help them succeed in meeting their action items. In this way, action and effort are focused where they are most likely to bear fruit, and freedom and autonomy become the rewards of high performance. Plans should detail the specific actions to be taken (generally no more than three), the means of achieving them, who is responsible, and when they will be completed. Not surprisingly, we have found that action items that meet the SMART criteria (**S**pecific, **M**easurable, **A**ction-oriented, **R**ealistic, and **T**ime-bound) tend to be the most effective and the most likely to deliver results. For underperforming units in HS1, a "SWAT team"[1] approach has proven to be an extremely effective intervention. In this case, a "performance recovery team" made up of poor performers' top peers and corporate process experts is engaged on-site to develop a detailed action plan for immediate implementation with time-defined improvement targets. Because of their poor performance, underperforming units shouldn't be allowed to direct their own improvement efforts, but they shouldn't be thrown to the wolves either. If they manage significant improvement under the tutelage of a high-performing manager, they can earn the right to direct more of their improvement efforts.

Action-Planning Review. Though action planning is often a staple of organizational change programs, it's surprising to us how often local-level action plans are implemented without prior review and approval. It may seem obvious, but carefully reviewing, critiquing, and modifying a unit's action plans can increase its likelihood of success and reduce the likelihood that the process will frustrate the team. The review need not be particularly formal, but it should be regular and thorough. Senior managers with good practical knowledge of the circumstances faced by the particular team developing the action plan do the best reviews. So, for example, a core part of a regional manager's responsibilities could be reviewing and adjusting the action plans for business units within his or her region. Most of the time spent reviewing these action plans should be in conversation about what is planned, why it was suggested, and how changes are progressing. We have seen companies bury this idea in bureaucracy by worrying about what forms and systems are used to submit and store the action plans and how best to measure the amount of manager "activity." Done poorly, this kind of review system comes across very much like a corporate function looking to legitimize itself and can require more time and energy from local managers than it's worth. Done well, though, it can encourage and strengthen the action-planning process. Other uses of the system must be subordinated to this simple mission.

Customer Advisory Boards. True actionability can't be obtained by crafting better and more precise survey items. Instead, it's far more effective to use survey data to identify broad areas of opportunity and then supplement those data-driven insights with deep conversations with customers *and* customer-facing employees about potentially productive local solutions. But how can local units regularly engage in these conversations in a cost-effective way? A simple solution is for each unit to form a customer advisory board that meets on a regular basis. These don't need to be large groups, nor do the meetings need to be formal. But they do need to include local customers who can comment on the units' performance. Think of these meetings as ersatz focus groups in which the topics of conversation are guided by hypotheses gleaned from survey data. The idea here is to do a deep dive into the opportunity areas identified by the data *as they play out at a local level*. It's often a good idea to empanel several of these groups so that different groups may meet more often. At the very least, however, it's critical to supplement the insights provided by the data with explanations, examples, and solutions offered by the local customer base. Why local customers? The answer here is simple, but an example will illustrate it best.

For one company we worked with, the customer engagement survey data revealed that a key customer issue was "being easy to do business with." As each local team wrestled with what customers meant by that, they decided to ask them. Not surprisingly, their customers were delighted to provide insight and detail. But what *was* surprising was that the identified solutions to the same opportunity — that is, being easy to do business with — differed from location to location. One unit defined it as having appropriate staff available to answer questions. Another unit defined it as simplifying the paperwork necessary to open an account. It was the same revealed opportunity, but with different local solutions. The bottom line is that there is no substitute for engaging your customers directly to formulate solutions to drive local improvement.

We hope these suggestions will help organizations improve something we also hope they are already doing: measuring performance and regularly discussing and brainstorming ways to enhance it. With some of your highest-performing groups, measurement, discussion, and brainstorming may very well be sufficient to help them maintain their high performance. But the poorest performers will need more encouragement and support, and they will need much more time to make improvements stick. This is significant because our research shows that current poor performers represent one of the greatest opportunities for HumanSigma improvements.

TRANSFORMATIONAL ACTIVITIES IN INTERVENTION

If done correctly, you will reap considerable benefits just by improving how you implement the kinds of transactional intervention activities we have described so far. But just as seeds planted in rich, fertile soil and nourished with sunshine and water will grow faster, stronger, and healthier than seeds sown on barren land and left to languish on their own, so too will your improvement efforts gain greater traction if you plant them in a more "fertile" organizational soil. The goal of transformational interventions is to create this kind of environment within your company.

Though it's important to hold poor-performing units accountable for moving their HumanSigma results up a level or more, it's equally important to hold high performers accountable for maintaining their already high results. Creating a culture of accountability is one of the most important transformational interventions any company can implement, if they haven't done so already. But, once you've defined acceptable performance standards, it's also important to provide groups with the assistance and incentives they need to improve if you're going to hold them accountable to those standards. Transactional interventions include communication and orientation activities, strongly directed action planning with external facilitation, reviews and coaching, creating customer advisory boards, and the occasional use of performance recovery or SWAT teams. If your goal is to "meet them where they are," however, the organization must assess the needs of each unit individually, considering performance *and* potential. One useful way of gauging the group's potential is to learn the unique talents and strengths of the individuals who comprise it. A second transformational activity is to supplement your existing workforce by selecting new associates who have an increased likelihood of success and performance at excellence. We will address each of these transformational interventions in turn.

BUILDING A STRENGTHS-BASED ORGANIZATION

When we use the word "strength," we're actually referring to something specific — an ability to provide consistent, near-perfect performance in a specific activity. The first step to building a strength is to identify your greatest talents — the ways in which you most naturally think, feel, or behave as a unique individual. Talents are inherent predispositions that exist deep within us, like a burning desire to win, a natural tendency to assume command of groups of people, or an instinctive sense of the feelings of other people. Strengths are created when your most naturally powerful talents are combined with more learnable skills such as knowledge of how to program a computer or the ability to drive a truck. The important distinction here is between talents, which naturally exist in you and are quite difficult to change, and knowledge and skills, which you can acquire with relative ease through education and training. Talents develop over long periods of time, and being much more resistant to change, are our more defining characteristics as individuals. Gallup has researched this topic for more than 35 years, studying more than 6 million people in the process, and we have found that individuals and organizations have much more potential for growth in areas of great talent than areas of weakness.[2]

For this discussion, it's important to know that we all have unique talents and that understanding them helps us master them. That awareness can also help us work more effectively with our coworkers, many of whom will have talents different from our own. For example, both of the authors of this book are highly analytical by nature; we prefer objectivity and empirical discourse. We search for patterns and connections and tend to be highly rigorous and logical in our approach to things. We always ask, "Why?" Having a common language that helps us explain these natural tendencies to our coworkers and friends has made it much easier for them to understand that our habitual skepticism of their ideas is not personal, but a natural response from someone who always wants to ask "Why?" It also helps our spouses understand why our first response to a problem or issue is to search for its causes and a solution rather than to empathize and listen.

Knowing your employees' most naturally powerful talents helps you understand how best to position them for success. This is another instance where The Terminator School of Management gets it wrong by assuming employees are interchangeable parts that can be placed into virtually any job if provided with sufficient training. The surprising thing about this assumption is not that it's false — most of us have known people who were not fit for certain jobs, no matter how much training they got. No, the incomprehensible thing about this is that many leaders actually know that some employees are a poor fit for certain roles, yet they manage their organizations as if it weren't true. A strengths-based approach, on the other hand, starts by taking a look at the unique talents of each member of the team and then figuring out how best to use those talents to maximize the group's — and the individual's — performance.[3]

Terminator Management systems are designed to remove as much of the variability and individuality among employees as possible — to reduce most jobs to the lowest common denominator so that just about anyone can perform them. Strengths-based management, instead, capitalizes on each employee's uniqueness to maximize the team's output. Teams that operate this way are more engaged and, as a consequence, more productive. Our research shows that an employee whose supervisor focuses on her strengths is significantly more likely to be engaged than one whose supervisor focuses on her weaknesses. Even worse off is the employee whose supervisor ignores him: He has virtually no chance of being engaged at all.

A strengths-based approach not only improves team engagement and cohesion; it also generates better results. In 2002, Gallup conducted a study of more than 2,000 managers, comparing the high-performing managers to their lower-performing counterparts. We found that high performers were more likely to indicate that they spent time with their high producers, matched an individual's talent to the tasks assigned, and emphasized individual strengths versus seniority in making personnel decisions. The probability of the manager being a high performer was 86% (or 1.9 times) greater for managers with a "strengths versus non-strengths" approach.[4] At an individual level, our studies have also shown that a strengths-based approach to development increases self-confidence, direction, hope, and altruism, all of which enhance productivity and overall performance.[5]

Most importantly for companies that invest in employee develop-ment, a recently completed study shows significant financial returns on those investments. The study included an estimated 90,000 em-ployees in 900 business units from 11 different organizations, rep-resenting five different industries. In addition to large increases in employee engagement, teams whose managers received a strengths intervention had productivity measures that were 12.5% higher (post-intervention) than teams whose managers received no inter-vention, and 8.9% higher profitability. Individual employees who learned to apply their strengths were also less likely to terminate their employment; their turnover rate was 14.9% lower than employees who did not learn their strengths.[6]

YOU IN REVIEW

To illustrate how a strengths intervention might produce these superior results, let's consider something most of us have experienced — the performance review. In our experience, here's a script for a typical review: First, you were rated on some kind of survey, say one that gives you 360-degree feedback. During your review, your manager honed in on all the lowest ratings and then spent most of the meeting coming up a strategy to remediate your shortcomings. Does this scenario sound familiar?

Let's start with those ratings. First, where did the set of things to be rated come from? Did they come from a systematic study of the necessary outcomes of your job, or did they come from a committee of people who described all the things they think you should do in your role? Does the list mix hard financial and operational outcomes with fuzzier ratings that sound good but may or may not have any bearing on how well you do your job (as compared to how others think you should do your job)?

We have observed many companies that have thrown as many measures as possible at the wall, hoping that a few would stick. Companies that use this laundry list approach seem to do this for two main reasons: First, it preserves the illusion of control. For example, when managers aren't trusted enough to achieve key financial or operational outcomes in the best way they see fit, accountability measures often are more about "style points."

Second, the organization does not understand that HumanSigma is the causal underpinning of many of the included measures and would thus be a better area to focus on. We have found that most workgroups and managers can be optimally measured with only two classes of metrics: the critical financial and operational outcomes that are the purpose of that business unit and the HumanSigma level of that unit.

Just as we each have our own powerful talents, we, of course, also have talents that are less powerful in us — and we can choose to focus on either one. Let's examine the strategy of "fixing" your lesser talents. Everyone has them — even Superman would have a difficult time meeting or exceeding the laundry list of desired behaviors outlined in many performance reviews. Once your manager has identified your "deficiencies," how much of your review is spent discussing them and how to fix them? Now compare this with the amount of time you both spend discussing the ways in which you most naturally and powerfully think, feel, and behave, and how better to capitalize on that.

Is it starting to become clear how this kind of review can inhibit building a productive, trusting relationship with your manager and suppress engagement in general? We have found that there is a much better way to meet the desired outcomes of the typical performance review while simultaneously helping managers forge better relationships with those they manage, and as a result build engagement among the team.

The first step is to set clear expectations about *what* each employee is supposed to accomplish, not *how* he or she is supposed to accomplish it. So, don't rate employees on whether they seem to "drive for results," but on whether they actually produce results. The second step is to get to know the employees' greatest talents and therein their potential for strength. Beginning a performance review with a discussion of an employee's talents sets a very different tone for the review. Most people naturally prefer to talk about what they like to do, and steering the discussion toward what they naturally do well as opposed to what they do poorly builds a better relationship between managers and employees. The discussion during the review focuses on how employees can use their unique talents to perform their roles with strength, and it helps managers understand the many possible ways of achieving a successful outcome.

Done correctly, a strengths-based performance review will make it much clearer what the organization means by "success" — and whether the employee is succeeding. It helps remove much of the anxiety inherent in the more typical performance review; it also helps build the attachment between employee and manager that is a necessary precursor to engagement. Finally, it should help managers understand how to motivate individual employees to do their best. It's one thing to know what we do well; it's another thing entirely to do it to the best of our abilities every day.

SELECTING FOR TALENT

One means of improving productivity and engagement in your workplace is to replace struggling employees with better ones. There are many wrong or harmful ways to do this, but there is a method that works if applied with diligence and care. First, let's cover some of the less successful ways. One well-known method for changing the talent of an organization is the forced stack-ranking and purging of employees perhaps most commonly associated with Jack Welch and GE. We have found this to be one of the laziest manifestations of performance management. We will focus here on contrasting this "de-selection" approach with an approach based on an understanding of employee talents and how it can be used to reliably hire new employees in a way that obviates the need for regular purges.

When we talk about "talent," we mean those natural tendencies that exist deep within us. These are the aspects of our personality or behavior most resistant to change. This is a much more precise usage of the word "talent" than is generally meant in common parlance where one's natural abilities and traits are considered together with acquired skills, experience, and attitudes.

Our research shows that some traits do not change much over time. There is ample evidence supporting the genetic or developmental basis for many of these traits.[7] Does this mean that a given talent or trait is absolutely fixed? Not necessarily.[8] But it does mean that our genes and our physical and social development all impose some boundary conditions on what we either can or choose to learn easily. In some respects, those relatively fixed talents are what define us as individuals in that they represent the product of all the billions of choices and circumstances that brought us to the present moment.

In hiring and managing individual employees, it's important to understand what is difficult to change (talent) *and* what is more easily changed or acquired (knowledge and skills). Once you hire someone, you are largely stuck with their talents, whereas you can still impart new skills and knowledge. Without a clear understanding of these two different aspects of ability, you will have an incomplete picture of how talents play into hiring decisions and could become more prone to making hiring errors.

Consider, for instance, an example from education research. Students with more ability often report studying less than, yet perform better than, their less-gifted peers. Given two students of equal ability, however, the one who exerts more effort performs better. If we ignore study habits, we might be tempted to think performance is all about raw talent. If we ignore that raw talent, we might be tempted to think performance is instead all about effort. But when we remember to consider both aspects, we begin to understand how talent and effort contribute to results in combination.

We have met resistance to using a talent-based selection method in a number of organizations. The objections to this approach generally fall into one of three categories. Talents, the objectors contend, cannot be perfectly identified; they are not fixed; and we all have talent and can do anything we want to if we work hard enough. We will now consider each of these objections in turn.

TALENTS CANNOT BE PERFECTLY IDENTIFIED

Though it's true that talents can't be perfectly identified, this is not saying much. There are a many things in life that we can't perfectly distinguish yet are perfectly useful to do. Selection instruments are not accurate enough for certainty, but they are reliable enough to have practical usefulness. This is no different from the clinical evidence for pharmaceuticals and medical procedures — often, they are not 100% effective either, especially when used incorrectly. Talent assessments need to be used intelligently with an understanding of the domains of talent one is trying to address and the accuracy with which one can measure them. If this is done, a well-constructed and psychometrically sound selection interview will reliably predict how job applicants will perform. Two major studies of selection interviews have been published since the mid-'90s.[9] In each study, hundreds of independent studies were aggregated, and we found that individuals with high interview scores had higher performance, whether measuring that performance in terms of sales volume, production records, or supervisor ratings. The interview scores did not perfectly predict performance, but they did a good enough job to be extremely useful.

TALENTS ARE NOT FIXED

Performance is not merely a function of talent. Performance is also dependent on motivation and experience, on how a person is managed or led, and on having the right materials and equipment to do the job at hand. Talent, employee engagement, and experience are interrelated, and together have a multivariate relationship to performance. But this does not imply that our core talents are not stable over time. There is growing evidence that we develop stable traits at relatively young ages,[10] and that personality traits at a broad level are universal across a wide array of cultures.[11]

We must also emphasize the importance of "practice." Having an exceptionally powerful talent does not invalidate the need for practice that will refine the talent so it can contribute to the consistently near-perfect performance of strength. In fact, highly talented individuals who practice excel more often than less-talented individuals who practice a similar amount. To use a familiar example, Mozart's hard work paid off a lot more for him than it would have for an average music student because Mozart had more intrinsic passion and talent for music than most, and because his father constantly motivated him to attend to that passion and talent.

Examples like this prove particularly fascinating in light of some recent research into the neuroscience of music. "Music is among the most distinctive features of the human race," writes Daniel J. Levitin.[12] "No known culture now, or anytime in the past, lacks music, and some of the oldest artifacts from archeological digs are musical instruments."[13] As such a universal human endeavor, music serves as a good example of how our talents develop under different circumstances. Levitin points out that memory and a person's emotional involvement in the instrument he is striving to master play a crucial role in developing expertise.

> Neurochemical tags associated with memories mark them for importance, and we tend to code as important things that carry with them a lot of emotion, either positive or negative. . . . Caring may, in part, account for some of the early differences we see in how quickly people acquire new skills. . . . It's impossible to overestimate the importance of these factors; caring leads to attention, and together they lead to measurable neurochemical changes.[14]

Levitin goes on to emphasize the importance of practice and that it takes 10,000 hours of practice to truly master just about anything in life.

> In study after study of composers, basketball players, fiction writers, ice skaters, concert pianists, chess players, master criminals, and what have you, this number comes up again and again. . . . Of course, this doesn't address why some people don't seem to get anywhere when they practice and why some people get more out of their practice sessions than others. But no one has yet found a case in which true world-class expertise was accomplished in less time. It seems to take the brain this long to assimilate all that it needs to know to achieve true mastery.[15]

This argument in favor of practice has led many to believe that it's the sole route to success, whether great talent exists or not. But this is an incorrect understanding of the way our minds work. Though practice is essential to the building of mastery, it's not enough by itself. Some people just get more from that practice than others do. For example, both of the authors are musicians and have experienced the improvement that comes with practice. But one of us has a sister who is a classical pianist who exhibited more interest and aptitude in music at a very early age. The greater interest spurred her to practice a great deal, and the greater aptitude helped her benefit more quickly from that practice — so the interest and the aptitude reinforced each other. It was likely the same in our Mozart example above; as Levitin notes, Mozart's father "was widely considered to be the greatest living music teacher in all of Europe at the time,"[16] so Mozart's precociousness had assistance in being developed into mastery. Both examples illustrate talent's significant contribution to strength. Without application and practice, talent languishes, and without talent, the practice does not have as much benefit.

HARD WORK VERSUS TALENT

Everyone has some stable dispositions that we can evaluate and discuss. But no two individuals share the same array and levels of talents, and some of the talents that are most naturally powerful in a given individual could be the most difficult for that person to change. Can an individual with low conscientiousness be conscientious occasionally? Sure. Some aspects of personality are dependent on the situation. Many of us can exhibit a degree of discipline when we really need it, but for some of us, it's not a reliable trait. When we talk about great talents, we are really talking about one's most reliable dispositions, the ones that best represent that person's core personality. These traits can be reliably measured and used to select candidates who are better fits for the job at hand, and thus much likelier to excel.

The benefits of hiring employees using psychometrically valid[17] talent assessments are numerous and substantial. Because a candidate who passes such an assessment has talents that are known to be predictive of success in the job of interest, the odds of this candidate being successful are much higher — he or she is less likely to quit and more likely to produce superior results. In a recent meta-analysis of selection instruments[18] — including 55,234 observations from 386 studies — results showed that hiring the top 20% of candidates recommended on the basis of their talents relates to more than a 20% gain in sales performance per person.

No reasonable amount of training or hard work will likely ever make up for the performance gap that can be attributed to having talents that fit the job. It has been our experience that more talented individuals also learn and adapt faster in situations that fit their talents, so it is likely that additional training and experience will instead widen the performance gap between those with talent and those without. Understanding the talent requirements of a given job makes it much easier to hire candidates that are likely to succeed in those circumstances. It also helps clarify existing employees' perceptions of the role and the extent to which those perceptions match who they are as individuals. If the role is a good fit talent-wise, then any deficits in performance are likely the result of a lack of skills, knowledge, or experience, all of which can be changed with relative ease. If the role is a poor fit, then deficits in performance may be difficult to overcome, and the employee should find a more suitable position.

The final judgment in these cases should always be the employee's performance. There are many routes to success; talent assessments merely find the most common ones associated with excellence and raise the odds of high performance. This is the best way to think about talent — as one factor among others, including experience, skills, and knowledge. Using structured selection interviews to hire individuals with more talent for a particular job is a powerful way to build a stronger HumanSigma culture.

"TRY SOMETHING"

We began this chapter with former President Roosevelt's observation that when faced with a need to change, the act of trying *something* is as — if not more — important than *what* you try. The simple truth is that without focused and disciplined action, even the best evaluation tools are nothing more than information without context. It is by taking action on that information that companies begin to imbed HumanSigma principles into the fabric of their organizations. Some of your actions will bear considerable fruit; others may be less effective. In these cases, it is crucial to admit the failure frankly and go and try something else. But above all, *try something*. This trial-and-error process is how children learn, it is how science progresses, and it is how your organization will begin the journey to higher human systems performance. Of course, you can improve the likelihood that your actions will bear fruit by targeting actions to teams whose performance indicates that they are prepared to execute them, by using an adaptive intervention process to tailor interventions to the performance levels of teams and units with the company, and by deploying the full range of transactional and transformational intervention activities available. But few activities will lay the groundwork for sustainable success better than providing ample reward and encouragement for progress made. We turn now to the crucial task of motivating your employees to improve their HumanSigma performance.

CHAPTER **FIFTEEN**
THE DEMAND FOR ENCOURAGEMENT

"Correction does much, but encouragement does more."

— Johann W. von Goethe, German playwright, poet, novelist, and dramatist, 1749-1832

In the helter-skelter pace of our day-to-day business lives, it's all too easy to forget the adage that you can attract more bees with honey than vinegar. But we should all strive to remember that success must be encouraged, celebrated, and rewarded. To that end, high-performing HumanSigma units should be recognized — and not just the managers or executives who run the units, but the entire team. And because the financial payoff of HumanSigma management accrues to those units that improve their HumanSigma position as well as those that consistently perform at very high levels, it's also important to recognize those that improve the most.

Celebrating successes helps institutionalize improvement by establishing the language and culture of engagement. Consistent enterprise-wide support is necessary to maintain positive momentum, and cheerleading and emphasizing initiative are important means of sustaining enthusiasm for the change process. In our work with companies that have improved the most, we have identified a number of transactional and transformational activities that motivate employees to improve.

TRANSACTIONAL ACTIVITIES IN ENCOURAGEMENT

Again, we consider transactional activities to be regularly recurring efforts that are more short-term in focus. Because most organizations have some form of regular rewards and a recognition system in place, adding a HumanSigma component to that system is a logical first step. We have some well-formed opinions on how a company can add a HumanSigma component to its recognition system.

Preferred Recognition. No two employees are alike, and not every employee desires to be recognized in the same way. Financial compensation or formal awards and plaques motivate some employees. A personal letter, a note, or an e-mail from a senior leader encourages others; while still others enjoy the more informal thanks they receive from their peers. Sadly, however, few managers embrace an individualized approach to the ways they recognize excellence. Take for instance, the story of Rachel, a salesperson who was to be recognized for exceptional achievement in sales growth. Part of the recognition ceremony required her to make a short speech to the worldwide sales force. Unfortunately, she was terrified of public speaking, so what was intended to be a high point of her career, turned into a situation filled with anxiety and dread — hardly the kind of recognition she desired or deserved. A first and important step in meeting the demand for encouragement and recognition is to sit down with your employees and ask them how they would prefer to be recognized. You may be surprised by what you learn.

Performance Communication/Celebration. Top-performing units should be identified and recognized from the first HumanSigma measurement. Lower-performing units shouldn't be announced until some time later to give them an initial opportunity to catch up, but at some point, the performance of all units should be made public within the company. Organizations benefit by not being punitive too early in the process because it keeps fear-based conditioning from narrowing employee mind-sets and stifling creativity. Also, from a practical standpoint, a single measurement — just one data point — does not provide any sense of whether the situation is improving.

Local Celebrations/Recognition. Many teams best express their identities and aspirations through local celebrations of achievement and excellence. Some of the totems or rituals they develop might seem strange to outside observers, but those group characteristics help cement the behaviors that produced superior results and provide a rallying point for future efforts. These local celebrations run the gamut from individual call outs or lineups during regular team meetings all the way to extreme rituals such as contests to determine whether the store manager dyes his hair blue or shaves it off.

Formalized Rewards. A specific reward structure may be formalized, taking into account numerous factors including company culture and existing compensation plans. To keep these activities from degenerating into either beauty contests or revolving doors, they need to maintain internal validity to remain useful while balancing competing behaviors. In other words, they should be based on performance outcomes rather than a sense of equity

("Everyone should win at least once.") or popularity ("Everyone likes Bob."). If a majority of a company's employees or business units can easily achieve the rewards, then the criteria are probably not stringent enough.

It's essential to remember, however, that human nature dictates that employees will always follow the money: They will do what they are rewarded for doing. Any incentive or reward structure must ensure that only desired outcomes are recognized and rewarded, and that financial incentives do not crowd out other motivations by occurring too frequently. Trying to micromanage behavior with frequent, small incentives can create a culture of employees who will not do anything without an inducement, much like rewarding a dog for learning a new trick. And like that dog, employees may continue doing that new trick long after it is desired in hopes of getting another treat. For an incentive to send the right signals, it should be large, targeted, and difficult enough to achieve to be meaningful.

TRANSFORMATIONAL ACTIVITIES IN ENCOURAGEMENT

Transformational activities that respond to the demand for encouragement should build an infrastructure that recognizes the best performers for their accomplishments. These activities should also lay a foundation for sharing next practices within the company. Next practices are intended to help create a culture of celebration and recognition that continually drives successively higher levels of performance and give struggling managers and teams the support they need to succeed.

Peer Group Mentors. Top performers should be encouraged to mentor their lower performing peers. Mentorship should represent an important contribution, not a burden, and thus it should be strongly recognized. Additional compensation should also be part of the mentorship program. There are skills and tactics that managers can learn best from their peers, and they are generally going to get more from discussions with others who have been in their shoes. A mentorship program can also be a good pipeline for managers who want to ascend to leadership positions within the organization by giving them a chance to learn and demonstrate crucial leadership skills. Our experience suggests that in its initial stages, the mentor-mentee relationship should be a private one to encourage open and frank discussion. Should performance fail to improve as a result of the partnership, the mentor's evaluation of the mentee's strengths and weaknesses may need to become part of his or her formal record, with an eye to *recasting* the floundering mentee if need be.

HumanSigma Level 5 and 6 Summit/Retreat. Special gatherings intended exclusively for top managers and managers whose units show the most improved performance should be scheduled regularly. This provides significant recognition to high achievers and fosters sharing of success stories and practices. It's important, however, that these gatherings be extremely focused on strategies and tactics for improving HumanSigma performance lest they degenerate into something substantially less useful.

It's worth noting that similar, though less celebratory, gatherings for level 1 and 2 performers can also be an effective tool for driving improvement in poor performing units. Attendance at these off-site gatherings should be mandatory for poor performers, and each attendee should be required to identify and present on a targeted area for improvement as well as a plan for driving change. The ultimate goal for any attendee of this summit is not to be invited back.

Performance Linked to Advancement/Promotion. A formal linkage of rewards and recognition to SMART objectives or other performance contracts can be instrumental in driving continued success. General accountability for performance is essential. All too often, there is a disconnect between what is measured and what is actually rewarded. To be effective, HumanSigma performance must be consequential to everyone in the organization from top to bottom.

Case Studies. A featured article in a company publication highlighting specific success stories and actions can serve to provide recognition and praise. Many readers may find this an obvious tactic, but it's one that we have seen all too infrequently. Even when these kinds of case studies are written, it's not always clear how one team's story illustrates a strategy that might be replicated by other teams. Instead, many case studies we have reviewed dwell on an aspect of a team's success that is difficult to replicate. Instead of highlighting responses to unique circumstances, case studies should focus on how and why a team developed its exceptional response.

Consider, for instance, a store that energized its employees every morning by marching around the parking lot in formation behind a banner that they received for outstanding performance. This ritual provides a nice photo opportunity, and it's a clever example of the kind of odd tactics managers develop to motivate their employees. But, it's not easily transferable. For one thing, this store is situated in a warm climate; a store in Minnesota or Düsseldorf, Germany, might have a little more difficulty making this work. More importantly, the drill formation is just a goofy thing the local manager came up with to remind his employees that they are high performers and are expected to meet high standards. He also discovered that local customers found the exercise amusing, which provided another reason to keep doing it.

What does this story teach us? It shows that perseverance pays off: The manager tried a few things until he found one that worked. It also demonstrates that local cultures will embrace different things: The daily march idea worked well in the sports-crazy town that was used to parading its accomplishments in front of everyone else. It shows that little things such as a daily parade can build esprit de corps and energize employees. It shows that innovations come in all sizes. It doesn't show how following a flag around a parking lot will improve your store's performance.

CHANGE IS POSSIBLE

Over the years, many executives we have talked to suffer from "flatline skepticism" concerning their company's ability to improve their employee and customer performance metrics. They have become frustrated by the lack of significant and sustainable improvement in those metrics and have resigned themselves to lives of quiet desperation, unable to move the numbers. Some have even shut down or de-emphasized their employee and customer measurement programs. But our experience with organizations all over the world clearly demonstrates that dramatic — and sustainable — improvement in a company's human systems is achievable if you apply focused and sustained effort to the task.

Sometimes change requires an earth-shattering or disruptive act. Sometimes the actions required are very basic and simple. But all successful HumanSigma efforts we have seen have involved a range of transformational and transactional activities at the enterprise (top-down) and local (bottom-up) levels. All of this effort has generated substantial increases in performance for the companies involved. Perhaps more importantly, however, those are not one-time rewards, but rather sustainable improvements in productivity that are expected to continue long into the future.

Are you suffering from flatline skepticism? Or do you believe real improvement in your company's human systems is not only possible but also likely when the appropriate activities are applied to the task?

CONCLUSION

"A journey of a thousand miles begins with a single step."
— Lao Tzu, Chinese philosopher (c. 604 B.C.–531 B.C.)

We began Chapter 12 by quoting Aristotle to emphasize that nothing gets better until you start trying to make it better. This is an old idea, and its continued truth speaks to its importance. The tools and tactics we have discussed in the preceding chapters are all about helping you start using HumanSigma to make changes for the better in your company. HumanSigma focuses on accepting our human nature and capitalizing on it to manage employees, motivate them, accelerate their development, and unleash innovation and productivity all to ultimately engage the emotions of your most valuable asset — your customers.

We hope that it's now clear that the most important thing is to get started and keep working at it. Improvement takes time and mindful attention to the everyday facts of our lives. Each team needs to sketch out a vision for its future and work hard to build toward that vision. You will make mistakes, so your system needs to be tolerant of missteps if your organization hopes to optimize its performance for the long haul. To paraphrase Nietzsche, what does not destroy you will make you stronger. The Apostle Paul provides a more positive spin on this same idea in his letter to the Romans (5:3-5a) in the New Testament:

> And not only that, but we also boast in our sufferings, knowing that suffering produces endurance, and endurance produces character, and character produces hope, and hope does not disappoint us.

As Jonathan Haidt points out,[1] ancient thinkers were not very good scientists, but many provided extraordinary insights into moral psychology and social relations that still hold true today. St. Paul was particularly insightful with respect to problems of will power or the ability to persevere in an effort to change. By using this ancient advice as a guide and applying some modern science, Haidt provides the following advice[2] on how to make a resolution and stick to it:

1. Train your emotional mind. Most of our cognition is automatic and intuitive, and it connects directly to our brain's motivations and reward centers. Haidt refers to those more automatic and intuitive processes as the mind's "elephant,"[3] and our more conscious, controlled will is the rider on that elephant. We can guide the elephant, but when it really wants to do something, it is difficult to control. Training our elephant involves changing our daily habits through behavioral conditioning, meditation, or some other purposeful redirection of our most basic impulses. It also takes time (about 12 weeks) for our brains to learn new habits.

2. Change the elephant's surroundings. Everyday stimuli impose the most important boundaries on our behavior, and the people we associate with are the strongest sources of these stimuli. We have observed this time after time in our research on employee engagement and well-being: Friends and coworkers have an enormous effect on us, and we should therefore involve them in our efforts to change.[4] If not all the members of a team are rowing in the same direction, it's difficult to accomplish any meaningful or long-lasting change.

3. Get to know your own elephant. Once you learn to identify your elephant's strengths and weaknesses, you will know when to follow your instincts, and when they might lead you astray. The kinds of strengths interventions we described in previous chapters excel at helping us learn these things about our coworkers and ourselves.

So there you have it — the map of the terrain that we call HumanSigma. We have described a multiyear program of research and discovery to map the employee-customer encounter. We have presented the best evidence we've seen in the research literature to help you better understand the inner workings of the hearts and the minds of customers and employees and, importantly, the kinds of behaviors that can result when those inner workings are better understood. We have described the best examples we've observed from companies that have already been down this path and that have brought these principles to life. And we hope that we've demonstrated the immense economic return that is the result of a disciplined application of HumanSigma principles. But there are no silver bullets, no magical levers to pull, and no mystical pills to swallow that will instantly solve all of your company's challenges. Managing the employee-customer encounter is just plain hard work. It involves measuring the right things in the right ways, taking deliberate and disciplined action to improve each local team's performance, and celebrating your successes. However, when approached correctly, all of this hard work can really pay off. What works best for your organization must ultimately be determined by the employees who work there. The answers are not easy, and some organizations can find this frustrating. But we've also noticed how the need to own your own improvement makes people more innovative, productive, and confident. Are there a better set of characteristics for companies facing an unknown future? We think not, and millions of employees and customers agree.

L E A R N **MORE**

To read more about the in-depth research behind *Human Sigma* and to stay up-to-date on Gallup's latest discoveries in employee and customer engagement, visit the Additional Insights area in the *Human Sigma* Book Center on the *Gallup Management Journal* Web site (http://gmj.gallup.com).

Readers of *Human Sigma* can receive a complimentary six-month trial subscription to the *Gallup Management Journal*. Go to https://commerce.gallup.com/ma/code and follow these instructions:

- If you already have a Gallup membership, enter your user name and password, then click "Log In."

- If you do not have a Gallup membership, click "Create an Account." Enter the required information, click "Submit Registration," then log in to continue. Enter your user name and password and then click "Log In."

- Enter the promotional code **HumanSigmaBook** and then click "Continue."

- Review your order and click "Submit Order" if the information is correct.

For questions or assistance, e-mail galluphelp@gallup.com.

ABOUT **THE** AUTHORS

John H. Fleming, Ph.D., is a Principal of Gallup and Chief Scientist for Gallup's Customer Engagement and HumanSigma practices. He consults with Gallup's global clients to help them improve customer engagement and enhance their business effectiveness. Fleming is a coauthor of the *Harvard Business Review* article "Manage Your Human Sigma."

Prior to joining Gallup, Fleming spent six years as a member of the psychology faculty at the University of Minnesota. He received his doctorate in social psychology and master's degree in psychology from Princeton University and his bachelor's degree from the College of William and Mary in Williamsburg, Virginia. He lives near Princeton, New Jersey, with his wife, Robin, and their daughters, Allison and Emma.

Jim Asplund is a Principal of Gallup and Chief Scientist for Strengths-Based Development. He leads Gallup's global research on the science of human strengths and how to apply them to improve organizational performance. Asplund is also one of Gallup's leading methodologists, specializing in complex research and development efforts.

Prior to joining Gallup, Asplund spent eight years as a policy expert and lobbyist at the Minnesota Legislature, representing clients in the areas of taxation, education funding, and economic development. He earned his master's degree in public policy with emphasis in mathematical demography from the University of Minnesota and his bachelor's degree in mathematics from Grinnell College in Iowa. Asplund lives near St. Paul, Minnesota, with his wife, Susan, and their sons, Jakob and Jonas.

APPENDIX A

The set of 11 customer engagement items that were used for the reported analyses are listed below. They provide the means for measuring and monitoring the strength of the relationship that exists between a company (a brand) and its customers.

The metric consists of three "attitudinal loyalty" items, which employ a 5-point scale that ranges from "extremely" (5) to "not at all" (1):

- *Overall, how satisfied are you with [Brand]?*
- *How likely are you to continue to choose/repurchase/repeat (if needed) [Brand]?*
- *How likely are you to recommend [Brand] to a friend/associate?*

Copyright © 2000 Gallup, Inc.

These three attitudinal loyalty items are combined with a standard set of eight emotional attachment items that also employ a 5-point scale, one that ranges from "strongly agree" (5) to "strongly disagree" (1):

- *[Brand] is a name I can always trust.*
- *[Brand] always delivers on what they promise.*
- *[Brand] always treats me fairly.*

- *If a problem arises, I can always count on [Brand] to reach a fair and satisfactory resolution.*

- *I feel proud to be a [Brand] [customer/shopper/user/owner].*

- *[Brand] always treats me with respect.*

- *[Brand] is the perfect [company/product/brand/store] for people like me.*

- *I can't imagine a world without [Brand].*

For product-marketing situations that don't involve a service component or human touchpoints, the two Integrity scales ("treats me fairly"; "if a problem arises, . . .") are adjusted as follows:

- *[Brand] always treats their customers fairly.*

- *If a problem arises, I can always count on [Brand] to stand behind their products.*

One of the two Pride scales ("always treats me with respect") is also adjusted as follows:

- *[Brand] is a highly respected brand name.*

The set of 12 employee engagement items that were used for the reported analyses are listed below. They provide the means for measuring and monitoring the quality of a local workplace.

The metric consists of 12 items, which employ a 5-point scale that ranges from "strongly agree" (5) to "strongly disagree" (1):

- *I know what is expected of me at work.*

- *I have the materials and equipment I need to do my work right.*

- *At work, I have the opportunity to do what I do best every day.*

- *In the last seven days, I have received recognition or praise for doing good work.*

- *My supervisor, or someone at work, seems to care about me as a person.*

- *There is someone at work who encourages my development.*

- *At work, my opinions seem to count.*

- *The mission or purpose of my company makes me feel my job is important.*

- *My associates or fellow employees are committed to doing quality work.*

- *I have a best friend at work.*

- *In the last six months, someone at work has talked to me about my progress.*

- *This last year, I have had opportunities at work to learn and grow.*

END**NOTES**

INTRODUCTION

1   Hurd, G. A. (Producer), & Cameron, J. (Director). (1984). *The terminator* [Motion picture]. United States: Orion Pictures Corporation.

2   Pyzdek, T. (2003). *The Six Sigma handbook: A complete guide for greenbelts, blackbelts, & managers at all levels* (Rev. ed.). New York: McGraw-Hill.

    Gygi, C., DeCarlo, N., & Williams, B. (2005). *Six Sigma for dummies*. Indianapolis, IN: Wiley Publishing.

3   Six Sigma is a strategic tool that is supported by a well-defined set of tactics for process improvement. The strategic component of Six Sigma is called Business Process Management (BPM). The Six Sigma methodology focuses on the strategic goal of process improvement and process integration aligned to achieve the organization's strategic business objectives, whatever those might be.

The basic tactical methodology of Six Sigma is abbreviated and referred to as *DMAIC (Define, Measure, Analyze, Improve,* and *Control).* Each of these steps has some well-defined activities for process improvement as well as a set of milestones that must be accomplished as the process unfolds.

The first step, *Define,* is when a team charter is drawn up and a project team is impaneled, the specific process requirements are identified, and a high-level description of how the process currently works — called a process map — is generated. The second step, *Measure,* is when the team actually goes about collecting some data to assess the efficiency and effectiveness of the process in terms of how well it's meeting customer requirements. It's on the basis of these data that the project team will identify the critical improvement issues — the vital few — they will focus on as the process moves forward in the next step.

The *Analyze* step is when the team uses the data collected in the *Measure* step to identify the sources (or root causes) of inefficiency and ineffectiveness in the process. Root causes are usually classified as belonging to one of six types: *Machines, Materials, Measurement, Methods, Mother Nature,* and *People.* The identification and validation of specific root causes provides a road map for subsequent process improvement activities.

The *Improve* step is when the rubber really hits the road. This is when the team brainstorms potential solutions for the root causes of process inefficiency and ineffectiveness. The team then selects a subset of those potential solutions to implement. It's essential in the Improve step to demonstrate that the implemented actions have actually had the desired, positive effect on the process. Consequently, reassessing the performance of the process is critical. The final, or *Control,* step is when the proven improvement solutions from the previous step are permanently incorporated into the process so that the enhanced efficiency and effectiveness that were generated by the implemented solutions hold up over time. This is also where the changes to the process are documented and the "new and improved" process is formalized.

There is, of course, a great deal more detail behind the specifics of the Six Sigma methodology than what we have presented here, and readers are encouraged to consult some of the sources we identified earlier for additional information. Nonetheless, understanding the basic structure of the DMAIC methodology will prove useful as you begin to identify and discuss opportunities to improve your company's performance.

4   Cameron, J. (Producer/Director). (1991). *Terminator 2: Judgment day.* [Motion picture]. United States: TriStar Pictures.

'CHAPTER 1

1   In manufacturing companies, value is created on the factory floor when finished goods of acceptable quality are made available for sale. But in sales and service organizations, value is created (and ultimately enhanced or destroyed) when an employee and a customer meet and interact. This employee-customer encounter is the equivalent of the factory floor in sales and service companies.

2   Lev, B. (2001). *Intangibles: Management, measurement, and reporting.* Washington, D.C.: Brookings Institution Press.

3   Intangible assets are by and large not traded in organized markets, and the property rights over these assets are not fully secured by the company, except for intellectual properties such as patents and trademarks, so their magnitude is difficult to measure. And it's this difficulty in consistently measuring the magnitude of a firm's intangible assets that has proven so nettlesome to accountants and financial analysts valuing investment projects. This, in turn, has prevented intangible assets from forming the core of a company's valuation.

We are not trying to pick on accountants here. In fact, it has been our experience that they understand all this better than anyone else does. But it remains that an insidious side effect of this inability to measure intangibles is that accounting systems basically treat employees as expenses — not as valuable assets.

Lev and others, however, are beginning to make strides in creating a foundation for consistent, intangible asset valuation. Lev's methodology for measuring the value of intangible assets, for example, is based on the economic concept of the "production function," where a firm's economic performance is stipulated to be generated by the three major classes of inputs: physical, financial, and intangible assets. Thus:

$$Economic\ Performance = \alpha(Physical\ Assets) + \beta(Financial\ Assets) + \gamma(Intangible\ Assets),$$

where α, β, and γ represent the relative contributions of a unit of asset to the enterprise's performance.

Lev and his colleagues derive the value of the third performance driver — intangible assets — as the solution to the above production function for the one unknown (intangible assets). What remains from this subtraction is the contribution of intangible assets to firm performance, which Lev defines as "intangibles-driven earnings." [Gu, F., & Lev, B. (2003). *Intangible assets: Measurement, drivers, usefulness.* (Working Paper No. 2003-05). Boston: Boston University School of

Management. Hand, J., & Lev, B. (2003). *Intangible assets: Values, measures, and risk.* New York: Oxford University Press.]

The general superiority of intangible assets is not immediately apparent from this equation. But consider that physical assets such as superior store locations become commodities after the market leaders have reaped supernormal profits, and everyone else has imitated them. The same phenomenon occurs with some intangible assets, as well; one can purchase or outsource some R&D functions, for example. But one class of intangible assets is difficult to commoditize because they are hard to replicate or purchase outright. Lev refers to these kinds of intangible assets as *Organizational Capital (OC),* and they are things such as organizational designs or processes that are unique or idiosyncratic to firms (like the Internet-based supply chains at Wal-Mart), or the organization's human systems — the engagement of employees and customers that has accumulated over years of repeated engaging experiences. By virtue of its idiosyncratic nature, this OC can be thought of as the main competitive advantage of most firms. [Lev, B., & Radhakrishnan, S. (2004). *The valuation of organizational capital.* (Washington Evaluation Research Network paper).]

The Nobel Prize-winning economist Robert Solow developed a model that showed how country level growth relates to changes in investments in capital and labor. However, when tested econometrically, it only explained 20% of the variation in countries' GDP. That means that 80% of the variation in GDP was due to something besides investments in capital and labor. Statistics refer to this unknown "other" category as the "residual." The particular residual in Solow's equation came to be known as "Solow's residual" (who says economists have no imagination?) and was widely assumed to be due to country differences in innovation and advances in technology. In a variation of Solow's approach, Lev and Feng Gu have added research and development to the equation and attributes the residual amount to intangibles [Gu, F., & Lev, B. (2003). *Intangible assets: Measurement, drivers, usefulness.* (Working Paper No. 2003-05). Boston: Boston University School of Management.]. So:

Firm Performance = f (Capital, Labor, R&D, Residual)

In a study of thousands of companies — in which Capital, Labor, and R&D are all held constant — OC explains the remainder of performance at the firm level. Adding OC to the model significantly increased the explanatory power of the model.

In a perfectly competitive market, where all this information is available, companies' stock prices should reflect these differences in organizational capital. Consider Company #1, an extremely innovative company with highly engaged employees and customers, and Company #2, which has an actively disengaged workforce and customer base. If the market truly reflects these two companies' future prospects, they should have similar risk-adjusted returns over time. The market price of Company #1 should be high enough to reflect its bright future, and the price of Company #2 should be discounted enough to reflect its dismal prospects.

The problem for the market, however, is that the quality of information disclosure on OC components is inadequate. Few companies disclose how engaged their employees or customers are, or how effectively they are leveraging their employees talents, skills, and knowledge. To validate that the information OC captures is not filtering its way to the markets and stock price, one simply needs to run a test of market efficiency. This involves looking at a portfolio of high OC stocks versus a portfolio of low OC stocks and measuring their risk-adjusted performance over time. When Lev performed exactly this kind of test, the analysis revealed systematically higher returns to companies with higher OC [Meeting with Baruch Lev, Gallup Manhattan offices, April 25, 2003]. Clearly, there is information on these firms that is not used to predict future performance but could — and arguably should — be.

4   Gallup scientists conducted an extensive study of the earnings per share trend of the publicly traded companies in its databases. Researchers compared the engagement levels of publicly traded organizations for which census engagement surveys were conducted (average 83% response rate). Top quartile organizations' EPS was 2.4% above the competition in 2001-2003 and improved to 18.0% above the competition in 2004-2005. Below-average organizations' EPS was 2.9% below the competition in 2001-2003 and improved to 3.1% above competition in 2004-2005 (the companies in the below-average group also worked on improving engagement). Relative to the competition, the growth trend for top quartile engagement organizations was 2.6 times that of the below-average organizations.

5   An exceptional counterpoint to the "How Big Can You Get Before You Get Bad?" issue is exemplified by the dabbawallas of the Nutan Tiffin Box Suppliers Association in Mumbai, India's largest metropolis. For more than 100 years this 5,000 person-strong network of semiliterate tiffin- (lunchbox-) toting delivery specialists has managed to deliver more than 175,000 hot, made-at-home lunches every working day throughout the greater Mumbai metro area with stunning accuracy. They also get the empty tiffin boxes back home every night. Not only do they never make mistakes — their error rate is something around 1 in every 6 million transactions (a little less than 7 Sigma or 0.16 DPMO) — but they deliver their gastronomic cargo affordably, averaging between $4 and $7 per month for the service. For more information, please see:

Anderson, B. (2004, August 18). Fast food delivers lunchtime lesson. Retrieved March 20, 2007, from http://edition.cnn.com/2004/BUSINESS/08/16/mumbai.dabbawallahs

Vora, R. (2005, May). Mumbai dabawallas: The amazing story of the Nutan Tiffin Box Supply Charity Trust better known as dabawallas. Retrieved March 20, 2007, from BPIC Web site: http://www.bpic.co.uk/articles/dabawallas.htm

6   Heider, F. (1958). *The psychology of interpersonal relations.* New York: John Wiley & Sons. Fritz Heider was a German social psychologist whom many consider to be (along with Kurt Lewin) one of the major forces in shaping contemporary social psychology. His *Psychology of Interpersonal Relations* was a watershed work that spawned countless research programs and influenced social psychological theory for more than four decades. Two of the topics that Heider dealt with in the *Psychology of Interpersonal Relations* were personal causation and purposeful human behavior. In this work we also find Heider's discussion of balance theory as well as the naïve perception of action, a forerunner of modern attribution theory.

7   Plato. (2001). *Plato's Republic.* (B. Jowett, Trans.). Millis, MA: Agora Publications. (Original work published 1873)

END**NOTES**

CHAPTER 2

1   Dunning, D., Johnson, K., Ehrlinger, J., & Kruger, J. (2003, June). Why people fail to recognize their own incompetence. *Current Directions in Psychological Science, 12*(3), 83-87.

2   Kaplan, R. S., & Norton, D. P. (1992, January-February). The balanced scorecard: Measures that drive performance. *Harvard Business Review, 70,* 71-79.

Kaplan, R. S., & Norton, D. P. (1996). *The balanced scorecard: Translating strategy into action.* Boston: Harvard Business School Press.

3   Heskett, J. L., Jones, T. O., Loveman, G. W., Sasser, W. E., Jr., & Schlesinger, L. A. (1994). Putting the service-profit chain to work. *Harvard Business Review, 72*(2), 164-174.

Heskett, J. L., Sasser, W. E., Jr., & Schlesinger, L. A. (1997). *The service profit chain: How leading companies link profit and growth to loyalty, satisfaction, and value.* New York: Free Press.

CHAPTER 3

1   Thomas, W. I., & Thomas, D. S. (1928). *The child in America: Behavior problems and programs.* New York: Alfred A. Knopf.

2   Bruner, J. S. (1973). *Beyond the information given: Studies in the psychology of knowing.* Oxford, UK: W. W. Norton.

3   Tversky, A., & Kahneman, D. (1974, September 27). Judgment under uncertainty: Heuristics and biases. *Science, 185,* 1124-1131.

4   Kahneman, D., Slovic, P., & Tversky, A. (Eds.). (1982). *Judgment under uncertainty: Heuristics and biases.* Cambridge, UK: Cambridge University Press.

Kahneman, D. (2003, December). Maps of bounded rationality: Psychology for behavioral economics. *American Economic Review, 93,* 1449-1475.

5   Gilbert, D. T., Pelham, B. W., & Krull, D. S. (1988, May). On cognitive busyness: When person perceivers meet persons perceived. *Journal of Personality and Social Psychology, 54,* 733-740.

6   Simons, D. J., & Chabris, C. F. (1999). Gorillas in our midst: Sustained inattentional blindness for dynamic events. *Perception, 28,* 1059-1074.

7   Darley, J. M., & Gross, P. H. (1983, January). A hypothesis-confirming bias in labeling effects. *Journal of Personality and Social Psychology, 44,* 20-33.

Snyder, M., & Swann, W. B., Jr. (1978, March). Behavioral confirmation in social interaction: From social perception to social reality. *Journal of Experimental Social Psychology, 14,* 148-162.

Word, C. O., Zanna, M. P., & Cooper, J. (1974). The nonverbal mediation of self-fulfilling prophecies in interracial interaction. *Journal of Experimental Social Psychology, 10,* 109-120.

8   Loewenstein, G. (2000, May). Emotions in economic theory and economic behavior. *American Economic Review, 90,* 426-432.

Loewenstein, G. F., Weber, E. U., Hsee, C. K., & Welch, N. (2001). Risk as feelings. *Psychological Bulletin, 127,* 267-286.

9   Ashraf, N., Camerer, C. F., & Loewenstein, G. (2005, Summer) Adam Smith, behavioral economist. *Journal of Economic Perspectives, 19*, 131-14510

10 Damasio, A. R. (1994). *Descartes' error: Emotion, reason, and the human brain.* New York: G. P. Putnam's Sons.

    LeDoux, J. E. (1996). *The emotional brain: The mysterious underpinnings of emotional life.* New York: Simon & Schuster.

11 National Institute of Neurological Disorders and Stroke. (2005, December 8). *Brain basics: Know your brain.* Retrieved March 6, 2007, from http://www.ninds.nih.gov/disorders/brain_basics/know_your_brain.htm

12 Damasio, A. R. (1999). *The feeling of what happens: Body and emotion in the making of consciousness.* New York: Harcourt Brace.

    LeDoux, J. E. (2002). *Synaptic self: How our brains become who we are.* New York: Penguin Books.

13 Lovallo, D., & Kahneman, D. (2003, July). Delusions of success: How optimism undermines executives' decisions. *Harvard Business Review, 81*, 56-63.

    Thaler, R. H. (1991). *Quasi rational economics.* New York: Russell Sage Foundation.

    Thaler, R. H. (2000). Toward a positive theory of consumer choice. In D. Kahneman, & A. Tversky (Eds.), *Choices, values, and frames* (pp. 269-287). New York: Russell Sage Foundation.

14 *Roethlisberger in 2005: '... The safest rider I can be.'* (2006, June 12). Retrieved March 6, 2007, from http://sports.espn.go.com/nfl/news/story?id=2481004

15 A comprehensive review of this academic literature is beyond the scope of this book, but the interested reader will certainly want to read the expanded version of Kahneman's Nobel Prize acceptance speech published in the *American Economic Review* in 2003 in which the bulk of this work is summarized (Kahneman, D. (2003, December). Maps of bounded rationality: Psychology for behavioral economics. *American Economic Review, 93*, 1449-1475.).

16 Tversky, A., & Kahneman, D. (1974, September 27). Judgment under uncertainty: Heuristics and biases. *Science, 185*, 1124-1131.

17 One of those heuristics — estimating the likelihood of an event based on how typical the event is — is referred to as "representativeness" and it's extremely powerful. Imagine that you were provided with the following information about a graduate student called Tom W.:

> Tom W. is of high intelligence, although lacking in true creativity. He has a need for order and clarity, and for neat and tidy systems in which every detail finds its appropriate place. His writing is rather dull and mechanical, occasionally enlivened by somewhat corny puns and by flashes of imagination of the sci-fi type. He has a strong drive for competence. He seems to have little feel and little sympathy for other people and does not enjoy interacting with others. Self-centered, he nonetheless has a deep moral sense. (p. 49)

How likely would you be to guess that Tom is a graduate student in computer science as opposed to humanities and education? If you are like most people, you'd probably guess that Tom is a computer science grad student. But if you are like most people, you'd also be wrong. In an experiment that explored the use of the representativeness heuristic in decision making, Kahneman and his colleagues gave two groups of college students the same information about Tom W. that you just read. The first group of students was asked to rate how similar Tom W. was to a typical student in one of nine different types of college graduate majors (business administration, computer science, engineering, humanities/education, law, library science, medicine, physical/life sciences, or social science/social work). As you might expect, most of these students thought Tom W. was most similar to a computer science grad student and least like a grad student in the social sciences/social work. The second group of students was asked instead to estimate the likelihood that Tom W. was actually a grad student in each of the nine majors. Their probabilities matched the first group's assessments with a correlation of 0.97 (that is almost identical). A third group was asked simply to estimate the proportion of first-year grad students there were in each of the nine majors.

What is fascinating here is that computer science actually had among the fewest real (and estimated) number of grad students of all nine majors (only library science was estimated to have fewer). In spite of the fact that any randomly sampled grad student would be much more likely to be a social science/social work grad student than one in computer science, students judged Tom W. to be more similar to and more likely to be a computer science grad student. They did this because his description "fit" their preconceptions of what a computer science grad student should look like — how "representative" he was of the "typical" computer science grad student. Knowing nothing else about Tom W. other than the description that was provided, the students' smartest guess would have been that Tom was *anything* other than a computer science grad student.

A different heuristic explored by Kahneman and Tversky — using how easy an event is to imagine as an estimate of that event's likelihood of actually happening — is called the simulation heuristic. It, too, is remarkably powerful. Image you heard the following story:

> Mr. Crane and Mr. Tees were scheduled to leave the airport on different flights, at the same time. They traveled from town in the same limousine, were caught in a traffic jam, and arrived at the airport 30 minutes after the scheduled departure time of their flights. Mr. Crane is told that his flight left on time. Mr. Tees is told that his flight was delayed, and just left 5 minutes ago. (p. 203)

Who do you think would be more upset — Mr. Crane or Mr. Tees? Again, if you are like 96% of the participants in this research study, you would have guessed Mr. Tees. But why? Both men missed their flights, and both were identically delayed. But it just *seems* like Mr. Tees, who missed his flight by a mere five minutes, should be more upset than Mr. Crane, who missed his flight by a half an hour. The fact that it's easier to imagine how Mr. Tees might have been able to do things just a little differently to arrive in time for his flight makes the fact he didn't make it in time that much more frustrating. It's this ease with which we can imagine an alternative set of circumstances that frames our emotional response to these kinds of situations. Surprisingly, however, deliberately imagining these kinds of counterfactual situations, or "considering the opposite," can actually improve the decision-making process in everyday life. For more information, please see:

Kahneman, D., & Tversky, A. (1982). On the psychology of prediction. In D. Kahneman,

P. Slovic, & A. Tversky (Eds.), *Judgment under uncertainty: Heuristics and biases* (pp. 48-68). Cambridge, UK: Cambridge University Press.

Kahneman, D., & Tversky, A. (1982). The simulation heuristic. In D. Kahneman, P. Slovic, & A. Tversky (Eds.), *Judgment under uncertainty: Heuristics and biases* (pp. 201-210). Cambridge, UK: Cambridge University Press.

Lord, C. G., Lepper, M. R., & Preston, E. (1984, December). Considering the opposite: A corrective strategy for social judgment. *Journal of Personality and Social Psychology, 47*(6), 1231-1243.

18 Kahneman, D., & Tversky, A. (1979, March). Prospect theory: An analysis of decision under risk. *Econometrica, 47*, 263-292.

19 Coffman, C., & Gonzalez-Molina, G. (2002). *Follow this path: How the world's greatest organizations drive growth by unleashing human potential.* New York: Warner Books.

20 Around this time, the quality movement was gaining momentum and functional quality issues such as these were indeed paramount. No one can question the fact that quality has improved over the past two decades and this has largely been the result of a relentless focus on quality improvement methodologies such as TQM and Six Sigma. In addition, this kind of functional approach meshed quite well with prevailing rational-functional models of human decision making that viewed customers in simplistic terms as automatons that dispassionately evaluate product features, tangible benefits, price-to-quality ratios, and a host of other largely rational dimensions to arrive at a purchase decision.

21 Recent (and some not-so-recent, but overlooked) research and theory in social/ cognitive psychology and neuroscience lead us to draw a number of conclusions that have implications for business managers. A comprehensive review of this literature is beyond the scope of this book, but the inescapable conclusion to be drawn from this work is that non-rational and emotional factors play an enormously important role in human decision making and behavior and must be incorporated into our thinking about the metrics we use to assess the employee-customer encounter.

Most existing approaches to understanding customer requirements provide, at best, only a partial perspective on these important issues. Equally important, however, is the fact that it's possible to create relatively simple tools that allow managers to monitor and react to these factors and incorporate them into their existing business processes. For additional information, please see:

Kahneman, D. (2003, December). Maps of bounded rationality: Psychology for behavioral economics. *American Economic Review, 93*, 1449-1475.

Loewenstein, G. F. (2000, May). Emotions in economic theory and economic behavior. *American Economic Review, 90*, 426-432.

Loewenstein, G. F., Weber, E. U., Hsee, C. K., & Welch, N. (2001). Risk as feelings. *Psychological Bulletin, 127*, 267-286.

Lovallo, D., & Kahneman, D. (2003, July). Delusions of success: How optimism undermines executives' decisions. *Harvard Business Review, 81*, 56-63.

22 Jones, T. O., & Sasser, W. E., Jr. (1995, November). Why satisfied customers defect. *Harvard Business Review, 73*, 88-99.

Reichheld, F. F. (1996). *The loyalty effect: The hidden force behind growth, profits, and lasting value.* Boston: Harvard Business School Press.

23 Thurm, S. (2006, December 4). One question, and plenty of debate. *The Wall Street Journal,* p. B3. Also see: Morgan, N. A., & Rego, L. L. (2006). The value of different customer satisfaction and loyalty metrics in predicting business performance. *Marketing Science, 25*(5), 426-439.

24 Crocker, L., & Algina, J. (1986). *Introduction to classical and modern test theory.* New York: Holt, Rinehart, & Winston.

Wanous, J. P., & Hudy, M. J. (2001). Single-item reliability: A replication and extension. *Organizational Research Methods, 4,* 361-375.

Wanous, J. P., Reichers, A. E., & Hudy, M. J. (1997, April). Overall job satisfaction: How good are single-item measures? *Journal of Applied Psychology, 82,* 247-252.

CHAPTER 4

1 Schneider, B., & Bowen, D. E. (1999). Understanding customer delight and outrage. *Sloan Management Review, 41*(1), 35-45.

2 Ibid.

3 Maslow, A. H. (1943, July). A theory of human motivation. *Psychological Review, 50,* 370-396.

4 The 11 CE[11] items are presented in Appendix A.

5 For the statistically inclined, the 11 items have an alpha reliability of 0.94.

CHAPTER 5

1 Gonzales, M. H., Manning, D. J., & Haugen, J. A. (1992). Explaining our sins: Factors influencing offender accounts and anticipated victim responses. *Journal of Personality and Social Psychology, 62,* 958-971.

Gonzales, M. H., Kovera, M. B., Sullivan, J. L., & Chanley, V. (1995, February). Private reactions to public transgressions: Predictors of evaluative responses to allegations of political misconduct. *Personality and Social Psychology Bulletin, 21,* 136-148.

Chanley, V., Sullivan, J. L., Gonzales, M. H., & Kovera, M. B. (1994, July). Lust and avarice in politics: Damage control for four politicians accused of wrongdoing (or, politics as usual). *American Politics Quarterly, 22,* 297-333.

2 Goffman, E. (1959). *The presentation of self in everyday life.* New York: Doubleday.

3 Mazor, K. M., Simon, S. R., Yood, R. A., Martinson, B. C., Gunter, M. J., Reed, G. W., et al. (2004, March 16). Health plan members' views about disclosure of medical errors. *Annals of Internal Medicine, 140,* 409-418.

Vincent, C., Young, M., & Phillips, A. (1994). Why do people sue doctors? A study of patients and relatives taking legal action. *Lancet, 343,* 1609-1613.

Kraman, S. S., & Hamm, G. (1999, December 21). Risk management: Extreme honesty may be the best policy. *Annals of Internal Medicine, 131,* 963-967.

Aronson, P. (2002, June 24-July 1). "How not to be sued: Lawn mower maker Toro moves quickly to mollify victims of accidents." *National Law Journal,* p. A19.

4   Witman, A. B., Park, D. M., & Hardin, S. B. (1996, December 9). How do patients want physicians to handle mistakes? A survey of internal medicine patients in an academic setting. *Archives of Internal Medicine, 156(22),* 2565-2569.

    Tanner, L. (2004, November 11), "'Sorry' seen as magic word to avoid suits." *Yahoo! News.* Retrieved March 7, 2007, from http://www.cs.indiana.edu/~dasulliv/sorry.html

5   Zimmerman, R. (2004, May 18). Doctors' new tool to fight lawsuits: Saying 'I'm sorry.' *The Wall Street Journal.* p. A1.

CHAPTER 6

1   Cialdini, R. B. (1988). *Influence: Science and practice* (2nd ed.). Glenview, IL: Scott, Foresman.

    Cialdini, R. B., Borden, R. J., Thorne, A., Walker, M. R., Freeman, S., & Sloan, L. R. (1976, September). Basking in reflected glory: Three (football) field studies. *Journal of Personality and Social Psychology, 34,* 366-375.

    Cialdini, R. B., & Richardson, K. D. (1980, September). Two indirect tactics of image management: Basking and blasting. *Journal of Personality and Social Psychology, 39,* 406-415.

    Hirt, E. R., Zillmann, D., Erickson, G. A., & Kennedy, C. (1992, November). Costs and benefits of allegiance: Changes in fans' self-ascribed competencies after team victory versus defeat. *Journal of Personality and Social Psychology, 63,* 724-738.

    Lee, M. J. (1985). Self-esteem and social identity in basketball fans: A closer look at basking in reflected glory. *Journal of Sport Behavior, 8,* 210-223.

2   Bem, D. J. (1972). Self-perception theory. In L. Berkowitz (Ed.), *Advances in experimental social psychology* (Vol. 6, pp. 1-62). New York: Academic Press.

3   Wicklund, R. A., & Gollwitzer, P. M. (1982). *Symbolic self-completion.* Hillsdale, NJ: Lawrence Erlbaum.

4   Using symbolic self-completion to close the gap between who we are and who we'd like to be may have an interesting side benefit: it may help insulate people from feelings of depression. Extending earlier work on the nature of the self, Columbia University Professor E. Tory Higgins and his students have studied the consequences of having a big gap between who we really are and who we'd like to be. Higgins describes three different types of "selves" that each of us carry around (figuratively) in our heads. For the sake of illustration, let's think of these three selves as different people who are either similar to one another or different. The first self — the "ought" self — is less relevant to this discussion and will be mentioned only in passing. The "ought" self is essentially a symbolic version or mental representation of your mother or other authority figure whose primary job is to represent who you ought to be. It's the moral compass of the self and the self that keeps you in line. The second self — the "ideal" self — is the mental representation of the person you would someday like to be. This is the aspirational self. The third and final self — the "actual" self — is, as the name implies, the mental representation of the self you really are, warts and all. The actual self is as close to a hard-nosed realistic appraisal as is possible.

    In Higgins' self-discrepancy theory, these selves can overlap completely, partially, or not at all. In other words, these three mental representations can be similar to one another or they can be different. How different they are is referred to as one's *self-discrepancy*. The interesting part of the theory is not the part that says that our actual and idealized selves can be different, because most of us have some degree of gap here. The interesting part of the theory is that the size of the actual ideal gap is a good predictor of one's mental health, especially one's likelihood to become depressed.

In a study of university undergraduates, Higgins measured their actual and ideal selves and estimated the size of the gap between them. He then assessed each student for symptoms of depression. The analysis revealed that those students with the largest discrepancies between their actual and ideal selves were at the highest risk for depression.

It stands to reason, then, that if a substantial gap between who we are and who we'd like to be is associated with relatively poorer mental health, then closing that gap — using symbolic self-completion as one means to that end — should be beneficial. It's not too great of an inferential leap to posit that building strong emotional connections with the companies we do business with not only helps customers feel better about themselves in general, but could have an impact on people's overall mental health. For additional information, please see:

Higgins, E. T. (1987, July). Self-discrepancy: A theory relating self and affect. *Psychological Review, 94*, 319-340.

Higgins, E. T. (1989). Self-discrepancy theory: What patterns of self-belief cause people to suffer? In L. Berkowitz (Ed.), *Advances in experimental social psychology* (Vol. 22, pp. 93-136). New York: Academic Press.

Strauman, T. J. (1989, February). Self-discrepancies in clinical depression and social phobia: Cognitive structures that underlie emotional disorders? *Journal of Abnormal Psychology, 98*, 14-22.

Strauman, T. J., & Higgins, E. T. (1988, December). Self-discrepancies as predictors of vulnerability to distinct syndromes of chronic emotional distress. *Journal of Personality, 56*, 685-707.

5   Kahneman, D., & Tversky, A. (1982). The simulation heuristic. In D. Kahneman, P. Slovic, & A. Tversky (Eds.), *Judgment under uncertainty: Heuristics and biases* (pp. 201-210). Cambridge, UK: Cambridge University Press.

6   Merton, R. K. (1948). The self-fulfilling prophecy. *Antioch Review, 8*, 193-210.

7   In 1968, social psychologist Robert Rosenthal and school principal Lenore Jacobson sent shock waves through the educational community when they published a study that had a profound effect on our understanding of the power of expectations to transform human behavior. In their research, Rosenthal and Jacobson gave an intelligence test to students at an elementary school at the beginning of the school year. Of these students, 20% were randomly selected to be in the so-called "late bloomers" group. Elementary school teachers were then told that the Harvard Test of Inflected Acquisition (a non-existent test) had identified some of their students as late bloomers and although they might start out slowly, they had unusual potential for intellectual growth and could be expected to show a spurt of academic achievement later in the school year. When the students were retested at the end of the school year, those who had been randomly identified as late bloomers indeed showed a significant increase in their test scores compared to students who were not labeled as having

unusual potential. Rosenthal and Jacobson concluded that the bogus expectation of superior intelligence led the teachers to treat those students differently and in ways that actually made them more intelligent.

Perhaps even more surprising are the results of a field study conducted by Carnegie Mellon University social psychologist Robert Kraut in 1972. Kraut had researchers fan out into the community ostensibly to canvas neighborhoods looking for charitable givers. Based on a brief checklist, the researchers randomly classified the individuals they talked to as either "generous potential givers," "not likely to give," or did not classify them. When different people later canvassed the same neighborhoods looking for actual charitable donations, those who had been randomly labeled as "generous potential givers" indeed gave more to charity than did those who had not been labeled. Those not labeled, in turn, gave significantly more than individuals who had been previously (and randomly) labeled as "not likely to give." Clearly the application of a label to a person can (rightly or wrongly) have a profound effect on that person's subsequent behavior and, ultimately, their sense of self. For additional information on these topics, please see:

Rosenthal, R., & Jacobson, L. (1968). *Pygmalion in the classroom: Teacher expectation and pupils' intellectual development.* New York: Holt, Rinehart, & Winston.

Kraut, R. E. (1973, November). Effects of social labeling on giving to charity. *Journal of Experimental Social Psychology, 9,* 551-562.

8   Fleming, J. H., & Manning, D. J. (1994). Self-fulfilling prophecies. In V. S. Ramachandran (Ed.), *Encyclopedia of Human Behavior* (Vol. 4, pp. 89-97). San Diego, CA: Academic Press.

Rosenthal, R. (1994). Interpersonal expectancy effects: A 30-year perspective. *Current Directions in Psychological Science, 3*(6), 176-179.

9   Hilton, J. L., Darley, J. M., & Fleming, J. H. (1989). Self-fulfilling prophecies and self-defeating behavior. In R. C. Curtis (Ed.), *Self-defeating behaviors: Experimental research, clinical impressions, and practical implications* (pp. 41-65). New York: Plenum.

In a study by John Darley and his colleagues at Princeton University, for example, college students were led to believe that their (actually non-existent) partner in an experiment either had a history of mental illness or did not. They then engaged in a free-form conversation with the other "student" over an intercom system from a separate room. Results revealed that those students who thought their partner had been mentally ill went out of their way to avoid talking about the mental illness during the conversation. And because of the anxiety and work they had to do to avoid this uncomfortable topic, they actually emerged from the interaction believing *more strongly* that their partner had indeed been mentally ill in the past. Not surprisingly, those who had not been told about the student's history of mental illness emerged from their conversation believing the student had never been ill. For additional information, please see:

Darley, J. M., Fleming, J. H., Hilton, J. L., & Swann, W. B., Jr. (1988, January). Dispelling negative expectancies: The impact of interaction goals and target characteristics on the expectancy confirmation process. *Journal of Experimental Social Psychology, 24,* 19-36.

10   Snyder, M., Tanke, E. D., & Berscheid, E. (1977, September). Social perception and interpersonal behavior: On the self-fulfilling nature of social stereotypes. *Journal of Personality and Social Psychology, 35,* 656-666.

CHAPTER 7

1   McClure, S. M., Li, J., Tomlin, D., Cypert, K. S., Montague, L. M., & Montague, P. R. (2004). Neural correlates of behavioral preference for culturally familiar drinks. *Neuron, 44,* 379-387.

2   Adapted from Thompson, C. (2003, October 26). There's a sucker born in every medial prefrontal cortex [Electronic version]. *The New York Times Magazine,* pp. 54-57.

3   Greene, J. D., Sommerville, R. B., Nystrom L. E., Darley, J. M., & Cohen, J. D. (2001, September 14). An fMRI investigation of emotional engagement in moral judgment. *Science, 293,* 2105-2108.

   Greene, J. D., Nystrom L. E., Engell, A. D., Darley, J. M., & Cohen, J. D. (2004, October 14). The neural bases of cognitive conflict and control in moral judgment. *Neuron, 44,* 389-400

4   Harenski, K., Meaux, J., & Kilts, C. (2004, June 14). *Medial prefrontal cortex activity distinguishes strong individual preferences.* Poster presented at the 10th annual meeting of the Organization for Human Brain Mapping, Budapest, Hungary.

5   Aron, A., Fisher, H., Mashek, D. J., Strong, G., Li, H., & Brown, L. L. (2005, July). Reward, motivation, and emotion systems associated with early-stage intense romantic love. *Journal of Neurophysiology, 94,* 327-337.

6   With studies like the Pepsi Challenge analysis, Montague and other researchers like him have helped usher in a new — and remarkably controversial — discipline called *neuromarketing.* Neuromarketing, described as the place where the brain and marketing meet, uses the methods of neuroscience to study the brain's response to marketing stimuli. And although neuromarketing *per se* remains controversial, the experimental techniques of neuroscience — like fMRI studies and PET scans — have opened a new window to how the brain works and how brain activity affects human behavior. Having read this far, it should not be surprising then to learn that Gallup researchers have also turned our attention to understanding how brain functioning relates to the employee-customer encounter and specifically to customer engagement. But we have done so in a way that deliberately attempts to sidestep much of the controversy surrounding neuromarketing. (For more information on the controversy surrounding neuromarketing, see Mitchell, A. (2007, January 5). Advertisers turn to science to get inside consumers' heads [Electronic version]. *Financial Times).* Retrieved April 1, 2007, from http://us.ft.com/ftgateway/superpage.ft?news_id=fto010420071740119781

   Much of that controversy hinges on the criticism (also leveled at so-called subliminally communicated messages decades earlier) that by knowing the correct sequence of words, phrases, colors, or images that make various parts of the brain (like the *medial prefrontal cortex* in the Pepsi Challenge study) "light up," marketers will gain an impenetrable upper hand over consumers who would be completely vulnerable to this new marketing know-how. In other words, if marketers can make our brains respond to advertisements without our conscious control or mediation, then we would all be completely helpless and unable to prevent those messages from having their desired effects.

Our work, on the other hand, sought to use the techniques of neuroscience to validate a measurement tool for assessing how emotionally connected customers are with your company. In other words, we sought to show that emotion plays a critical role in customer engagement and that a simple attitude scale could be used as a "proxy" for the complex neural processes that mediate that relationship.

7   This chapter is a somewhat expanded and revised version of a paper we presented that the 2004 annual meeting of the Society for Neuroscience: Pribyl, C. B., Nose, I., Taira, M., Fleming, J. H., Sakamoto, M., Gonzalez, G., et al. (2004, October). *The neural basis of brand addiction: An fMRI study.* Paper presented at the 34th annual meeting of the Society for Neuroscience, San Diego, CA.

8   Due to idiosyncratic differences in brain structure between men and women, fMRI studies are typically conducted on same-sex participants. In this case, all participants were female.

9   Siemens Magnetom Symphony 1.5T fMRI machine.

10 Elliott, R., Dolan, R. J., & Frith, C. D. (2000). Dissociable functions in the medial and lateral orbitofrontal cortex: Evidence from human neuroimaging studies. *Cerebral Cortex, 10,* 308-317.

    Gottfried, J. A., O'Doherty, J., & Dolan, R. J. (2003, August). Encoding predictive reward value in human amygdala and orbitofrontal cortex. *Science, 301,* 1104-1107.

    O'Doherty, J., Rolls, E. T., Francis, S., Bowtell, R., McGlone, F., Kobal, G., et al. (2000, March 20). Sensory-specific satiety-related olfactory activation of the human orbitofrontal cortex. *NeuroReport, 11,* 893-897.

    Rolls, E. T. (2000). The orbitofrontal cortex and reward. *Cerebral Cortex, 10,* 284-294.

    Rolls, E. T. (1999). *The brain and emotion.* Oxford, UK: Oxford University Press.

    O'Doherty, J., Kringelbach, M. L., Rolls, E. T., Hornak J., & Andrews C. (2001, January). Abstract reward and punishment representations in the human orbitofrontal cortex. *Nature Neuroscience, 4,* 95-102.

11 The average reaction time among disengaged subjects was 2.04 seconds compared to 1.89 seconds among subjects who were more engaged emotionally. The correlation between mean reaction time and CE[11] scores was -0.32 and -0.44 for A[8] scores.

12 Fazio, R. H., Powell, M. C., & Williams, C. J. (1989). The role of attitude accessibility in the attitude-to-behavior process. *Journal of Consumer Research, 16,* 280-289.

13 Fazio, R. H. (1995). Attitudes as object-evaluation associations: Determinants, consequences, and correlates of attitude accessibility. In R. E. Petty, & J. A. Krosnick (Eds.), *Attitude strength: Antecedents and consequences* (pp. 247-282). Hillsdale, NJ: Lawrence Erlbaum.

    Fazio, R. H. (2001). On the automatic activation of associated evaluations: An overview. *Cognition & Emotion, 15*(2), 115-141.

    Fazio, R. H., & Olsen, M. A. (2003). Attitudes: Foundations, functions, and consequences. In M. A. Hogg, & J. Cooper (Eds.), *The Sage Handbook of Social Psychology* (pp. 139-160). London: Sage.

Fazio, R. H., & Zanna, M. P. (1981). Direct experience and attitude-behavior consistency. In L. Berkowitz (Ed.), *Advances in experimental social psychology* (Vol. 14, pp. 162-202). New York: Academic Press.

Fazio, R. H., Williams, C. J., & Powell, M. C. (2000, March). Measuring associative strength: Category-item associations and their activation from memory. *Political Psychology, 21,* 7-25.

14 Damasio, A. R. (1994). *Descartes' error: Emotion, reason, and the human brain.* New York: G. P. Putnam's Sons.

15 Bruce, V., & Young, A. W. (1986, August). Understanding face recognition. *British Journal of Psychology, 77(3),* 305-327.

Griffith, H. R., Richardson, E., Pyzalski, R. W., Bell, B., Dow, C., Hermann, B. P., et al. (2006). Memory for famous faces and the temporal pole: Functional imaging findings in temporal lobe epilepsy. *Epilepsy & Behavior, 9,* 173-180.

Kanwisher, N., McDermott, J., & Chun, M. M. (1997, June 1). The fusiform face area: A module in human extrastriate cortex specialized for face perception. *Journal of Neuroscience, 17,* 4302-4311.

16 O'Craven, K. M., & Kanwisher, N. (2000). Mental imagery of faces and places activates corresponding stimulus-specific brain regions. *Journal of Cognitive Neuroscience, 12(6),* 1013-1023.

17 Gehring, W. J., & Willoughby, A. R. (2002, March 22). The medial frontal cortex and the rapid processing of monetary gains and losses. *Science, 295(5563),* 2279-2282.

18 Seifritz, E., Esposito, F., Neuhoff, J. G., Lüthi, A., Mustovic, H., Dammann, G., et al. (2003). Differential sex-independent amygdala response to infant crying and laughing in parents versus nonparents. *Biological Psychiatry, 54(12),* 1367-1375.

19 For more information on *The neural basis of brand addiction: An fMRI study*, visit the Additional Insights area in the *Human Sigma* Book Center at the *Gallup Management Journal* Web site (http://gmj.gallup.com).

20 Correlations ranged from 0.50 to 0.60.

CHAPTER 8

1 Berlin, L. (2005). *The man behind the microchip: Robert Noyce and the invention of Silicon Valley.* New York: Oxford University Press.

Readers interested in learning more about the origins of the unique business culture in Silicon Valley should read this book about the man the *San Jose Mercury News* called the Thomas Edison *and* Henry Ford of Silicon Valley. Noyce was a fascinating and farsighted man who did research that led to two Nobel Prizes, including the co-invention of the integrated circuit, which helped launch the electronic age. Leslie Berlin's wonderful and thoroughly researched book paints a compelling picture of this complex man. We would also like to thank Abbey Scheckter of Grinnell College for her insights regarding Noyce and for sharing a recording of Berlin's 2006 presentation at Grinnell College on her biography of Noyce.

2 Ibid.

3 Ibid.

4   Ibid.

5   Ibid.

6   Ibid.

7   Harter, J. K., Schmidt, F. L., Asplund, J. W., & Killham, E. A. (2005, August). *Employee engagement and business unit performance: A longitudinal meta-analytic study of causal direction*. Omaha, NE: The Gallup Organization.

8   This example is substantially drawn from Rosenband, L. N. (2000). *Papermaking in eighteenth-century France: Management, labor, and revolution at the Montgolfier mill, 1761-1805*. Baltimore: Johns Hopkins University Press. We wish to thank Andre Wakefield at Pitzer College for recommending this excellent book.

9   Ibid.

10 Ibid.

11 Ibid.

12 Buckingham, M., & Coffman, C. (1999). *First, break all the rules: What the world's greatest managers do differently*. New York: Simon and Schuster.

    Coffman, C., & Gonzalez-Molina, G. (2002). *Follow this path: How the world's greatest organizations drive growth by unleashing human potential*. New York: Warner.

13 The 12 Elements are presented in Appendix A. These conditions have been described in detail elsewhere and form the core of our employee engagement approach. The reader is directed to the following sources for additional detail:

    Buckingham, M., & Coffman, C. (1999). *First, break all the rules: What the world's greatest managers do differently*. New York: Simon and Schuster.

    Coffman, C., & Gonzalez-Molina, G. (2002). *Follow this path: How the world's greatest organizations drive growth by unleashing human potential*. New York: Warner.

    Wagner, R., & Harter, J. K. (2006). *12: The elements of great managing*. New York: Gallup Press.

14 A good introduction to the field of positive psychology is available in Fredrickson, B. (2003, July-August). The value of positive emotions. *American Scientist, 91*, 330-335. The following are also recommended:

    Rath, T., & Clifton, D. O. (2004). *How full is your bucket? Positive strategies for work and life*. New York: Gallup Press.

    More academically inclined readers may wish to consult:

    Snyder, C. R., & Lopez, S. J. (2007). *Positive psychology: The scientific and practical explorations of human strengths*. Thousand Oaks, CA: Sage.

    Snyder, C. R., & Lopez, S. J. (Eds.). (2002). *Handbook of positive psychology*. New York: Oxford University Press.

15 Danner D. D., Snowdon, D. A., & Friesen, W. V. (2001). Positive emotions in early life and longevity: Findings from the nun study. *Journal of Personality and Social Psychology, 80*, 804-813.

16 A comprehensive treatment of each of the 12 Elements is available in: Wagner, R., & Harter, J. K. (2006). *12: The elements of great managing*. New York: Gallup Press. Wagner and Harter weave the latest Gallup insights with recent discoveries in the fields of neuroscience, game theory, psychology, sociology, and economics.

17 Giddens, A. (1991). *Modernity and self-identity: Self and society in the late modern age.* Palo Alto, CA: Stanford University Press.

18 Hamel, G. (2006, February). The why, what, and how of management innovation. *Harvard Business Review, 84*(2), 72-84.

19 Krueger, J., & Killham, E. (2006, September 14). Who's driving innovation at your company? *Gallup Management Journal.* Retrieved March 11, 2007, from http://gmj. gallup.com/content/default.aspx?ci=24472

20 Harter, J. K., Schmidt, F. L., & Hayes, T. L. (2002, April). Business-unit-level relationship between employee satisfaction, employee engagement, and business outcomes: A meta-analysis. *Journal of Applied Psychology, 87,* 268-279.

21 Harter, J. K., Schmidt, F. L., Killham, E. A., & Asplund, J. W. (2006). *Q^{12} meta-analysis.* Omaha, NE: The Gallup Organization.

22 Harter, J. K., Schmidt, F. L., Asplund, J. W., & Killham, E. A. (2005, August). *Employee engagement and business unit performance: A longitudinal meta-analytic study of causal direction.* Omaha, NE: The Gallup Organization.

23 For more information on the 89 companies we selected for this study from Gallup's Q^{12} database, visit the Additional Insights area in the *Human Sigma* Book Center at the *Gallup Management Journal* Web site (http://gmj.gallup.com).

CHAPTER 9

1 Readers are urged to consult the following books on how humans actually make decisions in real-life situations (as opposed to the very restrictive assumptions required under the rational choice theory espoused by early philosophers such as Jeremy Bentham, and implicit in many of the arguments underpinning classical economics):

Gigerenzer, G., & Selten, R. (Eds.). (2001). *Bounded rationality: The adaptive toolbox.* Cambridge, MA: MIT Press.

Gigerenzer, G., Todd, P. M., & the ABC Research Group. (1999). *Simple heuristics that make us smart.* New York: Oxford University Press.

These volumes describe the findings of research investigations into "bounded rationality." In their conception, backed up by several compelling studies, the contributors argue generally for a form of bounded rationality they call the "adaptive toolbox." This theory posits that most of our decisions are the product of a great many fast rules or heuristics that we choose from depending on the situation. This framework doesn't make unreasonable demands on our cognitive reasoning abilities or speed and incorporates emotions and cultural norms into a comprehensive decision-making theory.

2 Klein, G. (2003). *Intuition at work: Why developing your gut instincts will make you better at what you do.* New York: Doubleday.

This book is an excellent entrée into Klein's substantial work on intuition, and he makes a compelling case for how to understand our "gut instincts" and how to improve them. Central to our argument here is his emphasis on practice in his chapter on "Intuition Skills Training."

3 Ibid.

4 Siegel, D. J. (1999). *The developing mind: How relationships and the brain interact to shape who we are.* New York: Guilford Press.

5 Peterson, C., Maier, S. F., & Seligman, M. E. P. (1995). *Learned helplessness: A theory for the age of personal control.* New York: Oxford University Press.

Seligman, M. E. P. (1975). *Helplessness: On depression, development, and death.* San Francisco: W. H. Freeman.

6 Siegel, D. J. (1999). *The developing mind: How relationships and the brain interact to shape who we are.* New York: Guilford Press.

7 Ibid.

8 Dunning, D., Johnson, K., Ehrlinger, J., & Kruger, J. (2003, June). Why people fail to recognize their own incompetence. *Current Directions in Psychological Science, 12*(3), 83-87.

9 *Employee engagement database* [Data file]. (2006). Omaha, NE: The Gallup Organization.

CHAPTER 10

1 Eblen, R. A., & Eblen W. (Eds.). (1994). *The encyclopedia of the environment.* Boston: Houghton Mifflin.

2 In this example, we focus on customer engagement, but we could easily have focused on employee engagement or virtually any other performance metric for that matter. Exactly the same pattern of performance variability emerges on employee measures, as well, with similar implications.

3 Deming, W. E. (1986). *Out of the crisis.* Cambridge, MA: MIT, Center for Advanced Engineering Study.

Juran, J. M. (1988). *Juran on planning for quality.* New York: Free Press.

Juran, J. M. (1992). *Juran on quality by design: The new steps for planning quality into goods and services.* New York: Free Press.

CHAPTER 11

1 Fuller, R. B. (1969). *Operating manual for spaceship earth.* Carbondale, IL: Southern Illinois University Press.

2 Our meta-analytic work has demonstrated that the average correlation between employee engagement and customer engagement measured one year later is in the range of 0.30-0.35. This represents a moderate-sized but remarkably consistent and reliable direct relationship between the two constructs.

3 We encourage readers who are interested in a more detailed treatment of meta-analysis to consult the following sources for background information and detailed descriptions of the more recent meta-analytic methods:

Bangert-Drowns, R. L. (1986). Review of developments in meta-analytic method. *Psychological Bulletin, 99*(3), 388-399.

Hunter, J. E., & Schmidt, F. L. (1990). *Methods of meta-analysis: Correcting error and bias in research findings.* Newbury Park, CA: Sage.

Hunter, J. E., & Schmidt, F. L. (2004). *Methods of meta-analysis: Correcting error and bias in research findings* (2nd ed.). Thousand Oaks, CA: Sage.

Lipsey, M. W., & Wilson, D. B. (1993). The efficacy of psychological, educational, and behavioral treatment: Confirmation from meta-analysis. *American Psychologist, 48*(12), 1181-1209.

Schmidt, F. L. (1992). What do data really mean? Research findings, meta-analysis, and cumulative knowledge in psychology. *American Psychologist, 47*(10), 1173-1181.

Schmidt, F. L., Hunter, J. E., Pearlman, K., & Rothstein-Hirsh, H. (1985). Forty questions about validity generalization and meta-analysis. *Personnel Psychology, 38*, 697-798.

4   Harter, J. K., Asplund, J. A., & Fleming, J. H. (2004). *HumanSigma: A meta-analysis of the relationship between employee engagement, customer engagement, and financial performance*. Omaha, NE: The Gallup Organization.

5   For more information on the *HumanSigma* meta-analysis, visit the Additional Insights area in the *Human Sigma* Book Center at the *Gallup Management Journal* Web site (http://gmj.gallup.com).

6   The divine proportion was studied extensively by the Greek sculptor Phidias, hence the designation of the function as "phi."

7    $\varphi = (1 + \sqrt{n})/2$ For the HumanSigma quadrants, n equals 6^x and x is the number of human systems metrics (0, 1, or 2) on which the unit scores above the median. The observed impact coefficients for the HumanSigma performance bands also conform to the phi function. In this case, $\varphi_{HS} = (1 + \sqrt{(6k_{HS} + 1)})/2$ where HS equals the HumanSigma level (1 through 6) and k is a recursive function $k_{HS} = (HS\text{-}1) + k_{HS\text{-}1}$, given $k1 = 0$.

8   We are guided here by the thinking laid out by the noted biologist E. O. Wilson in his book *Consilience*. [Wilson, E. O. (1998). *Consilience: The unity of knowledge*. New York: Knopf.] Wilson's book is an attempt to describe the future synthesis of various fields of human knowledge. In his book, Wilson describes the qualities of a good organizing theory. One of those qualities is the principle of consilience, which means that organizing principles that conform to knowledge from multiple disciplines (such as the phi function's broad applicability across disciplines as diverse as mathematics, physics, art, and architecture) are superior to those that do not. In other words, a theory that can simply and effectively account for findings across a variety of different disciplines — like the phi function — is ideal.

One implication of Wilson's thinking that may not be immediately obvious is that bottom-up discoveries from more basic sciences have inherently more validity. This aspect of Wilson's work is not without controversy, but most scholars agree, for example, that there is such a thing as "human nature." Consequently, any attempt to explain what people do should at a minimum not fly in the face of our inherent human nature — our biological limitations. Although there will continue to be a debate about the relative strengths of our various biological traits and impulses, we cannot deny that they occur. So the psychobiological elements of human behavior — such as those we identified in our fMRI study of customers' emotions in Japan described in Chapter 7 — should carry a great amount of weight in explaining human economic activity and choice behavior. More generally, it is in biology and experimental psychology that the social sciences — including economics — should find theoretical guidance. The very specific knowledge of these scientific disciplines can illuminate the larger patterns we observe in human behavior.

What does this have to do with the phi function? It turns out that one of the places where phi pops up in mathematics involves the Fibonacci sequence. Most of us encounter the Fibonacci sequence in school: Fn = Fn-1 + Fn-2, where F1 = F2 = 1. The first few numbers in the sequence are 1, 1, 2, 3, 5, 8, 13, 21, 34, and so on. To find the next number in the Fibonacci sequence, one must add the previous two numbers. The ratio of two successive Fibonacci numbers approaches phi (1.618034 [rounded]) as n goes to infinity.

Fibonacci's sequence has wide applicability in mathematics and was identified by Indian mathematicians as early as 200 B.C. Fibonacci himself was an Italian scholar who described the sequence in 1202 in an effort to describe how fast rabbits could reproduce under certain conditions. His conclusion was that the number of adult pairs of rabbits in any given month would be equal to the sum of the number of pairs in each of the preceding two months.

9   Wolfram, S. (2002). *A new kind of science.* Champaign, IL: Wolfram Media.

10 Todd, P. M. (2001). Fast and frugal heuristics for environmentally bounded minds. In G. Gigerenzer, & R. Selten (Eds.), *Bounded rationality: The adaptive toolbox* (pp. 51-70). Cambridge, MA: MIT Press.

11 Ibid.

    Readers may also wish to consult Loewenstein, G., & Lerner, J. S. (2003). The role of affect in decision making. In R. J. Davidson, K. R. Scherer, & H. H. Goldsmith (Eds.), *Handbook of affective sciences* (pp. 619-642). New York: Oxford University Press. Tversky and Kahneman developed their prospect theory to explain cognitive biases and "irrational" economic choices.

12 Gladwell, M. (2005). *Blink: The power of thinking without thinking.* New York: Little, Brown and Company.

13 Simon, H. A. (1956, March). Rational choice and the structure of the environment. *Psychological Review, 63,* 129-138.

14 Dunning, D., Johnson, K., Ehrlinger, J., & Kruger, J. (2003, June). Why people fail to recognize their own incompetence. *Current Directions in Psychological Science, 12*(3), 83-87.

15 This concept and accompanying table are from Goldstein, D. G., Gigerenzer, G., Hogarth, R. M., Kacelnik, A., Kareev, Y., Klein, G., et al. (2001). Group report: Why and when do simple heuristics work? In G. Gigerenzer, & R. Selten (Eds.), *Bounded rationality: The adaptive toolbox* (pp. 173-190). Cambridge, MA: MIT Press.

16 Ibid.

17 Blanchard, K., & Glanz, B. (2005). *The simple truths of service: Inspired by Johnny the bagger.* Escondido, CA: Blanchard Family Partnership.

18 Isay, D. (Creator, Storycorps: Recording America). (2005, July 15). *In the Bronx, one passenger in a thousand* [Radio broadcast]. New York: National Public Radio. Retrieved March 21, 2007, from http://www.npr.org/templates/story/story.php?storyId=4755286

19 This example is adapted from Seeley, T. D. (2001). Decision making in

superorganisms: How collective wisdom arises from the poorly informed masses. In
G. Gigerenzer, & R. Selten (Eds.), *Bounded rationality: The adaptive toolbox* (pp. 249-
262). Cambridge, MA: MIT Press.

CHAPTER 12

1   Berlin, L. (2005). *The man behind the microchip: Robert Noyce and the invention of
Silicon Valley.* New York: Oxford University Press.

2   Eckes, G. (2003). *Six Sigma for everyone.* Hoboken, NJ: John Wiley & Sons.

3   Although the Chief HumanSigma Officer plays an essential leadership role for
the initiative and serves as a communication bridge to the corporate leadership
team, to be successful this person requires the support of a dedicated corporate
HumanSigma Steering Committee (HSSC), which he or she chairs. At a minimum,
this steering committee should consist of at least one senior representative from
each functional area that HumanSigma touches (at a minimum marketing,
operations, and human resources) to help coordinate and, in some cases, spearhead
activities throughout the organization. This team will drive accountability and
ownership, collate and publish results and rankings, and address enterprise-level
issues that need to be escalated. Other steering committee members include the
"systems owners" for the customer and employee engagement initiatives, as well
as one or more individuals who are responsible for the project management and
logistical elements of the customer and employee engagement measurement
programs. These systems owners are responsible for ensuring that the data is
collected on time. They work closely with one or more individuals whose primary
responsibility is driving culture change throughout the organization in response
to the measurement findings. These individuals are responsible for evaluation,
intervention, and encouragement activities. In some cases, the same individual
may play the logistical and change management roles, but because separate talents
and skills are involved in each function, different individuals may be required to
play these roles. In any event, this corporate HSSC is charged with the effective and
efficient implementation of the company's HumanSigma program.

To support local change efforts and to facilitate logistical issues at a local level,
the corporate structure should be "mirrored" as deeply into the organization
as is possible, ideally at a local level. That is, for each local business unit a
corresponding "champion" and local HSSC should be assembled. These local
structures report up to the corporate steering committee and the business
unit's senior management team and are the direct liaison between the frontline
managers, teams, and the initiative.

Because not every identified improvement opportunity resides at the local level (e.g.
shared services issues, centralized delivery or procurement channels, and product
development issues, among others), a second corporate team should be assembled
that has primary responsibility for addressing these enterprise-level issues on behalf
of the organization. Members of this "Enterprise-Level Escalation Team" should
include front- and back-office operations specialists, shared services owners, and
select members of the corporate HS steering committee.

1 A discussion of methods for identifying additional survey items is beyond the scope of this book.

2 We often recommend a three-tiered performance zone system comprising "green zone" units (typically those in HumanSigma levels 4 to 6), "yellow zone" units (HumanSigma level 3), and "red zone" units (HumanSigma levels 1 and 2). Depending on your company's particular HumanSigma performance profile, other designations may be possible or desirable, and, of course, the zone identifiers can and should be adapted to fit your unique organizational culture (e.g., gold, silver, bronze instead of green, yellow, red). The important point is that intervention activities you deploy in your company should take into account each local unit's current performance and resulting capacity for change; where intervention is concerned, one size definitely does not fit all.

3 Peterson, C., Maier, S. F., & Seligman, M. E. P. (1995). *Learned helplessness: A theory for the age of personal control*. New York: Oxford University Press.

Seligman, M. E. P. (1975). *Helplessness: On depression, development, and death*. San Francisco: W. H. Freeman.

1 SWAT stands for "Special Weapons And Tactics" and is police jargon for a team of officers with special tools and skills that is called in to help deal with particularly complex or difficult situations.

2 An overview of this research is contained in the book *Now, Discover Your Strengths* (Buckingham & Clifton, 2001). The book also contains a code that you can use to identify your own strengths via our Web-based assessment, the Clifton StrengthsFinder. Interested readers should also see:

Rath, T. (2007). *StrengthsFinder 2.0*. New York: Gallup Press.

3 It should be noted that a psychometrically valid instrument like the Clifton StrengthsFinder is needed to make an accurate assessment of one's strengths. Without this scientific foundation, one loses the common language that makes a strengths discussion productive. Also, a self-assessed strengths diagnosis can easily degenerate into a superficial discussion of flying kites or apple pie recipes, and research evidence shows that most of us are poor at assessing ourselves. To paraphrase Confucius so many centuries ago, "real knowledge is to know the extent of one's ignorance." This truism compounds the problem of self-evaluation because those who are most incompetent are also the least equipped to know this about themselves. Highly competent individuals, in contrast, tend to suffer from a bit of comparative humility because they are much better at realistically appraising themselves. This situation produces a paradox where the people most in need of self-appraisal are least able to do it. As recent researchers into this conundrum have observed, "if poor performers are given the skills necessary to distinguish correct from incorrect answers, then they would be in a position to recognize their own incompetence." But if these same individuals "had the skills needed to distinguish accuracy from error, they would then have the skills needed to avoid poor performance in the first place. They would no longer be incompetent." For additional information, please see:

Asplund, J., Lopez, S. J., Hodges, T., & Harter, J. (2007). *The Clifton StrengthsFinder 2.0 technical report: Development and validation.* Omaha, NE: The Gallup Organization.

Rath, T. (2007). *StrengthsFinder 2.0.* New York: Gallup Press.

Dunning, D., Johnson, K., Ehrlinger, J., & Kruger, J. (2003, June). Why people fail to recognize their own incompetence. *Current Directions in Psychological Science, 12*(3), 83-87.

4   Clifton, D. O., & Harter, J. K. (2003). Investing in strengths. In K. S. Cameron , J. E. Dutton, & R. E. Quinn (Eds.), *Positive organizational scholarship: Foundations of a new discipline* (pp. 111-121). San Francisco: Berrett-Koehler.

5   Hodges, T. D., & Clifton, D. O. (2004). Strengths-based development in practice. In P. A. Linley, & S. Joseph (Eds.), *Positive psychology in practice* (pp. 256-268). Hoboken, NJ: John Wiley & Sons.

6   Asplund, J., Lopez, S. J., Hodges, T., & Harter, J. (2007). *The Clifton StrengthsFinder 2.0 technical report: Development and validation.* Omaha, NE: The Gallup Organization.

7   See, for example:

Goldsmith, H. H. (2003). Genetics of emotional development. In R. J. Davidson, K. R. Scherer, & H. H. Goldsmith (Eds.), *Handbook of affective sciences* (pp. 300-319). New York: Oxford University Press.

Arvey, R. D., Rotundo, M., Johnson, W., Zhang, Z., & McGue, M. (2006). The determinants of leadership role occupancy: Genetic and personality factors. *The Leadership Quarterly, 17*, 1-20.

8   In *Genetics of emotional development*, H. Hill Goldsmith notes the greater similarity for identical twins of several traits, including "distress to novelty," "smiling and laughter," "social fearfulness," and "effortful control," among others (p. 303). This type of twin study is the generally accepted method of investigating the heritability of physical or psychological traits because monozygotic twins begin life with the same genetic inheritance. Without getting into the details of epigenetic development, the shared environment assumption, and so on, it can be safely assumed that a greater similarity between identical twins for a given trait implies a genetic influence at work.

Indeed, Goldsmith notes that "psychiatric epidemiology has yielded quite clear evidence of genetic input to common adult disorders such as schizophrenia, bipolar affective disorder, unipolar depression, and antisocial personality disorder" (p.315). He also notes that in most quantitative genetic research to date:

> heritability seldom rises above a figure of about 60% of the observed variance. In longitudinal analyses, much of the stability — in some cases practically all the stability — of these traits is due to the stability of genetic influences rather than stability of environmental factors. Both genes and environments seem to influence change in most emotion-related traits (p.315)

9   Schmidt, F. L., & Rader, M. (1999, June). Exploring the boundary conditions for interview validity: Meta-analytic validity findings for a new interview type. *Personnel Psychology, 52*, 445-464.

McDaniel, M. A., Whetzel, D. L., Schmidt, F. L., & Maurer, S. D. (1994, August). The validity of employment interviews: A comprehensive review and meta-analysis. *Journal of Applied Psychology, 79*, 599-616.

10 Low, K. S. D., Yoon, M., Roberts, B. W., & Rounds, J. (2005, September). The stability of vocational interests from early adolescence to middle adulthood: A quantitative review of longitudinal studies. *Psychological Bulletin, 131*(5), 713-737.

11 Terracciano, A., Abdel-Khalek, A. M., Adám, N., Adamovová, L., Ahn, C., Ahn, H., et al. (2005, October 7). National character does not reflect mean personality trait levels in 49 cultures. *Science, 310,* 96-100.

12 Small, M. (2006, Summer). It's only rock 'n' roll (jazz, funk, opera, etc.), but I like it. *Berklee Today, 18*(1). Retrieved March 28, 2007, from http://www.berklee.edu/bt/181/brainmusic.html

Levitin is a former gold- and platinum-selling rock musician and record producer who changed careers and became a professor of psychology, neuroscience, and music at McGill University in Montreal.

13 Ibid.

14 Ibid.

15 Ibid.

16 Levitin, D. J. (2006). *This is your brain on music: The science of a human obsession.* New York: Dutton. The authors would like to thank Amanda Hopson of DePauw University for recommending this book.

17 What do we mean by "psychometrically valid"? We mean that a selection method should produce results that are valid and reliable. Most selection interviews are developed by studying individuals who are already successful in the role, or via some other job analysis. In brief, validity is simply: Do the results mean what I think they do? Industrial/Operational psychologists concern themselves with several kinds of validity:

- Internal Validity: Whether the independent variable or intervention in a study is the actual reason for the outcome found in the study.

- External Validity: Can the results of a study be generalized to other situations? An analogy would be to think of this as taking lab or experimental results out into the real world.

- Content Validity: Does the measure cover the full range of a concept's meaning so all of the parts of the concept are measured?

- Criterion Validity: Can you compare the results to other measures of the same thing or use results to predict these other measures?

"Reliability" has several definitions. One definition of reliability, technically known as internal consistency, is the proportion of the score that is due to the aspects of the theme itself and not to irrelevant influences such as mood and fatigue. High internal consistency shows that a theme's items provide a consistent read with each other and do not reflect other influences. A second definition of reliability, technically known as test-retest, is the extent to which scores are stable over time.

Employment laws vary by geography, but most require hiring interviews to adhere to some standards of fairness relative to demographic traits such as race, gender, and age. This means that selection methods should use questions that have been validated against all of these populations so that the overall interview does not discriminate based on these factors.

18 Ibid.

END**NOTES**

CONCLUSION

1   Haidt, J. (2006). *The happiness hypothesis: Finding modern truth in ancient wisdom.* New York: Basic Books.

2   Haidt, J. (2006, October). *The happiness hypothesis.* Paper presented at the Fifth International Positive Psychology Summit, Washington, D.C.

3   Haidt, J. (2006). *The happiness hypothesis: Finding modern truth in ancient wisdom.* New York: Basic Books. This is an excellent book on moral emotions and the human condition. In it, Haidt uses "great ideas" from ancient philosophers and cultures to discuss some of the most compelling research in modern positive psychology.

4   Rath, T. (2006). *Vital friends: The people you can't afford to live without.* New York: Gallup Press. This book contains some groundbreaking research on friendships and includes a link to an online instrument that readers can use to identify which of their friends play each of eight vital friendship roles in their lives.

Gallup Press exists to educate and inform the people who govern, manage, teach, and lead the world's 6 billion citizens. Each book meets Gallup's requirements of integrity, trust, and independence and is based on Gallup-approved science and research.